"Parrish's latest is a quietly beautiful tale about learning how to accept the past and how to let go of the parts that tie you down. Readers can find a great deal to identify with in Liesl's life, from her tumultuous family background to her reluctance to accept love. All of this is entwined with a meaningful spiritual journey and amazing bread recipes that will appeal to the beginner and satisfy even the most seasoned baker."

—*ROMANTIC TIMES*, 4 ½ STARS, TOP PICK!

"The vitality of close relationships is powerfully depicted in Liesl's struggle to let go of her past and embrace the future right in front of her. Readers will definitely relate to her struggle of faith and confidence."

—*BOOKLIST*

"A beautiful story of love and friendship, of redemption and forgiveness, *Stones for Bread* is uplifting and hopeful. It satisfies like a warm loaf of freshly made bread."

—LYNNE HINTON, AUTHOR OF *SISTER EVE, PRIVATE EYE, FRIENDSHIP CAKE,* AND *PIE TOWN*

"Christa Parrish has once again proven herself to be a powerful voice in inspirational fiction. *Stones for Bread* is delivered in Parrish's trademark lyrical style, and its content—a mix of spiritual journey, history, love story, and cookbook—is expertly woven together with Truth. An excellent choice for book clubs and individual readers alike, *Stones for Bread* does not disappoint."

—ALISON MORROW, AUTHOR OF *COMPOSING AMELIA* AND *THE HEART OF MEMORY*

"No one knows how to plunge the depths of what our souls hunger for like Christa Parrish. *Stones for Bread* is a masterpiece, a story that is more than a story. You'll never look at a loaf of bread the same way again."

—SUSAN MEISSNER, AUTHOR OF THE GIRL IN THE GLASS

The Air We Breathe

"A fast-moving, suspenseful, enrapturing novel . . . Fans of Christian fiction with kick and psychological depth will be engaged and touched by Parrish's exciting third novel."

—BOOKLIST

"*The Air We Breathe* is a compelling and emotional novel about identity, redemption, and faith. Expect it to be popular among women of all ages."

—CBA RETAILERS & RESOURCES

"Parrish has created an exceptional look at trauma and its aftermath, as well as hope and recovery from grief at its best. Readers will love it for sure."

—PUBLISHERS WEEKLY

Watch Over Me

"Parrish's deft characterization pulls readers into a storyline filled with raw emotion . . . comes together seamlessly for an unforgettable conclusion."

—ROMANTIC TIMES BOOK REVIEWS

Home Another Way

". . . written with heart and soul. It is always refreshing to read books with imperfect characters; they seem more real."

—ROMANTIC TIMES BOOK REVIEWS

"Parrish . . . adeptly avoids the clichéd happily-ever-after ending while still leaving the reader satisfied."

—CINDY CROSBY, FAITHFULREADER.COM

"Christa Parrish manages the rare accomplishment of telling a very good story peopled with flawed and very human characters."

—LYNN SPENCER, ALL ABOUT ROMANCE (LIKESBOOKS.COM)

"With its vast array of richly imagined characters, its humor and its substance, this debut is sure to resonate with a wide and appreciative audience."

—PUBLISHERS WEEKLY

STILL LIFE

OTHER BOOKS
BY CHRISTA PARRISH

Stones for Bread
The Air We Breathe
Watch Over Me
Home Another Way

STILL LIFE

CHRISTA PARRISH

THOMAS NELSON
Since 1798

NASHVILLE   MEXICO CITY   RIO DE JANEIRO

Published in Nashville, Tennessee, by Thomas Nelson. Thomas Nelson is a trademark of HarperCollins Christian Publishing, Inc.

Thomas Nelson titles may be purchased in bulk for educational, business, fund-raising, or sales promotional use. For information, please e-mail SpecialMarkets@ ThomasNelson.com.

Scripture quotations are taken from:

HOLY BIBLE: NEW INTERNATIONAL VERSION®. © 1973, 1978, 1984 by International Bible Society. Used by permission of Zondervan Publishing House. All rights reserved.

The KING JAMES VERSION.

The Holy Bible, NEW INTERNATIONAL READER'S VERSION®. Copyright © 1996, 1998 Biblica. All rights reserved throughout the world. Used by permission of Biblica.

Library of Congress Cataloging-in-Publication Data

Parrish, Christa.
  Still life / Christa Parrish.
    pages ; cm
  ISBN 978-1-4016-8903-2 (softcover)
  1. Female friendship—Fiction. 2. Life change events—Fiction. I. Title.
PS3616.A76835S75 2015
813'.6—dc23   2014029129

Printed in the United States of America

1 2 3 4 5 6 RRD 19 18 17 16 15 14

For Joseph and Ann Parrish, my parents.
"But as for me and my house, we will serve the Lord."

PART ONE

THE WRECKAGE

CHAPTER ONE

She believes tragedy comes only in the night. It's her mama's two stillbirths and a toddler brother lost to a fever her father said would take him; Ada had kissed the listless boy good-bye with all the others in the room, gathered there to pray him home to Jesus, and bit her cheek against the rebellious words—*aspirin, alcohol bath, doctor*—pooling on her tongue. It's the Langley family cattle, bloated with a strange plague and struck down dead, nearly forty in all gathered from the muddy pasture the next morning and burned so whatever afflicted them wouldn't spread like fleas on toast. No one honestly believed the burning was necessary. Surely one of the Langley kin had somehow secretly sinned against God or man. Probably both. Not long after that the eldest daughter confessed these sins to the elders and was deemed restored to the fellowship after twelve strikes with the paddle and three days of solitary fasting in the woods. *We are all desperately wicked,* her father said over supper, though he would not tell them what Rebekah Langley had done. *It can be any one of us at any time, if we don't take captive our thoughts at the first hint of wandering.*

Ada hoped he couldn't discern her thoughts, even if he was a prophet of the Lord.

It's the shadows in her bedroom at night, the ones she'd been taught were demons and still may believe it, despite Julian's skin and scent and laughter beside her—all things to drive her past away. Garlic to vampires. Human hair to garden vermin.

The switch to a disobedient backside.

It's not dark now, though, and the knock comes on the door. She finds strangers in dark suits, perspiration on their brows, neckties askew. Two men, one young and one old. White men. The young one speaks while plucking the skin beneath his thumbnail, asks if she's the wife of Julian Goetz, flying from Cleveland to Albany on Union North Flight 207. She tells them she doesn't know the flight number, didn't pay attention to it since he plans to drive himself home from the airport, but yes, she is his wife and is there a problem? They want to know if she's turned on the television today, or the computer.

Now she's nervous. "Who are you? What do you want?"

"There's been an accident. A plane crash. Julian was on the flight."

"Don't say his name like that," Ada says. They're not allowed to be so familiar with him, these men of polyester and sweat. "You don't know him."

The old one apologizes, his voice streaked with too many of these visits, and asks to come inside.

She moves, allowing them to pass.

* * *

She hadn't been concerned he wasn't home yet, or that she hadn't heard from him. People are waylaid all the time, flights delayed in the gate, traffic on the highway. Cell phone batteries dead. She didn't bother to contact him.

She breathes easier when he's gone.

She loves him, she's fairly certain. There are moments she catches sight of him in the corner of her vision and is stunned by his bone-aching beauty. *Something* rushes around her, warmth at once, soft and sharp. Her father would call it lust, but she knows better, can *almost* put a name to it, the proper name; the word is there just outside her understanding. If she can feel this feeling a little longer, she'll be able to decipher it. But it's gone too soon and she's left with nothing, a sensation she's but a table leg, all one substance straight through, all one temperature, unable to be filled or emptied out.

He called her from the airport a bit before ten this morning. "My flight's overbooked. Why in the world airlines do that, I don't know."

"What does that mean?" she asked, phone beeping several times in her ear, not used to the sleek screen and how her cheek pushes against the buttonless images, turning the speaker on and off, dialing random numbers, muting her voice.

"I've been bumped to the nine-fifteen flight."

"Oh."

They have reservations tonight for her birthday. Julian's idea. He wants the day to be special. She's twenty-six and has never had any sort of celebration. The day came and went with unspoken recognition in her previous life; her mother allowing her an extra biscuit with butter and honey at breakfast, or perhaps adding peaches to her pancakes. Her father nodding as she ticked another line on the door-frame, documenting not her height but her years since she'd stopped growing. They might all forget how old they were if not for the Sharpie marks in the pantry.

She doesn't want the attention anyway. "It's alright."

"No, it's not." He sighed. She could practically hear him mashing his fingers against the soft tissue behind his eye-lids. "Look, just let me—I'll call you back."

He didn't call, but texted twenty minutes later: I'LL BE HOME IN TIME. BE READY TO PARTY.

* * *

The men speak at first in hushed tones to each other. The ditty of a text message, the electronic *tap-tap-tap* of a reply. The old one puts the telephone to his ear when it rings, nods over and over again, responds with a single, convictionless, "Okay."

She knows, now, she won't see Julian again this side of heaven.

What she doesn't know is if she should offer them a seat or a glass of water, if hospitality is in order, or efficiency.

So she waits, fingers interlaced and against her navel, body curved into the banister at the bottom of the stairs. The men's eyes flicker to the sofa and chair in the living room, to the photographs on the wall beside her. The young one steps forward to look at the first framed image. A protest in some country she'd never heard of when Julian told her of it—world geography wasn't important in her community—where the off-center face of a young boy, maybe nine years old, shouted his angry words against the crowd. Above him, a man's arm, in flames. The boy's hair is beginning to singe, to smoke, about to be set afire in the next moments, the ones not captured on paper. Ada remembers being horrified when she first saw it. Angry. "You stood there and took a picture, and did nothing to help him?"

Julian had turned his body slightly away from her. "He was fine. Someone in the crowd threw a blanket over him. And the guy's arm."

"But not you."

"It was taken care of, Ada."

"Two strong arms are better than a quick wit. Or a quick lens, in this case."

He turned away completely. "I've helped before."

She'd wanted to believe him.

The young one isn't repulsed, though. The photo pulls him closer until his nose is almost to the glass, and he reaches to touch the boy's twisted face.

"Mike," the old one says.

His hand dives into the pocket of his pants.

The old one introduces himself as Wright and the young one as Bowen. Airline liaisons. "May we sit?"

"Oh, yes, of course. I'm sorry." She fumbles with the words as Wright holds his arm out toward the leather living room set, as if it's his own home and she's the visitor. She turns sideways to squeeze between them, sits on the chair. They both take a place on the sofa, each on the end cushions, the middle one empty.

"You haven't seen the TV today, then," Wright says.

"We don't have a television."

"News websites?"

Ada shakes her head. "I'm not good with . . . those kind of things."

"Me either. Old dog and all that nonsense." Wright clears his throat. "As we mentioned, there was an accident. A crash. We don't believe any of the passengers survived."

She closes her eyes, nestling between his sentences. Her nostrils flare on their own volition. She hears Bowen's phone jingle again, Wright say, "Take it outside." Thumping of feet on the dark, shiny floor. Too dark and too shiny for her taste. Masculine wood.

"Mrs. Goetz?"

"Where?"

"On the border of New York and Pennsylvania, in the Susquehanna."

"I can smell it," she mumbles.

"No, not from here," Wright says, and his eyes glaze with piteous familiarity; he's seen others go half-insane in their own living rooms before. Ada wonders about his *everyday* job. Plane crashes are few and far between. What does he do in that in-between?

He waits seconds for a response, and getting none, says, "Is there someone you can call? You shouldn't be alone. Any family close by? Friends?"

"No."

"No one?"

"Julian's sister." That imaginary jet fuel smell thickens to a haze, filling her skull, dulling the speed of her synapses. "She doesn't live far. Two hours, I think?"

"Is there someone not so close. To Julian, I mean. Someone who—"

"I know what you mean."

She finds her phone on the dining table, where she dropped it earlier, and scrolls through the contact list Julian programmed there. All people he knows, people she's met once or a handful of times. Names he parades through conversations, expecting her to remember.

She chooses one.

Hortense.

"Happy birthday to you. Happy birthday to you. Happy birthday dear Ada, happy birthday to you," Hortense sings. "That man of yours has taste, taking you to The Waterfront. You think mine would? Nope. Not in fourteen years."

There's murmuring in the background, and Hortense says, "I don't care that it's only been open for three. You've never taken me anywhere remotely like it. Denny's is a fancy date to you."

Ada probes around her mouth with her tongue, feeling

for something to say, finding only sticky, dehydrated spit. Her hearing tunnels, Hortense at the end of a long, thin tube saying, "Ada? Ada, hey, are you still there?" But her vision grows sharp and she sees Wright, in glowing pixels, moving from the couch to her elbow, prying the telephone from her hand. His voice runs from the other end of the tube, to Hortense, as he explains what has happened to Julian.

"She's coming," he says.

In the twenty minutes between hanging up with Hortense and her arrival, Wright covers Ada in a gray chenille throw he gathered from somewhere in the house, brings ice water and microwaved tea to her—both set on the end table, untouched and without a coaster. She watches beads of condensation crawl down the side of the glass, puddling on the wood, and Wright with Bowen at the front door. Suddenly Hortense is above her, around her, and Ada thinks, *She will grieve harder than me, she's known him twenty times longer than I have.* But Hortense is iron, and she emerges from the hug with a tearless face and firm jaw. She knows pain. This is nothing. A blip. A nuisance.

Life.

Before Ada met her, Julian had said Hortense was the most beautiful woman most people would ever see. And she is. Even Ada knows it, despite growing up sheltered from the world of celebrities and *Cosmopolitan* and glossy lipstick. Some beauty is purely objective. No one needed to tell her Rachael was the prettiest of her sisters, prettiest in the community, really. No one needed to point out Ada's own eyes were too wide set, her nose too blunt, her lips too colorless and pillowy.

And then Julian told her, "She doesn't have hands," preparing her, and since it was summer Hortense came wearing a billowy but sleeveless blouse, arms ending at the wrists, three fleshy, bulbous nubs of never-to-be fingers stuck to the end of one of them. The right one.

Hortense speaks with the men from the airline. She nods and responds and gestures. Ada can't make out anything they say. Bowen takes an envelope from the inside pocket of his blazer, hesitates. Hortense holds out her arms and clamps the rectangle between her wrist bones. She sets it on the side table and leads the men to the door, locking up behind them. Retrieving the envelope, she sits on the sofa across from Ada's chair, maneuvering a folded sheet of paper from inside. Opens it.

"They're setting up some sort of meeting place for the families, at the Hilton Garden in Albany," Hortense says. "They give phone numbers. One for information. One . . . if you need to talk to someone. A counselor. Do you?"

Ada shakes her head.

"Mark's on his way. Bringing food. You need to eat."

"Okay," Ada says. She does well with orders; they comfort her since it's what she's known most of her life. Julian never told her to do anything. He asked. He offered. And she'd sit there with the choice between going to a movie or strolling the downtown, anxiety crashing over her, because she could not pick and wanted Julian to make the decision for her, and he refused.

She thinks for a second time, *I won't see him again this side of heaven.*

Hortense reads the thought from her face and for a moment her perfect mouth trembles. Ada wants to cry but needs permission to do so; if Hortense begins, so will she. The doorbell rings, then, and Hortense sniffles, stands. "That's Mark," she says, voice cracking. She coughs, straightening her shoulders, adjusting her armor. "We'll eat and then call Sophie."

CHAPTER TWO

Her heart hears the hotel telephone ringing before her ears do, so when she wakes completely, her chest is constricted, and Katherine thinks, *He's found me.* Next to her, Thomas stirs but doesn't open his eyes, and she knows from these past five months that he sleeps as soundly as if in a coffin. She exhales until she can no longer force breath from her lungs, which only deepens the pounding behind her rib cage.

The phone rings again.

She turns her head toward it, red light flashing with each wail, and notices her cell phone blinking as well. She turns it over. Unplugs the cord from the landline.

It's dusk; they'd left the blinds open. She hates this time of day, all the contrast draining from her surroundings, making it difficult for her to see much more than shapes, outlines. No details, and that's where the devil is, for sure. She lays in the semidark, semisilent room, listening to Thomas snuffle, hearing footsteps in the hallway, stopping at their room. A polite knock on their door. And relief comes. If it had been Will, he'd be pounding and shouting.

Soft rustling, the sound of paper, something she recognizes, dealing with forms and contracts and *sign on the dotted line, please* in her day job. She slips from bed and sees the folded page beneath the door, sees her naked body in the full-length mirror on the wall, years of gravity and mothering and ice cream tugging down her parts. She wraps a white towel around her middle and snatches the paper from the floor, opening it to read the handwritten words. *Please call your sister Jennifer as soon as possible. Important.* Katherine knows it must be. Jennifer wouldn't bother her otherwise.

Katherine dials her sister's cell phone, ignoring all the other notifications.

"Seriously, Kate. I've been trying to reach you all afternoon."

"I had the volume down on my phone," Katherine says. "What's going on? Is it one of the boys?"

"No, they're fine, but turn on the television."

"Why?"

"Just do it. The news."

"What channel?"

"Try fifty-two."

"I don't think the hotel numbers are the same." Katherine clicks through the stations until she finds CNN, bold yellow lettering scrolling across the bottom of the screen declaring BREAKING NEWS and NO SURVIVORS. On the screen, she watches footage of a flaming airplane wreckage submerged in a river. Rescue vehicles buzz around the scene, dozens of angry wasps vainly searching for purpose. "The plane crash?"

"Yes," Jennifer says. "Kate, that's your flight from this morning, out of Cleveland."

"Oh, God." Nausea pounces, and Katherine folds in half, one arm sandwiched against her belly, the other still pressing the phone to her ear. "I could have . . ."

"Will's going crazy. He's called here a dozen times. I told him you were shopping. You need to get in touch with him."

"Okay, okay."

"He's driving out here."

"Now? From New York?"

"He doesn't want you to step foot on a plane after all this."

Katherine's eyes find the clock. "When did he leave?"

"Don't worry. He won't be here for another five hours or so. After midnight, at least."

She swears softly, her queasiness pushed out by rising annoyance. "I'll be to your place by eight."

She hangs up, checks her other messages. From Will, mostly. A few from the boys and Jennifer. Shaking off the towel, she fumbles into the clothes she tossed onto the chair earlier, knocking Thomas's to the floor and leaving them there. She flops onto the corner of the bed, on his legs, and he finally wakes as she rolls on her socks.

"What are you doing?" he asks her, looking surprisingly boyish with his tousled hair and sleep-puffed eyelids.

"Going back to Jennifer's house."

"What? Why?"

"Will is coming."

Thomas struggles out of the blankets, sits upright now. "Does he—"

"No. It has nothing to do with us. It's . . . that." Katherine flaps her hand toward the television, as if trying to drive the images back into the screen where she can no longer see them.

"A plane crash?"

"My plane, Thomas. The one I was supposed to be on this morning."

"Oh, my God," he says. "Thank God, thank God you didn't get on."

He holds her, his arms both altogether familiar and unfamiliar, known for such a short period of time compared to the length of her marriage, but the only ones to come around her lately. His entire body is different than Will's—longer, hairier, more blond, more freckled. She leans into him, trembling. "I could be dead. My boys could have been left without a mother."

"But they weren't," he says, stroking her hair. "Don't let yourself go there."

She rests in him, eyes closed, until she feels their bodies sinking toward the mattress and Thomas untucking her blouse, resting his hand on her bare stomach. Katherine jumps up, jams her shirt into her pants. "I have to go. I have to call my family. I can't do it . . . here."

They stare at one another and Katherine breaks first,

turning her head as if searching for something—her coat? her purse?—but really wanting to escape Thomas's gaze. Her outside life is encroaching on this life they've created, a place where spouses and children don't exist, where those things they've given up for the sake of family can be imagined again. Here, in this hotel room and others like it, they're allowed to be the people they've left behind, discussing all those things that make Will and Susanna roll their eyes and snort. But now she sees how Thomas asks, with his eyes, *Why do you choose to go back to that?*

Katherine belts her coat at the waist, noticing a smudge of something on the white fabric. She goes into the bathroom and dampens the corner of a washcloth, touches it to the bar of citrus soap, and scrubs at the spot. She can't tell, in the dark, if it comes clean, but won't turn on the light.

Her purse, she needs it, still on the desk beside the television. She turns on her realtor stride, her walk-with-purpose, and swings the green leather bag onto her shoulder. She doesn't look at Thomas.

"At least let me drive you," he says, her hand on the door handle.

She shakes her head. "I'll grab a cab."

"Is this it?"

She looks back; he stands with his pants on now, the televised crash scenes reflecting on his skin. An hour ago she would have abandoned her family for him, if he'd asked. Now he's dwarfed by the *what ifs* echoing back at her from the news.

"I don't know."

It's only when Katherine is at the elevator, after she's pressed the down button and waits, hands in her pockets, that she's pricked by the corner of the business card the man gave her. The one who wanted to get home for his wife's birthday. The one for whom she gave her seat up, plus a three-hundred-and-fifty-dollar airline credit and one more night with Thomas.

CHAPTER THREE

Mark brings Chinese food. *Little white boxes from the gods,* Julian had called it, causing her to flinch at the pagan reference. Ada's first ethnic food experience was only two days into their marriage; Julian bought some variation of nearly every dish on the long paper menu and after trying a taste of this and that, she ate mostly rice and the battered chicken without its red, syrupy sauce. Her virgin pallet couldn't handle the intensity of such unfamiliar flavors. She watched the chopsticks dance in Julian's fingers, tried propping the thin bamboo in her own hands but could not get them to obey no matter how she positioned them. *Like this,* he showed her over and over, until she simply speared a piece of chicken with the tip and bit it off. He laughed, taking the offending sticks from her, taking her to bed, his mouth full of spice and sugar and salt.

She uses a spoon now, licking off the few grains of white rice sticking to it, going through the motions often enough to appear as if she's eating more than she is. Mark has chopsticks but his hands are clumsy around them. Not like Julian. Or perhaps that's the dusty glitter of death coming over her memories already, making everything shinier and more perfect than in actual life.

Hortense has a fork, handle between her wrists, tines pointed toward her. She dips and scoops, bringing the chow mein neatly to her lips. Then she presses the fork into a boneless sparerib, takes up a steak knife, and leans forward to hold the fork with her chin; Ada has seen her cut things before, sawing the knife back and forth, each bite more work and more reward. Tonight Mark stops her, slicing her meat quickly and then touching her arm. The look they give one another says, *We're still here*. Then, as if programmed, they both turn and look at Julian's empty chair. Beneath the table, Ada slips her hand onto the seat.

So cold.

"We only have to get in touch with Sophie tonight," Hortense says, the first words since the meal began. "She can call the rest of the family. Mark and I will take care of the people we know tomorrow, the ones closest to us. Everyone else will hear about it when names are released."

Ada takes this opportunity to push back her plate. She nods, but surely there are other Julian Goetzes in the world. Will the television and newspaper reports show photos of the deceased? List family, age, occupation? She doesn't know how it all works. Hortense seems confident, though, and Ada has looked ignorant enough in front of her, and Mark, and Julian's other friends on other occasions. She doesn't want that tonight.

"What about clients?" Mark asks.

"I don't know. He always has that stuff with him."

"I guess we just tell them when they call looking, if they don't find out sooner."

"I guess." She looks at Ada. "Okay, then. Sophie."

Ada shakes her head. "I don't know how to say."

Hortense slumps, the news finally catching up with her. Ada knows she wishes she can be in her own space, grieving, instead of caring for her best friend's wife, a woman she barely knows and who has the resourcefulness of a day-old kitten—eyes closed still, able only to mew and wriggle and clamp on to its mother's nipple for milk. Hortense is doing all of this for Julian. Not her.

"I'll call," Hortense says. "Do you have the number?"

Ada gives her the cell phone and she passes it to Mark. He maneuvers around the touch screen and shows it to Hortense. She dials her own phone and hoists it to her ear. "Hi, Sophie, it's Hortense Travers . . . It has been awhile, a couple years, I think . . . No, I'm not calling about that, I'm afraid . . . Well, yes. I mean, geez, Soph, have you seen the news about that plane crash today? . . . Yeah . . . Yes . . . No, just him . . . She's here with me . . . Yeah, okay." She holds the phone out to Ada; it balances on the end of her arm, screen glowing. Ada hadn't realized night had come down; no lights are on in the brownstone.

She takes the call—"Hi, Sophie"—and hears only muffled sobs. She waits. Perhaps the tears of Julian's sister will dislodge her own. *Cry, cry, cry.* But nothing comes. Her eyes are open, her limbs move, her mouth creates words, but every other part of her sleeps, as if Julian's death injected Novocain into her soul.

You won't feel a thing, he'd told her. *They give you a shot to numb your gums. But you need to go to the dentist. That cavity's so big your tooth is practically gone.* That's all she'll have of him for the rest of her life, bits of conversation appearing and disappearing in her memory, like white rabbits. Another first with him, the magic show outside Quincy Market. Every day their marriage brought firsts. He made certain of it.

Finally Sophie said, "Ada, are you okay?"

"I don't know yet."

"No, I suppose not. There's no other information yet? No, of course there wouldn't be. Too soon. Still working on finding bodies. Identifying them. That could take days. Weeks. Like with that other crash, TWA—you wouldn't know anything about that. Don't listen to me. I'll go ahead and call family, if that's good with you?"

"I don't have numbers for anyone anyway."

"I'll take care of it. Something to do. Something to do. You need to keep doing, Ada. Don't let the sadness get you. It will, if you sit there. It grows over you."

Ada has no idea what she's babbling about. It makes her nervous. She passes the phone back to Hortense.

"Soph, I'm back . . . I promise, I'll call you with anything we find out . . . I will . . . Yeah . . . Bye." She shovels the phone onto the sofa. Mutters the Lord's name beneath her breath.

Mark and Hortense clear the food, moving like a couple married more than a decade. She and Julian still stumbled around one another, not yet of one being, evenings full of awkward moments—his jokes she didn't laugh at, her attempts to serve him through cooking and cleaning for which he cared nothing. She would cry and he'd hold her, and she'd say, "I have no way to please you. I can't do anything but cook and clean and laundry. But you bring home take-away and send your clothes to the Laundromat, and you won't fire your maid. So what can I give you to make me worth the trouble?"

You. I have you. Just you.

She told him that made no sense. He told her she'd learn.

Seeing Hortense and Mark together continues to confuse her. Her own father would never wash dishes. Her mother would never dare ask him to. Yet Mark scrubs away duck sauce and Hortense leans her body against his back, her face between his shoulder blades, her arms belted at his waist. She makes no move to help. When he finishes, he turns and embraces her, whispers in her ear. Then he says, "Ada, I'll be back in a few. Need something while I'm out?"

She shakes her head.

"He has to walk Lucca," Hortense says. Their dog. "And he's bringing our television. We'll stay the night with you."

So they sit, Ada back in her chair—her chair? This is the first time she's thought of anything in Julian's home as hers. It's as if, when he died, his essence evaporated from all the physical things around her, freeing them to belong to others—and Hortense on the sofa. She thought they might stay in silence all night, but should have known better. Hortense doesn't do quiet. Instead of tears, words spill from her.

"I framed those for him," Hortense says, nodding at the five prints on the wall. The one of the boy aflame. One of another boy, a teenager, bald and emaciated, wearing only jeans and spread eagle on a lawn painted with dandelions. A soldier, lighting a cigarette with bandaged hands, leaning against a wall punctured with dozens of bullet holes. A gathering of homeless and less-than during a Sunday morning worship service beneath the Albany overpass, sharing a Communion of donuts and day-old bagels.

And the fifth, a tree on a hill, shot from a distance, the shadow of a woman clinging to it.

"He told me you made him hang them there."

"Made him? That's probably too close to true. I would have badgered him until he put them up, for sure. I mean, who hides their Pulitzer photos? Except for that one on the end. He changed out the picture I put in there for that one." Hortense shifts on the sofa, leather squeaking beneath her long, denim-clad legs. "He said that's you."

Ada nods. Hortense wants more, but she has no energy to think about the image, much less tell the story of it.

When she doesn't continue, Hortense does. "He was stupid humble. Not in a false modesty sort of way. It didn't matter to him if he won a thousand awards or not. He knew he had a gift. I told him Mark and I had to get together to even come close to half the talent he had. He just . . .

I mean, he was . . ." Her phantom hands float above her knees; Ada can almost see them twisting and tapping, desperate to cling to anything real. And she clearly sees how much Hortense cares for him.

They had met in college, Julian and Hortense and Mark, all majoring in photography. Somehow they fell in together, though Julian couldn't remember exactly how it happened. And when Ada wanted to know if any part of Julian had loved her, he said, "I could have. At one point, I wanted to. But I asked God and he told me no. I was meant to be with someone else."

Growing up in a community where she had been expected to live in a constant state of cheerful meekness, she became skilled at hiding emotions. But she has no mask of joy to wear now, and grief doesn't cover nearly as well. Hortense must notice something on Ada's face because she quickly says, "Mark and I are happy, Ada. It's been a long time since I thought of Julian as anything other than a friend. Not since junior year. I promise you."

"I know."

"Good. I couldn't handle it if you thought . . . you know . . . otherwise."

Hortense tells stories of their college shenanigans, of a young, puckish Julian Ada never knew and can't at all conjure, until Mark comes back and plugs in the television. Hortense finds a sheet and blanket in the upstairs hallway closet, covers the leather sofa, and she and Mark squish together there, even though Ada offers them the spare room. "We've slept in smaller spaces," Mark says, and the couple laughs gently at shared memories. She stays in the chair, arms strapped around her legs, and she dozes in the flickering of the muted news channel. Each time she wakes, both Mark and Hortense are still staring at the screen.

CHAPTER FOUR

There's no one beside her when Katherine wakes; she thinks first Thomas should be there, then Will. Yes, Will. He was to come to get her, driving from New York to Ohio, meeting her at Jennifer's house. She remembers returning from the hotel, swallowing down two glasses of wine, and closing herself in Jennifer's guest room. Despite the alcohol, she woke often during the night, waiting for Will to appear. But the pillow beside her remains perfectly puffed. Katherine punches the center of it, denting the goose feathers. She draws it against her body, curls around it, her face pressed against the sateen pillowcase until she can't stand breathing in her own hot breath.

She turns her head, gasps for air, and smells bacon.

She dresses before going downstairs, wears her smart clothes, her shiny shoes, the fashionable garb she puts on when she wants to be more than she thinks she is. She stops on the bottom step, presses her body against the wall so she won't be seen. Listens to the conversation from the kitchen—Jennifer talking about ungrateful patients and long nursing hours, Will talking of basketball games and new construction jobs. When Katherine enters the room, both become so still the only sound is the snapping grease in the pan. Then Will stands and hugs her.

Within his arms she's taut as rawhide, counting the ways he irritates her, the things she finds distasteful. His shirt is too rough, missing a button, worn at least three days without washing. His forty-something stomach is too large. There's a bit of dandruff on his shoulder. His hands are awkward on her torso; they don't remember where to touch her since it's been so long. She wants all these things to add up to a reason to leave him, or at least an excuse for her affair with Thomas. She cheated death. Now is the time to dump unwanted baggage and grab hold of her second chance to do what she wants.

Instead, she remembers the home she and Will have created together, with the tumble of stinky teenage boy sneakers at the front door, the aqua toilet he's been promising to change since they moved in eleven years ago. The strawberry patch by the front door Bryce helped her plant when he was six, overgrown with clumps of dandelions and clover, and enjoyed more by the chipmunks than the human residents of 18 Birchbark Road.

She hasn't been happy in her marriage for years. But she's not been unhappy, either. They've both been wandering quietly through their own worlds and those of the boys, nodding at one another as they pass, no hostility, no fireworks. They live in the dry spell, as she imagines so many other married couples must do. When did the rain stop coming?

Thinking back, it was after Evan had healed and they settled into their new normal. When she and Will first married, it was all passion and shouting and spending more than they made. They were young and had no idea how to be husband and wife, their examples while growing up quite broken: his parents fiery and violent toward one another, her mother cold and her father absent. When Bryce was born, things between her and Will smoothed down, their first son's smiles a balm softening both of them. And then another boy, Evan. Only hours after his delivery Katherine noticed a blue tinge to his lips. His breathing grew labored and he was rushed to the PICU. Tests found a misshapen heart, beginning six years of surgeries, extended hospital stays, feeding tubes, doctors, therapies, appointments, sleepless vigils, fast food, and more worry than most parents have in a lifetime. They survived because there was no other choice, managing with the bare minimum, constantly exhausted and never allowing themselves the smallest hope things would get better. But things did improve. Evan's heart began functioning well enough to keep him from needing a transplant, and their marriage functioned well enough to keep the family from splintering. Wounds scarred over and grew numb to the touch.

And life continued on.

She allows her body to relax into him. Will feels it, says, "Let's get you home."

"I'll get my things. Upstairs."

Katherine leaves the bed unmade. Let Jennifer deal with it. She dumps her cosmetics bag into the suitcase, throws her toothbrush in the trash can. Zips her luggage, does what Will calls the *idiot check*, looking in drawers she didn't use for things she never unpacked, under the bed, in the closet—"Just in case," he'd say. She has everything except her white coat. Looking at it makes her swell with the guilt only a survivor can feel. Wearing it again would be like buttoning into a body bag. And *his* card. In the pocket.

Jennifer can keep the coat.

* * *

She offers to drive but Will says no, despite making the eight-hour trip for the second time in less than a day. He's always the one to drive when they're in the car together, a pattern from very early in their marriage, and she wonders if most couples fall into this, the man in control at the wheel, the woman submissive by his side. Katherine hates being in the passenger seat. It bores her, staring out the window at road signs and burger joints. She and Will aren't much for conversation, though they try. Life has moved beyond small talk. They've been very good at it previously, giving the boys and friends the illusion they communicate about everything, and without conflict, but the teeth never break the skin. Their relationship has shifted on its axis, both of them wanting to reconnect but not knowing which words to begin with. The airplane crash hasn't been mentioned yet, but it fills the inside of the Subaru as if the wreckage had fallen around them.

Katherine reclines her seat. Closes her eyes.

"Are you okay?" Will asks.

"In one piece, at least."

"Kate." His voice breaks.

"I know."

"I was so ticked you got off that flight. I thought, why doesn't she put us first for a change? And then this."

She doesn't put them first? She hears this and her mind reels. She *always* puts everyone else first. She changes her schedule to drive Bryce to every sport practice and pick Evan up from yearbook club. She shows dozens of homes each week so her family can have money for vacations in Florida and new car payments. She does the majority of the housework, the laundry, the cooking. Will comes home from the job and sits his gypsum-covered rear in his recliner, not bothering to change his dirty clothes, eating in front of the television and falling asleep there most nights.

"That's right. I'm the selfish one."

"I didn't say selfish."

"Last time I checked, not putting others first is the definition of selfish."

"That's not what I meant, Katherine."

They were bloated with the adrenaline of the past day, the pressure cracking the mortar with which they patched their marriage—for her, Thomas and her business; for him, food and gadgets and cable news—and years of unspoken wormwood seeped through the gaps.

"Then what did you mean?" She pauses a moment, and then for emphasis, "Will."

"Nothing. Forget it." And then he sighs. "I'm sorry. We shouldn't be fighting now. I'm . . . tired. And unsettled. It's like after we found out about Evan's heart. Everything's spinning. I can't make sense of it."

"I was just thinking of that. When things were so hard, I mean." Every stress point brought them back in time to the worst of their son's illness. Whatever problem they were going through was held up and squinted at in the light of *those days*. Always, always, the problem was found to be so much less than Evan's fight for life. But this situation came close to eclipsing it, at least in the immediacy of it. She adjusts her seat, bringing the back up so she's no longer reclining. "I'm sorry too."

Will steers the car onto the shoulder of the highway, switches on the hazard lights. He curls his fingers around her chin, as if she's wearing his fist for a beard. "We'll figure it out."

"Okay." She draws out the word in uncertainty. To her, there is nothing to figure. She wants only to get home to the boys and begin living as if the past twenty-four hours never happened. She'll gladly take her not-so-wonderful marriage if it keeps her guilt away.

CHAPTER FIVE

Morning comes and Julian is still dead. Ada has the briefest of seconds to consider it may have all been a dream, but then her eyes open and see the television, still broadcasting images of the crash site, of divers beginning their work again now that the sun is up, interviews with nosy bystanders and frantic loved ones. She moves slowly, one continuous spring of rigid muscle from spending the night in the chair. Each movement brings another shooting pain somewhere in her body. Her feet are numb. Her neck turns only to the right. A shower may unravel it all.

Hortense is on the telephone. Mark snores on the couch. She limps upstairs and sits in the hot water, skin turning red, reality seeping in. She's in a crash-induced limbo. Julian was her one connection with this strange world she'd been birthed into five months ago. She's hardly learned to sit up on her own, to crawl. How can she navigate life without him?

This is my punishment, isn't it?

Not a prayer but a moan of defeat.

Her father's God takes vengeance—it is his, he has said so—smiting the wicked and those who veer from the way of the righteous. He is the God Ada continues to go back to because he is the God she recognizes, and the known is safe even if it brings blows of judgment. Julian's God of grace, who is he? Surely no one Ada has ever met.

She dries and dresses in yesterday's long-sleeved tee and favorite cargo skirt that falls midcalf and is full of pockets. She keeps her hair wrapped in a towel, for now. She hates the ends dripping against her shoulders. As she brushes her teeth she remembers someone else who needs to be called—Julian's pastor. Hers, too, she supposes, though it's difficult to think of Ray Washington as something other than a *son of Ham*, as her father would call him. Cursed with dark skin.

The first time Julian took her to Holy Zion, she had nearly fainted upon seeing a congregation comprised mostly of blacks, with a sprinkling of college-aged students here and there. In fact, this was the demographic of Julian's entire neighborhood, three universities within walking distance of his inner-city row house, which is why Ada rarely ventured outside alone. When Julian asked her about it and she told him what her parents had taught her, his face grew so dark with anger Ada feared he would strike her; she'd seen the same look come over the prophet and end with someone backhanded for their rebellion. She cowered and apologized, and Julian had reached out for her slowly, as if offering his hand's scent to a frightened street mongrel, and then pulled her against him. "That man has the devil in him," he told her. She never mentioned her father again. Neither did he.

Her phone is stuck in the cushion of the chair where she slept. She digs it out and takes it back upstairs into the bathroom, despite Hortense waving for her attention. Dials. The church secretary answers and puts her through to Ray Washington.

"Ada, good to hear from you, sister. What can I do you for?"

She has to say it. "Julian's dead."

"Oh, sweet precious Jesus. That plane."

"Yes."

Ray's chalky baritone calls on the Lord again, and he prays in his rapid-fire way, his words sometimes indistinguishable from breath, perhaps not even English. He continues and Ada lets his voice wash over her, as soothing as a teacup of hot honey lemonade, and while her sadness and fear haven't been at all diminished, she almost feels as if she can stand up under it.

"What can we do for you?" Ray asks after his, "Amen."

"I'm not sure right now."

"We'll start with meals."

"No, please don't. It's just me. I couldn't finish one casserole in a week. Food would only go to waste."

"Do you need some folks to come sit with you?"

"Julian's friend Hortense is here now. And her husband."

Ray clucks his tongue. "Sister. Sister. Let us come alongside you."

"I will. I honestly just don't know what's next."

"I got that. I'll ask here and there and call you later tonight."

Ada nods even though Ray can't see her. She finds Hortense waiting for her at the foot of the stairs. "Do you want to go to the hotel where the families are meeting?"

What good will it do, sitting in a room with strangers, waiting for news she can get from the television? "I don't think so."

"We should fill out these forms, then."

"What forms?" Ada asks.

"From the envelope they left yesterday. It's to help them . . . identify people."

They sit together at the table, Hortense rereading the papers, not turning toward Ada even as she stares at Hortense in profile. Her silky, black hair is short as a boy's. Her pixie chin. Her eyes, shaped like teardrops with large red-brown irises. Her complexion, smooth as onionskin and nearly the same color. The genetic roulette of her Korean mother and Haitian father.

"Okay, we're supposed to draw any identifying marks Julian has, you know, in the spots he has them. Scars, birthmarks, tattoos, previously broken bones. Any sort of dental work, those sorts of things," Hortense tells her.

Ada looks at the paper, two simple black-line drawings of bald, androgynous figures—face up and face down—and watches as Hortense clamps the pen between her wrists and draws a jagged line across the left shin, labeling it with the number one. *Broken leg,* she writes on the first line. "From that incident in Darfur. You know, when he was attacked."

Ada doesn't know. She can't even say with certainty what Darfur is. A place, yes, obviously. But where? And what happened there? Hortense knows an entirely *other* Julian.

"Okay, we good?" Without waiting for an answer, Hortense folds the paper.

"Wait, no," Ada says. She shakes the form open and smoothes it against the table. Slowly, she adds a short, dark line on the left side of the figure's abdomen, just beneath the navel.

"What's that?" Hortense asks.

"A scar. He had some sort of surgery when he was a baby. On his intestines, when they got twisted up. He used some name for it but I don't remember what it was called. Do you?"

Hortense sucks her lips together. "Just write a two by it and call it a surgical scar."

She doesn't know about it. Ada fills in the information as Hortense directs but she feels enlarged. This is a part of Julian only she has, a place only a wife's eyes have seen. Touched. How many times had they been in bed, her fingers tracing that fine, ghostly line? It doesn't matter if they were married five months or five decades. Her relationship with Julian is beyond friendship. It's mystical, spiritual, the very image given by God of Christ's love for his own body, the church. It doesn't matter how many common experiences or inside jokes Julian and Hortense and Mark shared.

He's mine.

Ada caps the pen. Rushing now, Hortense more rolls than refolds the form, tries to cram it into the envelope but can't quite manage it in her haste. She sweeps the papers into her open tote bag, slinging the straps over her shoulder. "I'll fax it from the gallery. Mark's there. We have some work we have to get done."

"Okay."

"Do you need me to come back tonight? To stay?"

Shaking her head, Ada says, "No, I think I'm good."

Hortense nods. "Yeah, then. I'll check with you tomorrow." Her footfalls are heavier than Ada has heard them before, her lithe body gawkily striding toward the front door. And when she goes, Ada turns on the television and watches strangers moving with ant-like frenzy over the crash scene, collecting the wreckage of her life.

CHAPTER SIX

Even before Will turns the key and hustles her through the back door, Katherine hears a thunder of too-large teenaged feet on the stairs and then she's consumed by boy arms and scent—Axe deodorant, pizza sauce, denim, Clearasil cream. She can't breathe in the melee, dwarfed by both her sons' bodies, but holds onto them as they migrate into the kitchen, one multitentacle organism of mother-child bond.

"We wanted to come, but Dad wouldn't let us miss school," Evan says, still with his arm around her shoulder even as Bryce has taken two steps away. "What's so important about algebra when your mother almost died?"

"I'm fine," Katherine says. "It wasn't all that close to an almost."

Bryce gives his younger brother a light shove in the shoulder. "That's what I keep saying. Almost implies, like, actually being on the plane and surviving. This was more like potentially a possible almost, or something like that." He's the king of qualifiers, of precision in all things. He's most like Katherine, which is why they have the most contentious relationship of the household. Eighteen, a senior this year, ready to be a man but still so much a child who will eat frosting from the container before heating up real food, and sleep on his bare mattress instead of changing the sheets.

Evan scowls. Fifteen, bony, always smaller and weaker because of his damaged heart, he resents the correction and will have none of it. "She almost died," he repeats.

"Whatev," Bryce says. "I'm starving."

"I'll throw something together," Katherine says. "Give me a few minutes to change and wash up."

"Kate, seriously." Will flips open his phone, an ancient model he refuses to upgrade because he doesn't want to learn a new system. "I'll order pizza."

She wants to cook, wants to provide something for her family and return to normalcy in doing so. Will is already asking for mushrooms and green peppers, and she feels displaced, as if she's not there in the house but still in Cleveland, in the airport, waiting to board her flight. She moves into the L-shaped corner of the faux–butcher block laminate counter, her corner, between the dishwasher and stove, where she prepares food, eats lunch, opens mail. This feels like home, she thinks, counter pressing into the skin below her rib cage. The kitchen is the nucleus, the most worn room, the last one to be updated. Peel-and-stick tiles curl in front of the refrigerator and in the threshold between the kitchen and living room, where it changes to wood; how many times has she tripped in that very spot? She despises the wallpaper, hunter green and dotted with apples and hearts. The cabinets are oak, dark and dated, but she has great plans to paint and antique them, once she finds some empty time.

She still has the chance to find it.

"I'm going to take a bath before the food gets here," she says. "Unless you want the shower first."

Will shakes his head. "Go ahead."

"Thanks." She carries a wine glass and the half-full bottle of Shiraz, and drags her feet up the carpeted stairs.

The master bathroom has been renovated, and she loves it, from the natural stone tile to the modern plum tones, to the deep, welcoming tub. And, yes, she did sit in every tub at the Home Depot to see which was most comfortable, thank you very much. She runs the water hot, clears a ball of hair from the drain, and plugs it. Dumps a carton of Epsom salts into the whirlpool beneath the spigot. She pours the wine, undresses, and settles into the bath. When the water is high enough, she pushes the faucet with her foot and turns it off. Takes several long swallows of Shiraz. And then she burrows neck-deep into the water, knees sticking up and cold, the rest of her skin stinging with salt and heat. Closes her eyes.

She exhales, emptying the past two days with each breath until a knock comes on the door. "Pizza's here," Will says through the wood.

"Okay, thanks."

"Want us to wait for you?"

"No, don't bother. I'll be a bit more."

"Can I come in?"

"Yeah, okay."

Will's eyes stay averted. "It's your phone," he says, holding it out to her. "It's been buzzing like a fiend."

Katherine sits up, back arched in a C-shape, breasts hidden against her knees. She reaches over the edge of the tub and finds her towel, dries her one hand, and then reaches for the phone. He drops it into her palm. "They're almost all from Robin."

She settles back in the bath and Will shuts the warped door with an extra tug so it closes all the way. Her phone's blue light winks at her, like yesterday evening at the hotel. She shakes her wet hand, rubs it over her hair, and swipes the screen. Seven missed calls, six from Robin Wilcox and one from Unavailable. No voice mails.

Robin is her business partner; she calls Katherine all the time, but not from this number. It's Thomas; Katherine had entered his cell phone number under Robin's name, as a safeguard.

She can't talk to him now, doesn't know if she'll talk to him again, ever. She dips beneath the bathwater, a baptism of forgetting, holding her breath as long as she can, cheeks puffing out, eyes closed. She washes Thomas away in a soup of burning salt and soap scum and her own impurities. She sends him down the drain in a whirlpool of regret. Then she wipes any lingering thoughts of him away with a dank-smelling towel, clean but left too long in the washer.

Dressing in yoga pants and one of Will's warm sweat-shirts, she joins her family in the kitchen for pizza. They're counter eaters, all of them, standing and holding food over their hands instead of plates, the boys wiping drips of grease from the floor with the toes of their socks. Katherine grumbles about stains and napkins, and tears a paper towel off the roll for each of them. Will laughs and drinks Pepsi straight from the bottle. It's as if yesterday never happened; at least for the moment, there's enough melted cheese to cover it all.

CHAPTER SEVEN

His body is identified after four days. Wright shows up on the steps of the brownstone, alone, with a photograph and asks Ada if it's Julian. She nods. His face is bruised around the mouth and chin, but otherwise he could be sleeping. Wright hands her more papers and talks of claiming the body. Her eyes float from his face to the children playing across the street. Two of them, Alonzo and Marcus, foster children of the woman living on the third floor. They toss leaves and pebbles down the metal drain grate at the curb.

She's like a four-year-old, navigating this thing called death, with all its traditions and requirements. When someone passed away in her community, it's a pine box and four men with pickaxes and shovels digging a hole by nightfall. How much more complicated it is here. She's seen movies now. A fancy coffin and special burial outfit. Pictures of the deceased and flowers and lots of people talking about what a great guy the dead person had been.

Sophie volunteers to handle the funeral, seems honored and relieved she's able to oversee these last things, her anointing of the body with nard. Ada gives her Pastor Ray's number, but Sophie makes arrangements at St. Michael the Archangel. The Romanesque revival rises up around them, its arches pointing into heaven. Ada has never been in a church like this before, the air filled with the scent of melted wax and a spicy haze of incense. The voices of all those speaking around her are somehow both dulled and amplified by the vaulted ceiling and the cathedral's thick, stone floors. "But Julian's not Catholic anymore," Ada says, drawing a scowl from Sophie.

"You never stop being Catholic," she says.

The church fills rapidly. Ada recognizes very few faces— from Holy Zion, from the neighborhood, friends of Julian's she's met. The reporters, she thinks, must be here because the funeral of a plane crash victim is still newsworthy. But the others? Ada tries to survey the crowd discretely from her place in the front pew, Hortense and Mark on one side of her, Sophie and the rest of Julian's more immediate family on the other. She sees well-dressed people with tans and expensive jewelry, people in muted suits shaking hands, and a few thick men dressed in black with dark glasses and earpieces. Though she doesn't have a good memory, she's certain she's seen some of these strangers on the covers of magazines in the grocery line, or in search engine pictures.

"Who are all these people?" she asks Sophie.

Julian's sister stares at her. "They've come to pay their respects."

Ada wants to say *I know that,* since Sophie speaks as if she's what Grandmother would call a sandwich short of a picnic. But Hortense squints and nods a little, leaning around her to get Sophie's attention. "She doesn't know, Soph. I don't think Julian ever told her."

"Told me what?"

"How famous he is," Hortense says.

"Famous?"

Again, Sophie inspects Ada, her eyes so like Julian's Ada must turn her head away. "My goodness. He didn't, did he?" She shakes her head, the tiniest of smiles on her flaky lips. "That's my brother."

Hortense seems more agitated than amused. "Julian doesn't just take pictures. He's world-renowned for his photography. He's won a slew of awards, Pulitzers, AP, even recognition from the president. He's seen . . . *things.* He's brought images to people they never would have known, if not for him. He's risked his life, for pity's sake. He . . . he . . ."

Her voice trails away, and Ada, less surprised now by the crowd than by the urgency in Hortense's words, can only give a little shrug and stumble around for something to say. But nothing comes.

"That's why he didn't say anything," Hortense says. She's crying now. "He knew it would mean nothing to you."

Ada doesn't see Julian's photographs—any photographs, really, as she has browsed Julian's collection of photography books many times—as something more than images on paper. Beautiful images sometimes. But they don't evoke the kinds of emotions in her they seem to draw from everyone else. Vanity, her father would say, or worse, idolatry. Art is creation for the sake of creation, and that is only for Almighty God. Men must toil for their sanctification and their penance, in the briars amidst the sin of Adam.

She supposes, if she's honest, some part of her agrees, thinks it a bit silly to be taking pictures of everything from chewing gum on the pavement to politicians at their rallies when so much of importance is left undone. Then again, what does she know of doing important things? She worked at a farm store and waited with her family for Armageddon. And then she married a man she hardly knew and bumped around his home all day because she was afraid to walk down the street alone.

Hortense weeps now, face in Mark's neck, stump cupped in his hand. She has his name tattooed around her wrist bone, hidden in a garland of black wildflowers. Mark has similar ink on his ring finger instead of a wedding band. Sophie's back is to Ada as she speaks with her son and daughter. So she sits, a stranger in her love for this dead man, between the people who loved him best.

The funeral mass begins with pomp and organ and the condolences of a priest who'd never met Julian. Family members speak. Friends speak. Hortense sings to a slide show of his photographs; her voice matches the beauty of her face. She wears prosthetics in front of all these people, rubber hands growing from beneath the long sleeves of her black sweater. When they were in college, Julian said, Hortense would wear her hands to parties but after a time, take them off because she couldn't do much in them. Drunk frat boys would stumble upon them tucked between beer kegs or swimming in the bathroom sink. Startled cries periodically punctuated the music and Mark would say, "Someone's found Hortense's hands."

Sophie had asked Ada to say a few words but probably expected her to decline, and she didn't disappoint, not knowing what to say and realizing once again how much of a toddler she is in this life, still sticking random objects in her mouth in an attempt to understand the world around her.

Ashes to ashes. Dust to dust. Sophie had arranged to have Julian cremated, telling Ada those were his wishes. Sophie had spoken to her brother about it before, had all his funeral plans notated in her family organizer. "He didn't expect to get married, Ada. You caught him by surprise."

What a surprise.

The church has a huge parish hall, not attached but built beside it, and the reception takes place there. Ada stands with Sophie and family near the door as attendees shuffle through, touching her hands and shoulder, making introductions, giving those clumsy hugs of strangers, all arms and air between them. Eventually she disentangles from the crowd and locks herself in a bathroom stall, watching the feet of women come and go beside her. They chat as they fix lipstick at the mirror and Ada spins toilet paper into ragged, cigarette-like tubes.

"I haven't even seen the wife."

"They were only married a few months, you know."

"She'll make out big, with the airline settlement. I heard on the news they're talking over a million per person."

"And I heard Gary Sinise was here."

"I'd rather look for him."

Giggling. Water running. More conversation covered by the automated dryer. And then a knock on her stall. "Ada, I see your shoes."

She twists the handle and Hortense steps in to join her. In her sleek black boots, the woman stands a head taller than Ada. And when Hortense offers her arms to her, Ada goes into them, bone against bone, brow against clavicle. She was hugged this way as a child, before she grew taller than her mother. Before she grew too old to be comforted by the body of another.

"I'm lost," she says.

Hortense tightens her grasp. "We all are."

CHAPTER EIGHT

No one brings casseroles when someone almost dies, but plenty of people get awful nosy. "Excitement by association," Bryce tells Katherine as the phone calls come, mothers of the boys' friends, women she's nodded at a few times at the church, clients, and neighbors. The conversations begin the same, with an *Oh my goodness, how are you doing? Are you okay? You're so lucky.* Then, after a few brief sentences by Katherine about being fine and really, it's not that big of a deal because holding a ticket for a flight is not anywhere close to getting on an airplane, the caller launches into a story of how she almost died as well, so she totally understands how Katherine feels right now.

Eventually she lets the calls go straight to voice mail.

The *almost-isn't-really-almost* speeches do nothing to convince her. As much as she says it, she knows how close she came to getting on the airplane. Her solution? Refusing to consider the alternatives. She wondered and wallowed for a few days and then pushed it all aside. She can't dwell on the fact an affair saved her life. She can't act as if she were saved for a higher purpose and now has some noble mission to pursue. So she drops back into the same patterns from last week, last month, last year. Doing normal brings back normal. Even Will, for all his emotions the day after the crash, has settled into his own well-worn cycle of work and food and Fox News.

She picks up Evan from his photography club meeting and he's all a-chatter about his day, mostly the antics of friends in the cafeteria and little about learning. "Want to hear Andrew's joke?"

"This is what I'm sending you to school for?"

"It's funny. Just say yes."

"Okay. Yes. Tell me."

"How are a cigarette and a hamster the same?"

Katherine sighs. "I have no idea. How?"

"They're both perfectly harmless until you stick them in your mouth and light them on fire."

"That's very funny."

"You're not laughing."

"I am on the inside." She squints at the traffic light. "Is there an arrow?"

"Yeah."

She turns into the supermarket parking lot. "I have to pick up a few things. Coming in, or staying in the car?"

"That depends. Can I get a soda?"

"No."

Evan unstraps his seat belt. "I guess I'll come in anyway."

She doesn't need anything from the store, not really. She does it to continue deflating, releasing the stress and disbelief, and flattening to regular size. She works through her list. Pay the cable bill. *Check.* Vacuum the living room rug. *Check.* Make a meal everyone will complain about because they don't like kidney beans, and doesn't she remember that? *Check.* Schedule a house showing, wax her eyebrows, replace the mildewed shower curtain with the new one she bought on sale six months ago and stashed in the linen closet, forgetting about it until the other day when she refolded the fitted sheets. And now, a nice, mundane trip to Shop Rite.

Inside the store, Katherine asks, "Divide and conquer?"

"Sure," Evan says. He holds out his hand for his half of the list. She folds it neatly and scores it with her fingernail, tears it over the edge of the shopping cart.

"I'll be in produce when you're done," she says. She always finishes with produce. *Check.*

Evan has the bottom of the list—toilet paper, napkins, cream cheese—all things on the far side of the store. She begins in the middle and works her way to the deli counter, then the bakery, and then the fruit and vegetables. She's sifting through green beans when she hears, "Kate?"

She turns instinctually, and Susanna Bailey is there. They're not close, though they've known one another for years. She's mother to Seth, Evan's best friend since kindergarten.

And wife to Thomas.

"Susie."

"My goodness, how are you?" She gives Katherine a quick but sincere hug. Oh, so sincere.

"I'm fine, really."

"I've been meaning to call, but Thomas told me not to overwhelm you. He figured you were getting calls from everyone."

"I—"

"Mom, hey, there wasn't any Philadelphia fat free left, so I got the store brand. That okay?" It's Evan, with Seth riding on the front of the cart.

"Seth, get off there. You're not five," Susanna says, and when he steps down Thomas appears, just behind Evan, a blue basket hanging on his forearm.

"Katherine, good to see you," he says.

Her hands sprout perspiration; she squeezes the handle in front of her, the plastic slickening beneath her skin. The grocery list, pinched between two fingers, flutters to the ground. Both she and Thomas bend to get it and she smells his shampoo, so familiar because Will uses the same kind. How many nights has she been in bed with her husband, her face cradled in his pillow because she switched it with hers, that scent in her nostrils so she can imagine she's with Thomas and not Will? She pulls back, letting him crouch and rescue the paper. He offers it to her. When she doesn't reach for it, he sets it on the child seat in the cart.

"Thanks." She coughs into her shoulder.

"I know you've been busy with more important things," he says, "but is Evan going on the scouting trip?"

"That's right," Susanna says. She bites her knuckle. "I'm

glad you remembered. We were wondering if Will could take Seth along too. We'll be out of town that weekend. It's our anniversary."

"They're going," Katherine mumbles. "But you'll have to ask Will yourself."

"I'll call," Thomas says, his voice soft.

"Evan, let's go." She turns to Susanna and forces a bright smile. "So glad I ran into you. We'll have to do coffee soon."

Susanna nods. "Great, good. Don't be a stranger."

Katherine swings the shopping cart toward the checkout area and slows only when Evan bashes her Achilles tendons with his own cart. She swears, turns, and says, "Darn it, Evan, pay attention for once in your life."

He withers. "Sorry."

Her ankles throb. She stacks her groceries onto the conveyor belt, watches Susanna and Thomas two lines down; he stacks twelve packs of spring water in front of the cashier, something she knows makes him crazy, or at least he's told her he can't stand that Susanna insists on bottled when they have perfectly filtered well water of their own. He doesn't seem bothered by it now, making small talk with the young cashier as Susanna spins her wild curly hair into an elastic band and then fixes a button come undone on his plaid shirt.

A shirt Katherine bought for him.

She slices her debit card through the machine and mashes her pin code into the keypad, grabs all five of the bags, and stumbles to the car. After dropping the plastic sacks into the backseat, she turns the key in the ignition and sits, feeling the idle through her hands, breathing deeply. Her entire body stings. Evan climbs in beside her and sits quietly, contorting his double-jointed fingers into odd positions.

"Mom?" he asks finally.

"I'm fine. Just a sudden headache." She maneuvers the car out of its parking spot and, once home, she and Evan climb the back deck with grocery bags swinging from their arms. A box waits by the door, a stripe of decorative rainbow tape around the center, holding it closed. "That looks like something Aunt Jen would send," Evan says. He drops the bag and finds the package's shipping label. "It is from her."

"Bring it in," Katherine tells him. "And don't trample the eggs."

She has her way of unpacking food. All of it comes out of the bags, lined up on the kitchen island. Freezer items get put away first, and then things for the refrigerator. Pantry items. Toiletries, paper products, and cleaning supplies. She sends Evan to take out the trash and recycling, cuts through the thick tape with a steak knife, something Will hates. *Use a scissor*, he complains when he sees her. She has an idea what the box holds, and when she pulls back the flaps to plastic-wrapped marshmallow white, she knows she's right. Her coat. Jennifer sent it back to her with a note: *As much as I love it, I knew you wouldn't want to lose this. Call me when your head is on straight . . . J.* And a big smiley heart.

"What is it?" Evan asks, coming up from the basement.

"My coat. I accidently left it at your aunt's house. Wash your hands."

"I know. I know." He drizzles blue Dawn into one palm, rubs, and rinses with cold water. "Need help with anything else, or can I hit the Xbox?"

"Homework first."

"Don't have any."

"Fine, then." She sighs. "You can play for a little while."

Evan points at her with both hands, as if his fingers are guns, and makes a loud sucking noise. "Thanks, Mom. You're the best."

"Tell me that when you're not getting your own way." Katherine flips a bag of Doritos at him. "And take these. But don't eat them all. It's tacos for dinner."

"Kay-kay." He disappears into the family room.

She wants to think she's unpacking any garment, removes it from the static-charged plastic and shakes the fabric. Without looking, her hand finds the business card in the pocket. She opens the junk drawer and buries it beneath the chaos of loose receipts, Post-it note pads, old birthday cards, highlighters, and batteries that may or may not be dead. She takes a 9-volt and holds the terminals against her tongue, creating a sour twinge, and then drops it back with the others, slamming the drawer closed. The coat she tosses on top of a black trash bag of to-be-donated clothes in the laundry room. The box she kicks down the basement stairs; one of the boys will throw it in the recycle bin tomorrow.

CHAPTER NINE

Julian planned for her, should something happen to him. She doesn't know if this is because he had some sort of premonition, or because he knew she would be lost within the labyrinth of mopping up death. But he had taken all his important papers to Hortense and Mark—bank accounts, life insurance policy, a list of bills, the deed to Julian's building, and title to the Jeep—and they are able to go through it all with Ada, helping her fill out claim forms and catalog what needs to be done each month.

"We can take care of it all for you," Mark offers.

Ada shakes her head. "I need something to do."

"Are you sure you want to stay . . . there? Downtown, I mean. In the brownstone," Hortense asks. "You're welcome to come here with us."

Ada doubts either Hortense or Mark would want her in their home, but Hortense offered because Julian would have wanted her to. Perhaps he made her promise. Both their faces furrow at the offer, lines etched more deeply than they'd been four weeks ago. Ada rubs the rolled hem of her sweater; it needs to be steamed down and pressed but she doesn't iron anymore. That had been one of her chores in the community, keeping her father's clothes wrinkle free. She'd gladly never touch an iron again.

"Thanks for the offer, but I'll be fine," she tells them.

She thinks that's true, so far. She's been able to get what she needs when she needs it—groceries, cash, even fast food one afternoon at the Wendy's two blocks down, a baked potato and lemonade. She spends time reading through random articles on Wikipedia, fascinated by the world past and present. She considers again Julian's encouragement to try college, even a single class online, and studies the GED book he purchased for her because she needs a high school equivalency diploma before she can apply to one of the local universities. And she's made the spare room in the brownstone her own, though she's told no one about this, carefully scrubbing the cheerful yellow paint from her cuticles before meeting with Hortense so no questions will be asked. The walls are bright as dandelions, the bedding from Holy Zion's thrift store, the framed pictures torn from one of Julian's oversized art books. Van Goghs, all three. And her turquoise vase, the one she found in the free pile on the curb just weeks after she and Julian married.

She hadn't left the house without him. He took her someplace each day: a restaurant, a park, the bank, shopping, museums and college theater shows and the Saturday farmers' market. This particular day he'd been in his studio all morning and afternoon, clicking around on the computer. "Why don't you take a walk?" he asked her.

"Alone?"

"Yeah."

"I can wait for you."

"I'm swamped with work, Ada. These photos should have been edited, well, a while ago. I just need to get through them."

"It's because of me, isn't it?"

He sighs. "Not everything is your fault."

"But if we weren't married, you'd have time to—"

"Enough, okay? I'm not having this conversation again." His voice, usually no sharper than a butter knife, digs with tiny, serrated teeth.

"I'm sorry." She twisted the thin gold band around her finger. They didn't have rings when they married. Julian purchased these a couple weeks later. She chose.

Julian stopped clicking, spun around in his chair, and then stood to hug her. "No, I am. I shouldn't have snapped. I'm going to be at this all night, though. Really, take a walk. It's gorgeous out. I can call Hortense and see if she'll go."

"No, no." She wasn't comfortable with her husband's friend, the way she laughed so easily at everything, the way she sometimes looked at Julian like the women in her community looked at her father—in awe of the prophet, but also desiring him. "I'll try."

"Just walk straight in one direction on the sidewalk for ten minutes, then turn around and come back. Don't turn or cross the street and you won't get lost. But take your phone. Call me for any reason. I'll come get you." He suddenly looked more nervous than her. "You don't have to go. I'm not making you."

"I want to," Ada said, though she didn't. She thought he wanted her to, so she would do it. Because she interrupted his work. Because she was more of a child to him than a wife.

She tucked her cell phone into a small purse she slung across her torso. After groping with the doorknob several seconds too long, she stepped onto the sun-warmed stoop, down to the uneven sidewalk. Then she walked, head down, watching her sandals, occasionally seeing another set of feet pass hers. She checked the time at every corner, and after exactly ten minutes she stopped, planning to turn for home, but instead saw three children poking through a heap of household items at the curb. They loaded things into a plastic milk crate tied to the seat of a bicycle. "What are you looking at, lady?" the tallest boy, the one holding the bicycle upright, said.

"I, uh, well, nothing," she stammered. Her hand went into her purse for her phone.

"It's free, okay. See that? F. R. E. E. Free." He snapped his fingers at a small round boy. Pointed. "Show her."

The little one pulled the plastic sign from the ground. One side announced GARAGE SALE in orange letters. The other did, in fact, have the word FREE written on it in purple Magic Marker. "You want something?"

"I don't think so."

"More for us," the tall boy said. "Come on."

He pedaled away. The other boys followed, running, one waving a curtain rod in the air. Ada peeked at the mound. A box of dishes and coffee mugs and drinking glasses. A baby swing without the fabric seat cover. A nightstand, missing the drawer, a corner gnawed away. Another box of broken toys and little plastic Happy Meal figures. And a third box of this and that—acrylic yarn, placemats, panty hose, snowmen figurines, and something aqua. She took a few steps closer. A vase. She looked both ways and, seeing no one, took the vase from the box. It was the color of the sky, milky before the snow, the glass surface textured with raised bubbles. Trumpet shaped and only four inches tall, the top ruffled somewhat unevenly, and the bottom ended in a round base.

She walked home more quickly, clutching the vase. The glass warmed and seemingly disappeared into her palm, the tiny hobnails a reminder she still held onto it.

In the house she moved it between different surfaces before finding its place, on the front windowsill where the sunlight shone around it and she could see it from anywhere she stood or sat. It was the first thing ever that was hers alone, and the only item here in Julian's home that did not come with him. When he finally wandered downstairs to grab something to eat, his eyes flickered toward it but he said nothing, letting Ada have it all for herself.

* * *

She thinks people are looking at her differently as she walks to the corner market, and then does her best to shake the paranoia from her mind. She blames the weather, a drab, neutral day with equal parts sun and cloud, and the grainy air of impending rain. Normally she wouldn't go out on such a day, especially since she has no umbrella, but the refrigerator is empty except for bottles of catsup and relish, and a nearly expired container of Greek yogurt.

The automatic door swishes open and there's an initial blast of hot air on her head before she moves deeper into the store. Here the odd glances seem longer and accompanied by whispers. She checks the back of her skirt, the soles of her shoes, just in case she's dragging toilet paper, or worse. But no, nothing embarrassing goes on behind her. She uses her canvas market bag instead of a cart, fills it with apples and celery and bagels, and goes to the checkout line. A vacuum-like sensation surrounds her, as if all the customers have collectively gasped and then held their breaths, and there's no longer any oxygen for her to inhale. Her vision flickers, and she realizes she's looking at the cover of *People*. On it, the headline, The Final Moments of Flight 207. And there's a photograph of two women clinging to one another, eyes squished so tightly closed they fold beneath their fat cheeks, heads conjoined. At the bottom of the photo, in smaller but still bolded print, **The Last Photographs of Julian Goetz.**

Ada dumps the contents of the basket in front of the clerk, adding a magazine to the mess. Once she pays, she takes her bag and rushes out of the market, down the street, and locks herself into the brownstone. The grocery bag she drops next to the front door. She wheezes, leaning on the wall, magazine rattling against her thigh. Her joints lock; she can't bend to sit on the floor, but slides down the painted sheetrock until her tailbone catches on the baseboard molding, bumps over it, and settles against the oak plank flooring, legs splayed stiff and straight before her.

The pages are slick beneath her fingertips. She leafs through the table of contents and award show gossip before landing on the first photo, the one from the cover, the caption naming sisters, both in their fifties, returning home from visiting their mother. Ada turns the page. The next picture of a man kneeling in prayer in front of his seat, one stiff arm held toward the stewardess who appears to be trying to get him back into the chair. The man doesn't look at her, his forehead against his fist. His other palm is turned up toward the uniformed woman. *Stop*, it says. *Leave me.*

Another page. Another picture. This one of a young mother hugging her sleeping infant beneath her chin. Then a shot of the oxygen masks dangling from the ceiling, a twenty-something woman sobbing as she tugs it over her face, eyes and cheeks blackened with runny mascara. Three stoic men, eyes closed, hands clasped. Another man, mouth frozen in a terrified O. Another stewardess, helping an obese woman adjust her mask, touching the passenger's hair with her manicured nails, stroking it. *It will be okay*, her fingers say.

And then the photo meant only for her. An airline napkin stained with a half-moon of coffee and Julian's unmistakable lettering in ink:

A-
I love you
–J

Finally, the last picture—the back of seats and a flash in the upper left corner. The caption speculates this was the explosion that blew the plane from the sky, throwing it down into the river, ablaze, like Lucifer himself.

CHAPTER TEN

Katherine shows a house at ten in the morning, a charming Cape Cod with a two-car garage and gleaming oak floors. Great schools. Great street. The couple isn't in love with the upstairs bedrooms—too small, they say, and the slanted ceilings don't help—or the one-and-three-quarter bathrooms, as they really wanted two tubs rather than a tub and a tiny walk-in shower. She knows she's lost them when they learn the washer and dryer are in the basement, and tells them she has three more homes in their price range that might work better for them. They have to get to work, though, so they want her to send them links to pictures on the realtor website and they'll get back to her if they want to schedule showings.

She waves good-bye, knowing she won't hear from them, and locks the doors.

People used to be less particular about home buying. Good bones and a fair price in the right location were often enough to close the deal. People didn't mind putting in a bit of sweat equity or—God forbid!—buying what they could afford and slowly, room by room, improving the house as a little extra money became available. Not anymore. Now outdated meant appliances more than three years old and the living room walls painted in last season's trendy color.

She misses the feeding frenzy of ten years ago, when houses were purchased like fast-food meals, when she first began and couldn't believe how easy it was to make money. Now she's fortunate to sell two houses a month. Whoever said the poor couldn't afford to be picky had it wrong, at least in her experience. Those with the least to spend want more than the wallet allows because they know they'll be stuck with it for a long time.

Will thinks she walks women—dragging their husbands— through house after house as the ladies judge everything from the ceramic tile to the picket fence. She does more than that, though. She finds people *homes*. Single mothers who are forced to relocate after their marriages unravel. Newly wed couples expecting their first child, jittery with the responsibility of another life, the transition into adulthood. And she helps people say good-bye to pieces of their hearts when she pounds that FOR SALE sign into their property. The widower, downsizing, running from memories. The family in the midst of job loss or illness or crisis, desperate to find a way to cram two thousand square feet of stuff into an eight-hundred-square-foot apartment. The empty nesters, weeping as they scrape their name off the mailbox in front of the place they raised their family.

No more work to do today, except browse the new listings. Katherine drives to the office—a one-room storefront that used to be a hairdresser's studio—and instead of her business partner sitting at the other desk she finds Grace, Robin's daughter, clicking on the Internet. "Aunt Kate," the fifteen-year-old says, though they are unrelated by blood, "you've gotta see this."

"See what? And where's your mom?"

"Bathroom."

"No, I'm here," Robin says, wiping her hands on a paper towel as she emerges from the water closet. "Have you seen them yet?"

"Not yet, unless she's got the magazine," Grace says.

"What are you two talking about?"

"Kate, you won't believe it. There was some photographer on the plane that crashed. He was some big deal, I guess, though I never heard of him. He only lived three hours from here, too—"

"Mom. Not important."

"Don't be snotty," Robin says. Grace sinks lower in the oversized leather chair and wheels it from the desk. "Anyway, this guy, Julian Gotts, Goats—"

"Goetz." The girl swivels in circles.

"Right, Julian Goetz. He actually took pictures while the plane was going down."

Katherine moves to the computer. "What?"

"I know. Insane, right? He's about to crash. What's he doing with a camera? But the camera was found in the wreck and someone leaked them to *People*. They're horrible,

Kate. I can't describe it. You just have to see for yourself. I mean, I don't think anyone knew they were absolutely going to die. They look really scared but not desperate. But we know. And I keep thinking, you could have been in one of those pictures." Tears catch in Robin's mascara-clotted lashes; she blinks to dislodge them.

People's website is up and Katherine sees the first photo, two women in oxygen masks clutching one another. She brings up the second, a man in prayer. And a third, an airline napkin with a scribbled love note on it. "I can't look at these."

"There aren't many more," Robin says, wriggling next to Katherine to take the mouse. "Not on the site. They want you to buy the magazine. The rest are in there."

"No. I just—" She clamps her hand over her mouth as she runs to the bathroom, stands over the toilet, and swallows back her vomit. It burns going down, and she waits, still covering her lips, knowing no wall of fingers can prevent her from getting sick if her stomach decides to erupt again. She sees her reflection in the bowl, flushes it away, but it returns in the stillness of the blue water.

"Kate?" Robin asks.

"I'm going home."

"Wait—"

She doesn't.

Will's truck is in the driveway. Katherine figures he's home to eat lunch and does find him in the kitchen, but he paces, tapping a wad of rolled-up paper against his leg. He sees her and says, "Why aren't you answering your phone?"

"It's dead," she tells him.

"You think, by now, you'd be able to remember to keep it charged."

"If you want to talk to me like I'm an imbecile, I'm going upstairs to lie down."

Closing his eyes, he says, "It's just that I've been driving all over, looking for you."

"I'm here now. What is it?"

He shakes the pages open, bends them backwards; they crackle like the finger joints of an old man. "Have you seen this?" It's *People* magazine.

"Enough of it."

They've been living in the *almost* of the crash, both of them, but it isn't enough to push them toward the change both honestly want. *Almost* too easily becomes *not quite*, which slips into *barely*, which is effortlessly shrouded in routine and familiarity. *Barely* can be ignored.

Now, however, they've both put her face into those photographs. It doesn't matter that she never set foot on the airplane; the pictures transport her there, sharpening the focus on what could have been. And the guilt Katherine lives with, knowing she had been saved by choosing her lover over her family, swells with the images of those who did not have any choices to make.

She has to tell him about Thomas.

They are not a religious family. Yes, they go to church many Sundays, if there's nothing else more pressing to do and if they're all up on time. It's the same Methodist congregation they've been attending since Evan was five. They

didn't attend out of faith, but because of desperate promises both she and Will made to a vague notion of some
supernatural higher power while Evan was so sick. *God, if
you're out there, please save our baby.* Evan lived, and there
was an obligation to at least appear to make an attempt
at living up to their end of the bargain, just in case this
God really did exist and, if not appeased, would snatch
back their son's health from him. Throughout the years
Katherine, and probably Will also, continued to make
moral decisions based on some twisted *do ut des*. No
cheating on taxes, or only within the bounds of what was
deemed acceptable by the general population and the IRS.
No unethical business practices. Volunteer work here and
there, donations to the food bank at Thanksgiving and
Toys for Tots at Christmas. Shuffling the boys back and
forth to confirmation classes.

The affair surprised both her and Thomas, though that's
what people always say when they're having one. *We didn't
want it; it just happened.* In their case, it began with a five-
hour stint at the hot dog stand during the annual Boy Scout
fun fair. She'd known Thomas for years—scouts, birthday
parties, play dates, sleepovers—but rarely had any sort of
lengthy conversation with him. Small talk. A wave from the
car. She knew him as the busy but doting father, handsome,
professional, and making enough to live in one of the nice,
new subdivisions advertising homes from the mid-$300s.

Most of the things Will was not.

Susanna, she thought many times, was lucky.

Between slapping relish and mustard on buns, Thomas

listened to her prattle about work and the boys. He asked questions and seemed interested—those things she wanted but didn't get from Will. So when, six weeks later, she saw he had agreed to work the can drive from ten to two, she signed her name right under his. She smiled too big when she saw him. His touch lingered too long on her waist as he moved behind her to get more trash bags. She wasn't surprised when he showed up at her office with take-out Thai on a day he knew, because Katherine had told him—*wink wink, nudge nudge*—Robin had a doctor's appointment and wasn't coming in.

He'd had a business trip in Cleveland, and since her sister lived there, he asked her to come. Jennifer enthusiastically agreed to cover for Katherine because she was a seize-the-moment, do-whatever-makes-you-happy kind of gal. Will didn't suspect anything and probably was happy for three days without her.

The news may destroy her marriage in one verbal blast. But it's been decomposing a little each day for years, and whether love dies fast or slow, there's still a corpse in the ground eventually.

"Will—"

"Me first," Will says. He looks at her, pulls a stool out from the island. "You should sit."

"No, I'm good." Katherine's head suddenly aches. She removes the clip from her auburn hair and shakes it loose, then rubs the back of her scalp where the ponytail has been fastened. Her follicles sting as she manipulates the strands.

"I don't know how to start."

"Just say it."

"Okay. I've been having an affair. It's over. I ended it after the crash because I . . . I realized . . . God, this is hard."

The room tilts; she wriggles into her corner, grips the edge of the counter. This isn't right. Will is speaking *her* words.

"I realized it was a stupid thing to do and I wanted . . . us . . . instead. If there still can be an us. These pictures . . ." He holds the magazine by one thin page. Shakes it. It convulses, dark and glossy, reminding her of a dying bat she once saw as a child. The paper rips and the bundle of pages falls to the counter, slips to the floor. Will mauls the remains still in his hand, squeezing and crumpling and rolling them through his fingers. "Everything is more real now."

Katherine's fatty places—upper arms, thighs, buttocks—tingle with a cold, menthol-like shock. "Who?" she asks.

"Does it matter?"

"I don't know yet."

"Rosie Rimes. And then Meghan Parker before that."

"Both from work."

"Yeah. I don't know what I was thinking." He opens his fist and shakes the shredded magazine onto the island, gently, sowing seeds of regret. "You're going to leave."

"No." She scrunches her hands into fists and runs her thumbs over her fingers. Her wedding set cuts into her skin. "Because I was about to tell you the same thing."

He snorts. "Don't do that."

"I'm not joking."

He looks at her. Swears. "You are serious."

Katherine nods.

"Who?"

She hesitates, not because she wants to lie, but because of the families' close ties. A couple of coworkers Katherine may possibly see once a year at the company Christmas party is one thing. A man Will sits next to during scouting events multiple times a month is another. She doesn't want a confrontation, or even a conversation, to take place between the two men. "I'll tell you if you want, but—"

"Tom Bailey."

"Yes."

"You know, I . . . when Seth told Evan his dad was in Ohio on business the same time you were there, I thought . . . and then it was, 'No way. Not Straight Kate.'" Will chops at the bridge of his nose with his hand, shakes his head, and chuckles without humor. "You stayed the extra day for him?"

She nods.

"I guess screwing around can save your life."

"Don't do that."

"You're the one sleeping with him."

"Was! And you seem to be forgetting what you just confessed to me."

"You're my wife!"

"You should have remembered that when you were in bed with Rosie Red Lips."

They're shouting. Again. Always.

Will kicks the magazine; it skids over the vinyl, lodges beneath the refrigerator. "I can't talk about this now," he says, slamming the back door. His truck engine starts and revs, and then fades away as he speeds off down the street. Katherine doesn't care if he comes back or not, though she knows she'll see him again in a few hours, when the boys are home. He won't make her explain his absence. Neither wants their children to come face-to-face with the sins of the parents.

Katherine washes her face and changes from her clothes, all of them. Clothing holds memories for her. She remembers what she wore when going to the hospital for each child, when Will proposed, when she earned her real estate license, when she purchased her first vehicle—at thirty-six—with her own money, when her father died.

Her white coat.

She won't be able to wear these things again: the ivory cashmere sweater Will bought for their last anniversary; burgundy micro-wale corduroys that make her size twelve bottom look at least a ten; the socks, a stocking stuffer from one of the boys, probably Evan since they're colors she likes and he'd notice those things before his brother. She crams them in a Price Chopper bag. The panties she tosses in the hamper. They're white Fruit of the Loom bikini-style and she has dozens of the same. Once they're washed she won't know the difference. She pauses with her bra in hand. Her favorite. Cold, naked, she adds it to the bag and triple knots the handles. Redresses. Then she hides the bag beneath the others in the large trash can and drags it out to the curb. Pickup tonight, thank goodness. She doesn't have to wait for her misdeeds to be hauled away.

CHAPTER ELEVEN

The doorbell rings while Ada lies on the floor and she ignores the sound at first, focus shifting from one uncomfortable pressure point to another. Her hipbone, grinding against the wood. Her shoulder, twisted beneath her weight. Her neck contorted in an obtuse angle. She tries to feel all these pains at one time but her body won't allow it. The ringing comes again and now she moves because it's the only reason she has at the moment to get off the ground. The magazine sticks to her face; she wipes it away and kicks it toward the wall as she lurches forward, grabbing the doorknob for support.

She squints through the peephole. It's Wright, from the airline. "Mrs. Goetz. Please."

Ada cracks the door. "Why are you here?"

"Let me come inside."

"No."

He does anyway, gently, reaching his arm inside and

taking Ada by the elbow, steering her away from the door so he can move through it. She does nothing to stop him because, despite her words, she hasn't any *no* inside her. It was never allowed growing up. Hesitation brought a riding crop to the bare backside, five or ten whacks, dependent on who did the whacking. Outright disobedience garnered blue welts on the skin, cracked lips, loose teeth. *The wages of sin are death*, the prophet told them. *This is nothing.*

"You've seen them," Wright says.

"How could you?" She's crying, finally, for the first time since learning of Julian's death. Her thin form quivers and Wright stands, helpless, seemingly so far away from her, though if she reaches out her arm she can touch him.

"We didn't release the photos, I promise you. They were stolen. Leaked. We're doing what we can to find out who did it. It's a short list. He'll be caught."

"Why would someone do this?"

"Money."

Ada can't comprehend. "Please, go."

Wright looks at her. "Can I at least help you inside?"

She shakes her head. "Go."

He hesitates. A kind man, grandfatherly, he doesn't want to abandon Ada in the entryway alone in her current condition. And she knows, again, that she'd be unable to refuse him if he led her to the couch, tucked her under a blanket, soothed her with a cool washcloth on her forehead—all things she needs. But he's also an intelligent man, and the airline doesn't need any more problems, least of all a lawsuit from a dead passenger's wife who says a stranger refused to leave her home. Wright grimaces, his lips screwed up all sideways on his face. "Call if you need anything," he says, closing the door behind him.

Ada's trembling shakes her to the floor and she crawls, tears dripping from the tip of her nose, to the area rug in the living room. She can't manage to swing her body onto the sofa. She does try, but the leather is too slippery and her arm too gauzy, and her skirt twisted too tightly around her knees. She gives up, curling up on the floor instead, with her back against the legs of the couch, and pulls a cushion down to hide herself, the weight a comfort on her soul.

* * *

The lamp beside the chair flicks on, and she blinks at the pick-toed boots at eye level. Ada rolls her eyes upward, following the slick patent leather, the skinny jeans, the patterned blouse. Hortense. She reaches down and hooks Ada in the armpits, hoisting her with a grunt, easing her onto the end of the couch. Then she replaces the cushion, forcing it into position with her knee. "You should answer your phone."

"I don't even know where I put it." Ada's face cracks with dried tears.

"That Wright guy called. From Union North. He said you might need me."

"Have you seen them?"

"Ada, the entire universe has seen them."

"Not everyone," she says, thinking of her mother. Her

sisters. The women of Abram's Covenant weren't allowed to use technology, unless it was a phone, or the cash register at the farm store. They could type on the computer in a word-processing program if instructed by a man and overseen by a man—for their own protection, of course; the weaker vessels must be shielded from anything that may disrupt their purity. They couldn't drive, or bank, or manage money other than making change for customers.

Unless her father decides to show the photos to her mother, she will not know of them. She won't know Julian's dead. She won't be thinking of Ada, alone and full of mourning. But Ada thinks of her. She wants her mother.

She has no one else.

All those around her now are here only for Julian's sake. Mark and Hortense. Sophie. Pastor Ray and the fine, fine people of Holy Zion. Even the representatives from the airline. She wants someone to love her. Without Julian, all she has left is her family.

"I think I'm going home," she says.

Hortense drops an afghan on Ada's legs, stretches it around her. "This is your home."

"Home, home."

The microwave beeps. Hortense abandons the blanket, leaving Ada's frozen toes peeking from under it. She moves, tucking the edge beneath her feet, winding it over her shoulders until only her head is exposed. Hortense returns with two mugs of tea on Julian's rosewood cutting board. She sets the makeshift tray on the side table and takes one for herself before perching on the arm of the opposite end of the couch, the mug clenched between her wrist bones. She raises it to her lips. Winces. Then she balances it on her thigh. "When I was born, my parents were stunned, to say the least. The doctor who delivered me thought there could be more wrong with me than just my hands, things that couldn't be seen yet. He said I probably wouldn't be any smarter than a mongoloid baby, if I lived that long. Yeah, his exact words.

"They named me Hortense and told me they chose it because it was a family name. My father's great-grandmother. And that's true, but the reality of it was that my mother didn't want to waste her favorite girl's name on me." Hortense snickers. "In some grand cosmic justice, she never got pregnant again, never had the perfect child she wanted. She just had me, the handless freak with the ugly name. My father regretted it, I know. He's tried to make it up to me over the years. But I think to this day I can say with certainty that my mother doesn't love me at all."

"Why are you telling me this?"

Hortense picks up the mug again, rolls it between her forearms, transfixed by whatever it is she sees on the surface of the tea—the ripples, her reflection, the hovering steam—Ada can only guess. "Julian told me a little about your life . . . before," Hortense says. "Don't do it. Don't go back."

Ada's tea grows cold, untouched; she's yet to remove her arms from beneath the afghan, a granny-square pattern Sophie made for Julian. If he noticed the flaws, he never mentioned them to Ada. She knows crochet and sees them all, had planned to make Julian another blanket for their first Christmas together, not to compete (although part of her had hoped he'd see how much more skilled her handiwork was) or replace this one but to begin piecing together a life, a history, of their own.

The television—the one Mark brought the night Julian died and hadn't taken home yet—pops on. Hortense holds the remote between her knees pressing the up arrow, over and over, until one of Julian's airplane images flashes on the screen.

"Stop," Ada says.

Throughout the night they bounce from cable news station to local news station, to late-night television. The debates rage over Julian and what he did. Angry family members of the victims decry their loved ones' privacy in their last moments, feel violated by the photographs they could not help but see. Others are grateful for one last chance to see their friends and family, no matter the situation. Media specialists question ethics and integrity and the bounds of journalism.

"How is this any different than taking pictures in a war zone? During a riot?"

"An airplane isn't a public space. People have purchased the right to be there."

"Are you then saying all people in public spaces can be photographed without permission? I know parents who would vehemently disagree."

"Julian Goetz wasn't given a chance to get waivers signed. No one knew the plane would crash. Perhaps he planned to speak to passengers when the flight was over."

"He didn't know his pictures were going to be stolen, either."

"Come on, people. He was a Pulitzer-winning photojournalist. What would you expect him to do?"

That Ada understands. As death closes in, everything is stripped away until each individual's purpose on this earth remains, and their authentic self is laid bare. No more lies. No more façades. The brave risk their lives. The cowards hide in dark corners, eyes squeezed closed, holding their breaths so no sound will give them away. The generous give. The stingy withhold. Those filled with hate spill their emotional sludge onto the clean carpet, where it oozes over the toes of anyone standing too close. Those who love radiate love. For Julian, it was more than clicking off photographs. He was a truth-shower. In the end, he could be no other.

CHAPTER TWELVE

The little brass bell above the office door tingles, and even before Katherine peers around the computer monitor on her desk, she begins thinking of commissions and listings, a well-bred Pavlov's pup, salivating for success.

"Welcome to Hearth and Home Realty. How can I help—"

Thomas stands on the doormat, white paper sack in one hand, one of those county-specific, free real estate magazines in the other. This month's cover is red, for Christmas. "Kate."

"You can't be here."

"I brought lunch," he says, holding up the bag. Red-tinged grease soaks through one corner. *For Christmas*, she thinks again, and would laugh if it didn't mean her marriage might die in the process. She knows what's in there, Thai curry, the first lunch he brought that day, when they made plans to meet at his in-laws' empty house so Katherine could walk through, price, and list it. Susanna had asked Thomas to take care of the details; she was having a hard enough time with her father's death and her mother now living with them. He kissed Katherine in the back bedroom, the one with no windows—more a crib room than anything else, but Susanna's brother grew up in that room, the only boy in a family of five children and a three-bedroom, 1950s ranch. All four girls shared the largest room in two sets of bunk beds. Susanna's parents crammed their bed into the other one, where they could open the door almost all the way but their dressers took up residence in the narrow hall. As he showed Katherine the room, Thomas told her how his mother-in-law slept on the side of the bed against the wall, and climbed in each night over the footboard because her husband, a postman who woke at four in the morning for work, went to bed first and she didn't want to disturb him. Forty years, she did that, through pregnancies, arthritis, diabetes, a mastectomy. Even after he retired and sometimes went to bed late at night, even now, it was the only way she remembered to get into a bed. *That's love*, he told her. And they found a few worn polyester blankets in the linen closet, and covered the worn olive carpet with them, the one she told him minutes before would need to be torn out if he wanted the house to sell, and their affair began.

The property sold three weeks later, a bit over market value. So they met at the Holiday Inn a half hour from their town, or at business lunches in out-of-the-way restaurants, where she would bring her portfolio and he would bring photos of his family's summer cabin, and they spent hours talking about everything their spouses had no patience for. Only once had they met at Katherine's, but never again. It had been impossible to ignore the seriousness of their infidelity among the family photo collages, the half-folded pile of teen boy laundry on the rocking chair, the mound of sneakers and work boots at the door. And, for Katherine, the smell of years. She couldn't get it out of her nostrils. Showing houses, she'd long come to recognize it, all the *existing* in a home mingled together into this one, distinct scent—deep and peppery and unattainable.

Usually she only noticed it in the homes of others. There's an immunity that comes from steeping in one's own environment; people stop noticing all that's obvious to everyone else. That missing spindle on the staircase, cut out when Evan's head became stuck in the railing. The giraffe-shaped gouge on the wood floor, courtesy of Will's attempt to move the television without help and it tumbled from his arms, shattering, marring the oak; they walk over it every day without giving it another thought, but every visitor asks, *What happened there?* All the cobwebs and chipped paint and fingerprints on the light switches. But Katherine had, that one time, been able to smell it at Birchbark Road because it was only home when she was the wife to Will and the mother to her two boys. Being there with Thomas had made her someone else. A stranger.

"I'm not hungry," she says.

He ignores her protests, removes a round, dripping food container and, after flattening the bag to make a placemat, sets it on the desk in front of her. Napkins and plastic forks appear from his pockets like magic. This visit is all sleight of hand and manipulation, she knows it. *Keep your eyes here*, the illusionist says, *watch closely*, and he waves his hands while the real trick occurs behind his back. Oh, but Thomas looks so good, snow in his hair, legs long in slim Chinos. Katherine turns away from him, focuses on the framed picture beside her telephone, of the boys, taken four years ago at Sears, the last time they did family portraits. One of Bryce, one of Evan, this one of both, and one of all four of them. The woman behind the camera wanted to take another of her and Will, but Katherine said no. She always found it curious, adult couples having pictures taken together, without their children. Then again, maybe her discomfort stemmed from the fact she didn't want to be stuck forever at that point in time, with Will, knowing how she felt about him and her marriage.

"I'm here about a house. Really," Thomas says. He opens the catalog to a dog-eared page somewhere near the middle, folds the covers over, and points to a circled listing. "This one."

She gives him what he calls her irony look, mouth scrunched small, left nostril and eyebrow lifted, cheek twitching from the odd positioning of her face. He laughs quietly with longing, and she dives into realtor mode to avoid feeling the same. She brings the listing up on the computer, an exquisite 1928 Craftsman-style home with original details and recently restored to perfection. She knows the one, having done a walk-through when it first went on the market early last month, only days before she left for Cleveland. She told Thomas about it while they were together, before either of them knew about the plane crash.

"I didn't know you and Susanna were looking to move."

"Not her. Just me. And you, too, if you wanted."

Now she stares, and Thomas holds up both his hands as if to say, *Wait, stop, hear me out,* but she plows over his silent plea with, "Have you lost your mind?"

"No. Kate, listen. When you wouldn't answer my calls, I told myself it was over and to let it go. But I can't. I miss you. I want to be with you. We—"

"I told Will."

Thomas stops. "When?"

"A few days ago."

He swears. "What in God's name were you thinking? He could tell Susanna."

"Two seconds ago you were leaving her."

"Two seconds ago you weren't telling everyone in town about us."

"Good-bye, Thomas."

"Kate—"

"I want my marriage. I don't know if it can be fixed, but I'm sure as sugar going to try."

Thomas's jaw clenches; he shifts it beneath his skin, mouth closed, chin swinging to the right. And then, with a deep breath, he steps out the door, bell singing the same song with his departure as his entrance, as if coming or going it made no difference.

The house is dark, but she sees through the front window as she parks in the driveway, the television flickering in the living room. Will is in his recliner, glass of Diet Pepsi in one hand, plate of fried chicken in his lap, hole in the toe of his gray sport socks. On the screen some rerun plays, a detective show—there are so many now she can't tell one from another—two police in an interrogation room, questioning a suspect. Good cop, bad cop. Bryce once said they played those same roles, Katherine the shrew, Will the softie. If he wanted something he sought out his father; if he wanted something done, he went to his mother. He'd been eight at the time.

So perceptive.

She's tired of always moving toward completion, of her task-oriented life, but she's been so long programmed that way she can't imagine changing. It began with Evan, with his heart. Deal with the doctors, the therapists, the insurance companies. Order his feeding supplies, administer his medications, monitor his oxygen saturation levels. *Do, do, do.* She handled the medical end of things because Will was so easily overwhelmed—not by what had to be done, but by what it meant. *His son was unwell.* His empathy paralyzed him, and he'd tell Katherine to stop describing Evan's interventions; he could feel those things in his own flesh. Searing pain between his ribs when he looked at the baby's incisions. Tightening in his sternum as doctors showed them X-ray after X-ray of Evan's lungs drowning in fluid.

Nausea and cramping to the point of vomiting when Evan was unable to keep down his feeds. Eventually Katherine's reports to him consisted of a few key phrases. *Today was a good day. The doctors are concerned but for the moment are only watching. We have to go to the hospital immediately. There's improvement and it looks like we'll be discharged soon.* And Will stayed home caring for Bryce and working a job he hated to keep insurance for Evan's care while Katherine lived in a hospital room.

When the crisis passed, she continued to do; her body no longer remembered how to be still, and her doing overtook her relationships. Will wanted to sit with her and watch a movie? She had meals to plan, and couldn't concentrate in front of the television. A lovely night for a family walk around the block? Nope, she needed to finish planting her perennials. It wasn't only her frenetic compulsion to stay busy that damaged her marriage, but she can admit now—to herself, to Will—it had played a part.

They've not spoken in four days, since both admitted their affairs. She's not sure the boys noticed; they didn't mention it. *This is what our lives have become, so disconnected no one hears the silence.* If she hadn't been carrying around her guilt, she might not have paid any attention to it either.

Our normal.

They all deserve more than that.

She takes the glass from Will, sets it on the floor where she'll inevitably forget it's there and kick it over, and replaces it with her hand. Squeezes. He turns his head toward her, tiny television villains reflecting on his corneas. "I want this," she says.

Will reaches behind her head with his free arm, draws her close enough to kiss her forehead. Her eyebrows stick in his stubble. "Can it be fixed?"

When Evan was small, they had a book of nursery rhymes and once, peeking around the corner of the stairway so they wouldn't see her, she caught Bryce reading it to his brother in his bedroom. She wanted to delight in the sweet scene without them noticing so a shoving match didn't begin, which was what usually happened when she caught the boys together in a moment of calm. Bryce couldn't have been more than seven, so Evan was four and frail and still recovering from his most recent hospitalization. The older boy read the Wheels on the Bus with sound effects and motions, and his brother giggled for more. *Please, please, piggy please?* Bryce turned the page and began Humpty Dumpty.

The panic rising in Katherine startled her, so much so the ditty was over and Bryce had moved on to Five Little Monkeys before she reacted, rushing into the room, snatching the book from his hands, and screaming, "Don't ever read that again!"

Evan started crying. Bryce sat, cross-legged and confused, staring at his empty hands. When she touched him, he jerked away, cowering into the plaid dust ruffle. She dropped to her knees and lassoed her arms around both of them, pulling them into her body, crying with her youngest. "I'm sorry. I didn't mean to yell." And she made their favorite for dessert, Jell-O pudding, not the instant kind, but the one cooked on the stove. She let Bryce pour in the milk and Evan lick the spatula, and they ate it still warm with frozen Cool Whip on top. *And sprinkles?* Evan asked. Katherine found an almost empty bottle of hundreds-and-thousands in the back of her baking cabinet and added them to the boys' treat.

She never told them why she reacted as she did, but it was the rhyme.

Humpty Dumpty sat on a wall,

Humpty Dumpty had a great fall.

All the king's horses and all the king's men?

Couldn't put Humpty together again.

Evan. It made her think of her baby, broken, stitched together, and unable to be fixed. She tucked the boys into bed that night and Will found her, home from an over-time shift at the paper mill, tearing the Humpty Dumpty pages from the three books that included it, and scrambling through the others, looking, looking.

"What the heck are you doing, Kate?"

"I know he's in *Alice in Wonderland*."

"Who? What is all this?"

There were books sprawled over the floor where she'd thrown them, some spread-eagle, some in tepees, some in odd couplings, threes and fours, half under the ruffle of the wingback chair or on the slate hearth by the wood stove and freckled in ash.

"He could die," she said, and the sobs shook her so violently she heard her teeth knocking against one another, and she tucked her tongue to the back of her throat to keep from biting it. She hadn't cried like this since Evan's diagnosis as a newborn. She'd been knocked off her wall by a fictitious egg.

"I know." And Will had held her until she could see again, holding her hair back, wiping her face with weathered fingers.

Now, eleven years later, they face one another, his fingers just as rough, her hair not nearly as long, both their shells fractured and the pieces trampled together by life. She squeezes his hand again. "We're no Humpty Dumpty."

CHAPTER THIRTEEN

Ada doesn't tell Hortense she's decided to go, knowing Julian's friend will try to persuade her otherwise, knowing how easily persuaded she is. She has little to pack—three days' worth of clothes, a toothbrush, her aqua vase and inside it, bundled in a scrap of his shirt, Julian's wedding band, returned to her by the coroner. If she needs something else she can send for it later, though most of it won't be allowed in the community, if she stays.

She wants to take something more of Julian; since everything is him here, in his house, she has a difficult time choosing. She stands in the center of each room, spinning, eyes passing over each object. Upstairs. Then downstairs. Memories varnish each object. She finally lifts the five photographs from the hallway wall and wraps them in Sophie's afghan.

A storm is coming, according to the meteorologists. She's not confident in her driving and won't risk traveling in the snow, so she needs to leave soon. Within the hour. She hasn't used the Jeep since someone from Union North brought it back from the airport parking lot, but it starts; she doesn't know if there's a reason for it not to, but she's seen television shows where cars sputter and die from being left too long without attention, and from the cold—both circumstances at hand.

She doesn't know how to get home.

Her telephone has a navigation device. She types in the name of the town; the community has no actual address, but once she drives into Eastley, she'll be able to find it.

Drive point three miles then turn left.

She listens intently to the computer-like woman's voice, maneuvering out of the city and onto the highway. Her mind wanders then. She worries about what she's wearing. A skirt that isn't nearly long enough, falling midshin instead of to her ankles. A sweater tapered at the waist and not three sizes too large. Boots Hortense bought her because she didn't have footwear for the snow, brown leather with a one-inch heel, more stylish than she'd buy for herself. She admits to liking them more than anything she'd buy herself, too, and feels a bit Hortense-like when she slips them over her calves, like she can be beautiful too.

She is still wearing skirts, though. She tried pants but felt so confined, her legs extruded like toothpaste snakes through the denim. Even sweatpants and Julian's pajama bottoms.

Her hair has been cut, one of the first things she did on her wedding night. She'd wanted to shower before the bedroom part, soaped her body from face to feet, and when she stepped over the lip of the tub into the steamy room she saw her outline in the full-length mirror, hanging on the back of the door. Her hands trembled as she wiped the condensation, and when she stood nose-to-nose with her image, the first thing she noticed was her hair, the longest strands curling at the back of her thighs, the rest pasted to her back, arms, hips, like grapevine. She thought of her father, grabbing her long tail of hair and pulling her around while she was on her knees in the dirt, scurrying to keep up. She did not need her crowning glory anymore.

Julian's nail scissors were in the medicine cabinet, gold with balled points. She held them to her hair and let them chew, chew, chew away, bird-jaws opening and closing as she squeezed and released. It took time, the metal so dull, her hair so tough, and she thought of cutting through tree roots and umbilical cords.

"Ada? You okay?"

A knock on the door. She didn't answer so Julian opened it a crack and looked in. She was naked, dead hair twisted at her feet, using something of his without having asked first. She crouched, covered with her arms and hair, turning her head away from him. "I'm sorry. I didn't—"

He shut the door.

She shook and bit her lip, the hot tears squirming between her toes. Another knock, gentle this time, and Julian came in. He wrapped a towel over her shoulders like Noah's sons, lifted her from the floor. "Julian, I'm so sorry. I should have—"

"Shh," he said, touching a finger to her lips. "You'll never get the back straight. Let me help."

Ada nods and gives him the scissors.

"These wouldn't cut dental floss. I have better." He showed her the heavy steel shears he took from the pocket of his faded jeans. She thought he wasn't wearing anything else beneath them.

He spread a towel on the closed toilet lid, and she sat, gooseflesh bubbling on her legs and upper arms. Julian noticed, turned the shower on again, as hot as possible, and the bathroom warmed. He combed her hair smooth. "How short?"

"You decide."

"No. This is all you."

Still trembling, she touched her shoulder. "Here?"

And Julian tugged and snipped, and then stood her in front of the mirror, his turn now to wipe away the condensate so she could see. His arms roped her to him, one of his hands on each of her upper arms, the back of her skull nestled between his collarbones, his chin scratching the top of her ear. Her heart raced like a startled rabbit, slowing, slowing as the mist thickened over the looking glass again and they both faded away to outlines, to phantasms, and then disappeared.

"Do you like it?" he whispered in her ear.

She nodded, and he cradled her in his arms, lifting her over the mess of hair on the floor, twenty-five years of her life cut away and, the next morning, tied up with the garbage.

In point seven miles, exit right.

Eastley. She knows landmarks, and turns left at the turquoise barn, another left at the road leading to the water tower, and then she passes the main entrance to Abram's Covenant, where gawkers and organic produce seekers and tourists park to visit the farm store. Ada drives past, counts three gravel turnoffs. She takes the fourth, leading to her family's home.

Her mother comes out to the porch as Ada turns off the car, opens the door. Rosemary Mitchell holds her hand above her eyes, blocking the glare of the sky on the snow, and Ada wonders what her mother considers the greatest abomination—her daughter's hair, her clothes, or the fact she steered her own car to this sacred place.

Women can't drive in the community.

"Julian's dead," Ada says.

Rosemary gathers her oversized sweater more tightly around her. Ada hates that sweater. It was hers, at one time, the wool coarse and pungent with specks of dried hay woven into it. She'd been forced into it all winter, her only warm outerwear, and it would scratch her exposed skin until it bled. A wool allergy. She tied dish towels around her neck to keep the eczema from flaring, and to protect her blouses from the salve she needed to keep infections away.

"Come inside."

Movement stops when she enters the house. Her sister Judith freezes with a dish in her hands. Her youngest two siblings stop their penmanship lessons, copying Bible verses on blue-veined paper. And Micah, the eldest brother at home, appears from somewhere; he's always been so stealthy, a fisher cat among their family, solitary and fierce in his attacks. He takes ahold of her mother's arm and, from the grimace on her face, pinches it. "She can't be here," he says. He's fifteen the day after Christmas, old enough to be the man in authority when their father isn't around.

Her mother says, "The man is dead."

Micah's eyes grow large. "I'll get Father."

Ada doesn't move from her place just inside the doorway. In the waiting, Ada's mother tugs the bottom of her short hair, the same way Julian did when checking to make sure the cuts were even, but Rosemary seems to want to stretch it, make it grow faster to provide a covering for Ada's bare neck. "What have you done to yourself?" she whispers.

And then her father is here, Abram Mitchell the prophet, his gaze slipping over her, slug-like, a trail of accusation and shame left in its wake. He laughs in several rapid, dry puffs of derision. "My dear Ada. Did you honestly believe you would be allowed to keep him?"

She says nothing, staring at the toes of Hortense's boots, her bowed head too filled with fire to lift.

"Tonight we kill the fatted calf," her father says. "Tomorrow we discuss restoration."

CHAPTER FOURTEEN

Katherine prepares dinner, sautéing mushrooms and onions on the electric stove burner, the edges caramelizing, and she scrapes the vegetables from the bottom of the nonstick pan. She's an impatient cook, absentminded, the heat turned up too high. "Ma, it's burning," Bryce says, fiddling with his phone while leaning against the microwave. He's heating Swiss Miss, two packets to a mug, the torn pouches and spilled cocoa mix littering the countertop.

"No, it's not," she tells him, but he's right. She adds some water to the pan to loosen the food; it steams and browns, and then cools around the newly added frozen pepper strips. "See? All good."

"It doesn't smell all good."

"Take care of your mess."

He flicks the loose powder into the sink, turns on the water for half a second to rinse it away. Then he crumples the wrappers into one ball and shoots it into the trash can. "Three points."

"Two, at best," Katherine says, checking the sausages beneath the broiler. The topside is almost black, the bottom still blushing. She turns them. Setting the timer on the stove would help, but she's never learned how to use it and the manual disappeared years ago.

Bryce removes the cocoa from the beeping microwave, cuff of his sleeve pulled over his hand as insulation, and he stirs the liquid slowly. He wants to talk; usually he's in his bedroom after school, not skulking in the kitchen, taking too long to make a snack. Katherine knows to wait. He'll speak his mind when ready.

We are so alike.

Her relationship with Bryce is the hardest. While common interests attract, common personality traits repel. His fierce independence, like hers, closes him off from others. He's always been her I-Can-Do-It-Myself child. From tying shoes at three years old to running five miles a day at twelve, to AP physics homework, he's done it alone. She wonders, though, if some of that self-sufficiency isn't because, as a child after Evan was born, he had so much he had to do on his own. She couldn't be there for him the way she desperately wanted. Evan's needs were at the forefront of her existence. All else came second as necessity.

She's tried to make it up to him over the years, if that's at all possible. Special Mommy-Bryce nights out, taking him to all the Disney movies in the theater, topped with as much Fanta and Sour Patch Kids as he could eat, not to mention massive tubs of popcorn with butter. Allowing him to pick the restaurants almost every time the family went out to eat. Expensive electronic gifts, new video games, even a car for his eighteenth birthday—a used Sentra, but only four years old. She can't buy back those years, but she hasn't been able to stop trying to make him feel as though he has just as much value as his brother.

Cautiously lifting the mug to his lips, Bryce inhales the surface of his drink, slurping it, and winces. "Two minutes is too long."

"I could have told you that."

She shifts the frying pan to a cold burner and remembers the sausages. The tops are crispy but not too dark. With tongs, she moves each one from the pan to a platter and covers the mound with aluminum foil. Bryce rummages through the silverware drawer, finds a McDonald's straw saved from dinner last week. He taps the end on the top of the microwave until the straw breaks through, slips the remaining paper away, rolling it between his thumb and pointer before throwing it into the garbage. "Three points," he says again, "definitely," and uses the straw to hold each of the mini marshmallows beneath the surface of his cocoa until they melt away. "Chris Kennedy got into MIT."

"When did he hear?"

"Letter came yesterday."

"Did you apply at the same time?"

"I got mine in three days sooner."

"Bryce," Katherine says, "that doesn't mean anything."

"I know."

"Just wait."

He nods. "Yeah."

The back door opens and Will kicks the snow off his boots before stepping onto the braided rug where shoes get kicked off and tripped over. "It's really coming down," he says, unzipping his coat and hanging it on one of the pegs in the wall. Hat off next and shoved in the sleeve. "Smells good in here."

"Sausage and peppers."

"Did you get rolls?"

Katherine holds up the bag.

"Great," Will says. He goes to her, kisses her softly, breath warm and cola-flavored. "Hi."

"Hi."

They're trying, little things. Taking time to greet one another, not simply a peck on the cheek but connecting by looking each other in the eyes and acknowledging the return home, to family. He eats dinner with her, not in the recliner with the company of television. And he makes an effort to come up to their bed at night, not fall asleep in the chair. And she turns off the lamp instead of leaving the bedroom to finish a few more things downstairs—to avoid him—or reading while he covers his head with a pillow to block the light. And she touches him while they sleep, sometimes stomach-to-back and so close she wakes with her nightshirt twisted around Will's arm, or stuck under him so she can't get up to pee unless she wriggles away, which always wakes him. Sometimes they stay in their own space, holding hands across the invisible line demarcating his side and her side.

It's not enough. *After Christmas*, they say. *We'll really deal with this after Christmas.*

"Want to eat?" she asks.

"Are we waiting for Evan?" Will untwists the tie on the bag of rolls.

"He's after school for something."

"Photography club," Bryce says, and after dumping the cocoa down the drain, rinses the mug and pours in orange juice. He snags a hoagie bun and, with his fingers, adds three sausages. Bites away a quarter of the sandwich. "He's getting a ride home."

"I guess we're not waiting then," Will says, fixing three sandwiches with the fried pepper mixture and mustard on top.

"Save Evan at least four sausages," Katherine tells them.

"I'm done," Bryce says. He refills his mug and nods toward the stairway. "Homework."

"Don't spill."

The door opens and all three turn to watch Evan barge inside, red-cheeked, hair damp with sweat beneath his knit cap, coat open. Watery mucous drips from his nose. He sniffles, rakes his sleeve across his face. And he stands there, shoulders heaving, eyes bloodshot with exertion and fury. "I walked home," he says.

"Why didn't you call?" Katherine asks. She reaches to remove his hat but he flinches. "I would have come to get—"

"Mr. Bailey, Mom?"

"Evan."

"Seth told me. He heard his parents arguing. About you. About what you and Mr. Bailey . . . did."

She feels Will's arm come around her, hears him say, "Not now."

Bryce already has read their faces. "Holy crap."

"That's enough, both of you."

"They're getting divorced, Mom."

"I said that's enough," Will shouts.

"You know about this?" Evan creeps forward. "How can you both just stand there and—"

Will slaps him, a solid man-slap, full hand to the side of Evan's head. The boy recoils, stumbling backward, instinctively reaching for something solid to break his fall, finding the pan handle and yanking it from the stove. It overturns, soggy onions and peppers ooze down the oven, splatter Evan's pants, puddle on the vinyl. The pan follows, clattering to the floor. Evan's cheek glows red; he touches it.

"Go to your room," Will says.

He does, footprints of olive oil and melted snow trailing him.

"Dad," Bryce says.

"You too."

"But—"

"Now."

The older boy shakes his head in disgust and brushes by them, close enough to force Will out of his path. Katherine tears handfuls of towels from the roll and drops to her knees. She sops up the peppers, gathering the mess into nests of paper, and then fumbles in the cabinet beneath the sink, the one still with the child lock on it though it's long bent and opens with a good yank. She finds the Fantastik and sprays the stove front, the floor.

"Kate, get up."

"It needs to be cleaned." She wipes the oven, slips her hand beneath it, gathering several weeks' worth of crumbs as well as grease. She deserves to be down here, with the dehydrated corn kernels and the uncooked pasta and the peppercorns she spilled the other day but didn't bother to sweep, just kicked them under the broiler drawer to deal with later.

Will drags her up by the arm. She flaps away from him. "Don't."

He wrenches the bottle of cleaner out of her hand and throws it into the sink, and then tries for the towels clenched in her other fingers. She hides the wad behind her back, not allowing him to take it from her, and in his frustration he punches the refrigerator. Magnets loosen their grip on their orthodontist appointment cards, coupons, pay stubs, and take-out menus, dropping the paper items over Will's feet. He swears, and then grabs her and hugs her. She sobs and he doesn't let go.

Finally she wipes her face on his shirt. "I'll talk to Evan," he says.

"No," she says, shaking her head. "Let me."

Upstairs, she knocks on his bedroom door. "I know you're mad, Evan, but please let me in."

Nothing.

A draft whispers to her toes from beneath the door.

"Evan?"

She turns the knob. It's unlocked, and she pushes the door open without releasing it, leaning her shoulder into the wood and cataloging each slice of bedroom as it's revealed. The dresser first, Evan's gym clothes strewn atop, drawers open with socks and denim peeking out. The bed, unmade, same headboard he's had since he was five, dotted with glow-in-the-dark star stickers. His telescope, a Christmas gift three years ago, thick with dust. On his desk, in front of the open window, a magazine rattling in the wind. Katherine crosses the room and looks outside; the window is only a couple of feet above the roof of the porch. In the snow she sees footprints.

CHAPTER FIFTEEN

She wears a long-sleeved t-shirt as her covering, the band of collar holding back her bangs, the sleeves wrapped around her head and knotted at the nape of her neck, the body of the shirt trailing down her back in waves of yellow cotton hair. Her mother had offered her a bandana, but she did not want it.

Julian bought her this shirt.

She doesn't change from her inappropriate clothes, either. Instead she puts on the apparel of an outsider, an oversized black sackcloth her father keeps on hand, should someone come into the community as an observer or a potential convert. A symbol of mourning the old life, of submission to the new. It pools on the floor even as she sits at the dining table, the itchy rectangle of fabric so long around her.

Her mother serves venison stew for dinner. No calf had been slaughtered for the meal; she'd had the pot simmering on the stove when Ada arrived. Since no one cooks with salt—a worldly luxury, an adulterer of the God-made taste of the food he provides—the meat tastes soft and dark, like soil, and the vegetables have long lost their flavor to the stewing juice. There's cornbread and fresh butter and water. Eleven-year-old Tamar and eight-year-old Caleb stare at Ada, their food untouched. Micah sneers. And Judith, almost eighteen and betrothed since Ada left—she knows because her sister's ears have been pierced, a sign she belongs to another—shreds the deer meat with her fork, eating one thread at a time. Her mother blots her nose with her napkin; Ada had made them from a worn sheet when she was nine, hand sewing the hems with tiny pink stitching, and then embroidering the corners with snowflakes, a set of eight. The other place settings have mismatched napkins of various sizes and fabrics. Perhaps the rest of them had been used into rags or were mixed in with the washing, or perhaps her father ordered them all burned when she left, and Rosemary had held onto this last one, something of her daughter she refused to give over to the fire. Ada wishes for that last choice to be true.

Only Abram speaks, unimportant things at first, no more than gossip, about the happenings while Ada's been away. About her other siblings, married and with families of their own, who want to be here but there's no room for them around this table, in this home—"How blessed I am that my quiver is so plentiful!" he says with such mirth she can hardly believe it—but she will be reunited with them tomorrow. All of them. The entire community.

"Everyone will come together to welcome you home, Ada. And you are welcome. We will meet in the morning to begin your reconciliation to the covenant."

Judith's chin trembles.

"Father foretold his death, you know," Micah says.

"There will be time for all that later." Her father raises one calm hand and pats the air.

"She needs to hear it. She chose lust and debauchery over her true family, and her life here with a prophet of God."

"And now she is where she belongs, and it was and will be made right." Ada hates his voice, sing-songy and reasonable and very, very satisfied. She shivers, spoons the stew broth into her mouth, and swallows, but it does nothing to warm her. Her father centers his gaze on Micah, tilts his head downward while his eyes remain fixed, pupils dilated in the gloaming. Her brother shrinks, bites his cornbread wedge, crumbs dropping into his lap.

"Well, I think it is time for bed. You will all of you need your rest for tomorrow." Abram stands, as do the rest of them, following his lead, and on the way past her, he touches Ada on the shoulder. "Welcome home."

The house is simply built, a paradoxical pioneer home with all modern conveniences. The interior is wood plank, walls white, floors sealed with brown deck paint, ceilings natural. The main living area is a large, open eat-in kitchen and common sitting area. Off that is her parents' private bedroom. The children share the open loft above, divided by a wall down the middle—boys on one side, girls on the other—so there is privacy from one another, but not from those below.

Ada climbs the stairway, each step no wider than a cinderblock, slips off the black overgarment, and sits on the corner of her childhood bed. Tamar scrambles into night-clothes, tenting the gown around her before pulling it over her head, wriggling beneath it, and then emerging through the armholes and collar with her daytime clothes in hand. Her socks remain in place. She kneels to say prayers, which last less than *three Mississippi*, diving under the covers with an uncertain *amen*. Judith takes longer, unpinning her hair, combing it as the brittle ends *snap, crackle, pop*. The first time she ate Rice Krispies, it startled her how much they sounded like hair breaking during this nightly ritual. She's brushed so much hair so many times, but not tonight, even though she thinks Judith may want her to offer. She won't be sucked back into her old life, not this easily. Yes, she's here, and it's her father's victory, but for Julian's sake, it can't be her surrender. She's the resistance.

Or the prisoner of war.

Why did I come back here?

Because she knows nothing else.

Judith undresses with her back toward Ada, glides into bed with the grace of clouds, and flicks off the light. Ada's mattress squeaks and groans as she fights with the sheet tucked around it. She settles on her side, the shirt still on her head. She removes it, twists it in a ball, and hugs it.

On one side of her, Tamar mumbles with sleep. Judith hardly breathes at all.

"I saw your ears," Ada whispers. "Who?"

"Nathan Sumner." Her sister's voice smiles.

So does Ada. Of all the young men ready for wives, she would have wished Nathan for Judith. The eldest son of the Sumner family, he'd been an afterthought of many in the community—too quiet to be noticed, too baboonish in face to be desired, too steadfast to be exciting. But Ada had seen true kindness in him, trusted he was someone who would love her sister, protect her, nurture her.

Like Julian.

"I'm glad."

"Ada. Tomorrow . . ."

"What?"

"Mary Anderson tried to leave too. About a month after you. She wasn't gone four whole days. Father and the elders set up a restoration ceremony, like they're planning for you." Judith suctions her saliva through the gap between her front teeth. A nervous tick. "They drenched her with buckets of water mixed with lye, to wash the world off of her. She screamed, Ada. Her skin turned so red. And then they tied her to a post and left her there for the same amount of time she was away. They didn't give her food, only a spoonful of water here and there. She begged for-giveness and mercy, and everyone ignored her. And then she went blank, and they cut her down, and she's not the same now. She doesn't hardly talk, and when she does she won't look at you. She's just . . . broken.

"I'm afraid for you. It's going to be worse because you were gone longer, and they blame you for Mary's rebellion."

Ada swallows, hunching more tightly around the shirt she holds, now balled against her stomach. "It'll be okay," she whispers, licking the dry corners of her mouth.

"No, it won't." Judith rolls to face the wall, away from Ada, her movements so seamless and without sound or twisted blankets or her nightgown creeping over her knees. When she speaks again, her words bloat with tears. "Why did you come back?"

It's not the same question Ada asked herself minutes earlier; it's an accusation. In returning, Ada had stolen her sister's own hope of escape. Judith wants to run. Perhaps she talked of it with Nathan, and they had planned *something* for after the wedding. Even though Mary had returned, with Ada still gone, it meant it was possible to break free. Now, Judith only sees everything Prophet Abram Mitchell says is truth.

No one leaves.

How easily things come back. The sleep of her sisters arching over her, the snores from the boys beyond the thin plank wall. The wind outside, manipulating the trees, leafless oak marionettes, their gnarly fingers scraping the house's tin roof. The grandfather clock downstairs; how many nights did she sleep with her fingers plugging her ears because of the incessant *tick, tick, tick*. The smell, woodsy and smoky and human. Julian sometimes told her he smelled in color. She closes her eyes and tries to conjure the pigmentation of this place but there's only the blackness of her eyelids.

The familiarity is hypnotic. *Close your eyes. You are getting sleepy. You are crawling through an underground tunnel, deeper and deeper into the belly of the earth, to your old life, before defiance, before unclean thoughts, before Julian. On the count of three, when I snap my fingers, you'll be back there, given over to the teaching of your father. Obedient. Submissive. Ready to accept the consequences of breaking fellowship with the covenant and pursuing the lies of the ungodly. One . . . Two . . .*

She jolts awake as the clock chimes. Five a.m. The first ribbons of sunlight curl through the tops of the pines. She sits up, inhales thickly through her stuffed nose. Her head is soft with the cotton of sleep, but the remainder of her body has decided it will not stay. Pull back the covers. Stand up. She touches Judith's hair on the way past, still black in the not-yet-dawn. Ada's fingers feel its true color, copper, like not-quite new pennies, slightly tarnished from the warmth of someone's palm.

All her things are still packed in the Jeep. She'd left the keys there, as well, dangling from the ignition.

Despite her tiptoed gait and her shoes hanging from her thumbs, in her ears it sounds as if she's thundering down the stairs. As soon as she reaches the bottom, a light snaps on in the sitting area. There her father waits, feet up on the ottoman, hands resting on his lap, fingertips touching and pointing toward the sky.

"'But whoso shall offend one of these little ones which believe in me, it were better for him that a millstone were hanged about his neck, and that he were drowned in the depth of the sea.'" His reedy voice smears over the room, over Ada.

"Believes in who? God? Or you?"

The smallest grin tickles Abram's mouth, and he opens wide his arms. "I speak for God. There is no difference."

"It's not my fault Mary left."

"Oh, yes, my daughter, it is."

The longer she stays in this one spot, the more firmly rooted she'll become. So she takes one step backward, then another, until she bumps the dining table and begins feeling her way around it, knowing the front door is only around the next two chairs. Her father stands, raises his hand, and shakes it. Something jingles. Her keys.

"You'll need these," he says.

Back, back, hands frantic and searching behind her, and then she finds it. The doorknob.

"I don't need anything from you."

She runs from the house to the Jeep, kneels at the back bumper, and fumbles underneath it. *Please, be there.* And it is, the magnetic Hide-A-Key Julian left there, should he ever lock his keys in the car. When he showed her, she'd asked if it had happened before and he laughed and kissed her and said, *Why do you think I have one?* The driver's side is locked now. Ada manages to slide the cover off the box, open the door, and start the car. When the engine roars her father comes out on the porch, anger twisting his face, but it's too late. She jams the shifter into drive and steers onto the road, traveling toward the highway.

Only when she sees the on-ramp, and the gas station right before it, does she think she should have left a way for Judith to find her. At least her phone number, her address at Julian's brownstone. Tears overwhelm her vision and she needs to turn into the convenience store parking lot, jostling through several craters in the asphalt before coming to a stop with the Jeep still idling and crying with her cheek against the steering wheel.

Trust me.

The phrase startles her so much that, as she jerks back in her seat, she accidentally leans into the horn. A couple early morning truckers glance her way with creased brows. One flashes his middle finger at her. She ignores them, her limbs vibrating with some sort of electric pulse. She didn't *hear* those words, not coming from the outside and traveling into her ear canal, bouncing against the eardrum like a child on a trampoline. It was more as though the words had been embossed on her soul, raised to the touch but oh-so-subtle. This is what Julian meant by *in the Spirit*, she is certain of it. Why isn't he beside her to teach her more about his God?

Trust me.

It's more an echo this time, dim, swirled with the chaos of her other thoughts. She tips her head toward the dome light; the crack in the cover looks like a broken arrow. She belongs nowhere. Not with Abram's Covenant, not at the brownstone, not with Hortense and Mark. She's a nomad. If she drives around long enough, she'll cease to be. Forgotten in the minds of those who know her name, she will only exist on paper.

She's cold. Reaching over the front seats into the back, she unwraps the afghan from the picture frames she took off Julian's hallway wall. The face of the soldier stares back at her. These people all knew Julian better than she does.

Intreat me not to leave thee, or to return from following after thee; for whither thou goest, I will go, and where thou lodgest, I will lodge. Thy people shall be my people, and thy God my God.

An idea germinates, reverberating from the same place she heard those words. *Trust me. Do this.* She will find the ones in the photographs, and go to them, speak to them, and through them she will have pieces of Julian impossible to her without them. And, perhaps, when she staples those pieces together, she will see more clearly his God.

PART TWO

JULIAN

CHAPTER SIXTEEN

His writer friend Greg calls him and, without a hello, tells Julian he'll be in the area and needs a photographer. He's doing a story for the *Times* about pockets of separatist communities popping up with greater frequency across the United States. "They're like Amish, but not. Interested?"

"Where?"

"Massachusetts."

"I'm booked, Greg."

"Come on, man. I need you."

"Call Roberto."

"Seriously, Goetz, you have to come with. You buy into some of this sh– stuff. You'll be able to tell me what's the psycho cult bit and what's kosher."

"None of it's kosher."

"Don't be hating on the Jew, man." Greg laughs. "I don't know the Jesus lingo. That's why it's all you."

"You're an idiot."

"Tell me about it."

"Fine. But you're paying for gas."

Days later Greg picks him up and they drive ninety minutes across the border into the Berkshires, a place known for the arts and for liberals, such an unlikely home for an ultraconservative religious sect. Perhaps it was planned that way.

"What do you know about them?" Julian asks.

"Called Abram's Covenant, after the founder Abram Mitchell. Gotta love modesty. The guy's almost sixty, former lawyer. In 1985 he said God told him he would be coming back soon and to prepare by leaving behind the things of the world. So he and a few others settled in this place. It's grown to about 150 people here, but apparently there's some sort of loose network of like-minded communities. They ship their kids back and forth for marrying so no one has three-armed babies."

"Lovely."

"I just call it like I see it."

"How in the world did you get an idea for a story like this?"

"Mitchell contacted the *Times*. Thought someone might be interested in his freak show. Any publicity is good publicity. He wants to get his message out."

"I can't wait to meet him."

Others use photography to peer more deeply into life, to pull the focus from themselves and onto the objects of their pictures. Julian uses the camera as a buffer. His eyes are microscopes, the tiniest details assaulting him from all directions. Chroma. Objects. Imperfections. He sees too much, always has, even as a child when he'd close his eyes and cling tight to his sister's hand as she led him through the carnival, overwhelmed by the blinking lights whirling against the nighttime sky. Or the faces, each contorting in yet another expression, moving by him too quickly for him to decipher. The viewfinder blots everything out except the one thing at which he wants to look. There's silence in the aperture. Breathing room.

He rarely works in color. Colors not only distract him but they make his head ache with the sounds and smells. Blues crash over him like the ocean, reds are bright as cinnamon. Even his home is tone and shade, gray and wood and black.

Fortunately the day is muted, a heather sky dull with clouds, the sun tucked deep behind them. Julian closes his eyes, counting the rhythmic *thud-thuds* beneath the tires.

They stop to eat at a shiny retro diner, Greg darting from the car to use the restroom, Julian stretching, gathering his camera bag before going inside. Tall grass grows on either side of the pavement, hilly but mostly clear of trees or buildings. Something moves in the corner of Julian's vision. He thinks it's an animal streaking across the field, but he lifts his head and instead sees a woman, running, holding her long skirt in one hand so her feet won't tangle in it, other arm pumping her forward. He points the camera in her direction. Presses the shutter release. *Ch-ch-ch-ch-ch.* One photo after another, capturing her movements. She slows as she approaches the only tree in the field, an oak, reaching out toward the trunk. Julian thinks she's leaning against it to catch her breath, but as he zooms in he sees she's clinging to it, arms above her head, face pressed into the bark.

He's intruding in her private moment, one of sorrow, or perhaps worship. And while all photos at their most base are voyeuristic, Julian isn't comfortable being a peeping Tom right now.

Greg bangs on the diner window, waves at him to hurry. He clips on the lens cap and after flopping into the padded booth he orders a double slice of the diner's World Famous Humble Bumble Pie—or so the sign on the wall proclaims—*à la mode*, and a coffee. Greg wants bacon and eggs, decidedly not kosher, Julian points out. Greg says he hasn't been to temple since he was fourteen. "No offense, Goetz, but I look around and think, if there's some sort of higher power, he pretty much sucks."

When the waitress returns with their food, they ask about Abram's Covenant.

"Oh, well, I've been to the shop lots of times. They got great veggies at good prices, and sometime we use 'em here. They seem nice enough. Quiet, you know? The women and girls can't leave the property. Aren't allowed. But the men shop the local hardware stores and such. Won't eat here, that's for sure. This food ain't pure enough for them." She laughs. "Maybe not the help, either."

Greg drops a twenty on the table and, before leaving, Julian asks if he can take the waitress's photo.

"Sure, go right ahead," she says. "Don't know why you'd want to, though."

He snaps pictures of her balancing a pie on one hand. Her skin and teeth are abraded with the simple pleasures of life—chicken fried steak, sunshine in the perennial garden, comforting grandchildren in the night. Deep canals of laughter fan from her eyes. *Beaten down by happiness*, Julian thinks. Irene, the nametag reads. "Because I'm a photographer. I can't help it."

Then they're back in the car, Greg steering out of the diner parking lot and around the bend, stopping in a gravel driveway flanked by two short, splintery rail fences. Julian is suddenly reluctant to continue on this story, doesn't want to see a bastardization of his faith, a reason for critics to point and shout, *See, this is what Christianity does.* But Greg is already dialing Abram Mitchell's number, so Julian wanders toward the farm store. He expects the air to be different within the boundaries of this place, oppressive perhaps, weighed down with falsehood and insanity. He feels none of that, walking past baskets of spring onions and salad greens on the big front porch. Inside, women in long skirts and bandanas smile and assist a handful of customers.

"Can I help you?" someone asks, a girl about thirteen.

"I'm not sure. What's good?"

"Is this your first time here?"

"It is."

"I can tell. You have that look."

"Which is?"

"That you think you might catch something from us. Or we might bite you. Or convert you. All those are most likely equally awful, in your eyes."

Julian laughs a little. "You're good."

Now the girl grins. "I know. Prophet Abram tells me I have the gift of discernment."

"Mara, come away from there and stop talking that poor man's ear off," the woman behind the register says, something other than simple censure in her voice.

"I'm sorry, sir," Mara says, sparkle gone, expression as flat as week-old Pepsi, and she disappears into another room before Julian can say another word.

"She wasn't being a bother," he says, approaching the counter.

The woman looks up. She's too thin, but pretty with speckled gray eyes that remind him of house sparrow eggs, and dark eyebrows against pale skin. Pink, slightly raised lines embroider her cheek and the side of her nose. Scratches from the tree bark earlier today. It's the girl from the field. He's certain of it.

"'Seest thou a man that is hasty in his words? There is more hope of a fool than of him.'"

"A fool? Now that's somewhat harsh, don't you think?"

"They're not my words."

"Proverbs, yeah. But I think Jesus might have had something to say about that, too, recorded by our good friend Matthew somewhere around, oh, I don't know, chapter five, verse twenty-two, maybe?"

The woman meets his gaze. "'But I say unto you, that whosoever is angry with his brother without a cause shall be in danger of the judgment: and whosoever shall say to his brother, Raca, shall be in danger of the council: but whosoever shall say, thou fool, shall be in danger of hell fire.'"

"Sounds pretty serious to me," he says, a grin playing at the corners of his mouth.

"I believe, sir, you are mocking me?"

"I wouldn't dream of it. Mocking is decidedly old-fashioned. I'd say it's more like teasing."

"Or perhaps harassment."

Julian hesitates, startled by the woman's words. Then he sees she, too, has a little smirk on her lips, and he laughs softly at her nimble wit. "I'm Julian Goetz," he says, extending his hand. She shakes it, fingers cold and not much more than bone, releasing quickly. "A pleasure, I assure you."

The young woman snaps open a paper bag, the rustling loud and pointed. "I'm not assured that anyone could decide what's a pleasure and what isn't in such a short period of time."

"I'm fairly decisive."

She stops, stares at him with round eyes, as gray and glassy as sea stones, her body unmoving. Finally, when a customer slides her jars of preserves and bag of garlic scapes toward the register, she says, "I believe you are, Mr. Goetz. Excuse me."

Dismissed, Julian circles the store, pretending to read labels on the tins of maple syrup, comparing the varieties of brownies offered, and peeking over his shoulder at the clever young woman now trying not to look at him. He silently berates himself for his foolishness; he'd been flirting with her and has no idea why. It wasn't his way. He hasn't been on a date in four years, rarely thought about dating unless Hortense threatened to match him up with someone, and certainly didn't act with such unprofessionalism around anyone else. Something about the girl—she had to be at least ten, maybe fifteen years younger than him—made him feel like an awkward high school student trying too hard to win her over with his suave banter. *What a dope.* Still, he gathers an assortment of groceries in his arms and plops them down on the counter to pay. She shakes open the bag and punches numbers into the cash register. "I hope you enjoyed your first visit to our home, Mr. Goetz. Maybe we'll see you again?"

"Maybe." He crumples the bag closed. "Do I at least get a name?"

"Ada Mitchell."

"Any relation to Abram Mitchell?"

"Why?" Her voice sprouts briars of suspicion.

"Yo, Goetz, he's on his way," Greg calls, clamping his hand on Julian's shoulder. "Let's wait outside. I'm sweltering in here."

"Greg Eisen, this is Ada Mitchell."

His friend smiles, all teeth and dimples, and nods. "A daughter of the prophet, I'd guess."

Ada squints. "You're the reporter."

"Oh, the disdain with which you say that. Your daddy called me, not the other way around."

"I apologize. I meant no disrespect."

"Don't take me too seriously, Ms. Mitchell. My boy Julian will tell you the same."

"Are you a reporter too?" Ada asks.

"Photographer."

"Oh."

"You sound disappointed," Greg says. "But don't be. He may not look like much, but I promise he's the best. He'll make you beautiful, no worries."

"Thank you for your concern on my behalf, Mr. Eisen. Good afternoon."

Ada retreats through a door behind the register and Julian glares at Greg. "You'll lose this interview if you don't knock it off."

"What I say?"

"I'm going to get my camera."

Julian returns to the car, sits with his forehead against the dashboard, and prays. He and the Spirit have known one another long enough for Julian to recognize its urging. The encounter with the young woman has unsettled him. He asks for clarity and peace. Instead he gets the distinct impression this Ada person is to be his wife.

That's crazy.

He rubs his ears under his palms as if adjusting antennae for better reception. He's no charismatic, no fortune-teller. He doesn't claim to hear the voice of God and won't pretend his feelings are always right, and would never act upon a hunch like this without some sort of outside confirmation or biblical precedent. But this one has the paralyzing hallmark of authenticity in that it mimics all the other times it has been accurate. His entire body hums with it.

"Hey, Goetz, time's up." Greg opens the passenger side door, shrugs toward the farm store. "Mitchell's here."

Julian sees the man, lanky, horse-faced, dressed in navy pants and a matching long-sleeved shirt, the kind often seen on mechanics and factory workers. Laboring clothes. He's clean shaven and Julian blinks away surprise; he's been so certain Mitchell would have a beard, long and bushy and full of secrets.

They approach and the self-anointed prophet nods. "Mr. Goetz, so pleased you could join Mr. Eisen for our business today." He offers a skeletal hand. "I've seen your work."

"Thank you," Julian says, though Mitchell offers no praise. He allows the man to swallow his own hand in the extended grip and then fights the urge to snatch it back. Mitchell's palm is too smooth; Julian won't be surprised if it's lineless. The man releases him, finally, and behind his back he tightens his fingers into a fist.

"Yes, I like to know who I'm letting onto my property."

"Well, let's get this party started," Greg says, removing a digital recorder from his pocket, switching it on, and slipping it back into his shirt. "After you."

"No notebook?"

Greg waves a small, spiral pad in the air. "Got one of those too."

Mitchell leads them on a stroll around the community. Julian shoots and Greg scribbles, and they listen to the story of a lawyer-turned-prophet who claims, like Jacob, he wrestled with God and did not let go until God blessed him with the vision of Abram's Covenant, a place his family and others would be safe from the wickedness of the world, a place they could prepare for the second coming of the Lord.

"And when will that be?" Greg asks.

"Soon."

"Do you have a general time frame you're working with?"

"'But of that day and hour knows no man, no, not the angels of heaven, but my Father only.'"

"So, that's a no."

Mitchell raises his eyebrows. "Perhaps you should ask Mr. Goetz. I believe he has professed some . . . faith."

"I'm interviewing you."

"No, then. God does not give dates."

"And, what are you doing while you wait?"

The men work, Mitchell explains, once over the age of twenty. "In the wilderness, those who were twenty and older were cursed to have their carcasses scattered throughout the desert and would never see the Promised Land. They were, in other words, responsible for their actions. We show our men responsible as well. They take wives at twenty, move from their parents' homes and into their own. About half of the men are chosen to work jobs in the local towns and cities. We do need some income; the farm store doesn't meet all our financial needs. There are several professionals who have joined us, a physician and another attorney, and two men who are in technology fields. Of course, we make sure all outside employment is suitable for men of the Almighty. The other half farm the property and protect the women and children."

"Protect?"

"Oh, yes. We must give honor to the women as the

weaker vessels. They are much more easily tempted and corrupted, as we see clearly from Genesis to Revelation. If they are to remain the treasures the Lord God made them to be, we must be diligent in their protection."

"How does that look?"

"Vigilance, Mr. Eisen. Vigilance." Mitchell flaps his arm, motioning to some far-off place. "Out there, men are too busy seeking their own selfish pleasures to provide proper oversight, and their women are suffering for it, engaging in all manner of behaviors and activities they were not designed to do. So we minimize the possibility of that with a handful of . . . proprieties. Children are instructed in their roles from birth, boys as defenders, girls as damsels, and they are given ample opportunity to practice these roles. Women and children are never left alone without a man over them; should they have any needs or questions they will not have to make decisions on their own or worry about seeking out someone to help. In the homes, this is either the husband or eldest son, if he has turned thirteen. In the farm store, well, you've seen the overseers there. A father or brother will escort girls where they need to go, and be present for all courtship activities. Young ladies are married no later than twenty, but usually by eighteen. Giving them a husband, home, children to care for, it keeps them from idleness. Boredom only leads to mischief. No woman is given unbridled access to media. The men, of course, need to be aware of world happenings, but the sensitive sex must be shielded from it; women use computers only to help their husbands in their businesses or for the farm store, but—"

"—never without proper oversight," Julian interrupts. He aches for Ada Mitchell, a woman he doesn't know, and one who must be married; she is certainly older than twenty.

"You're offended, Mr. Goetz." Mitchell sighs as if he's burdened by this news. "I am not at all surprised. 'If the world hate you, ye know that it hated me before it hated you. If ye were of the world, the world would love his own: but because ye are not of the world, but I have chosen you out of the world, therefore the world hateth you.' Mr. Eisen has his little recorder in his pocket. I could choose to say only things readers of this news article will find acceptable. But at what cost? You will paint me in an unflattering light, that is unavoidable. But the Lord Almighty will use it to call those he has chosen to this place, and others like it. He will not come until all who are his have been collected into his flock."

"And how many families do you have here?" Greg asks it as if he cannot believe anyone would choose such a life.

"Twenty-two."

They continue through the footpaths, Mitchell speaking of less controversial things—organic farming, small game hunting, his grandchildren, the joys of a life unburdened by worldly demands. He introduces them to his wife; Julian takes photos of them together, in their modest home, his teeth overpowering his thin-lipped grin, her smile ragged around the edges. "How many children do you have, Mrs. Mitchell?" Greg asks.

She looks at her husband. He nods. "Nine," she says.

"And they have families of their own?"

She takes a picture from the mantel. Points. "Esther is the oldest, and then Rachael. They're both married. Rachael has three children, and is due with another at the end of the summer. Esther has only been blessed with one. Yet.

"This is Paul. And Zebulun. They're married as well. Paul has twins. They're two—and a handful and a half." She laughs, finally a smile with joy attached to it. "Zeb and his wife are only married six months, so no grandbabies yet, but there's time.

"Judith will be eighteen soon. Micah is fourteen. And then Tamar is eleven and Caleb eight."

"You love them," Julian says.

"You don't have children, do you, Mr. Goetz?" the woman asks.

"No." He squints at the picture, touches Ada's face. "You didn't mention her."

"That's Ada," Rosemary says.

"Does she . . . have any children?"

"She's unwed." Her voice quavers.

Julian has spent so long looking through the lens of a camera, collecting fractions of seconds, he sees things in frames, in stop motion, noticing the details in between changing expressions, those things the body tries to hide without the mind realizing they exist. Even without the release of the shutter, he watches this sequence unfold. Rosemary, a microcosm of distrust rising above her sorrow. *Click.* Mitchell takes the frame, her fingers tightening on it before letting go, and he turns it face down on the table.

Click. A patina of fear spreads over his gaze. *Click.* Did Julian see that correctly? Mitchell, afraid? Yes, he's certain.

"Well, gentlemen, I've taken enough of your time. If you haven't any more questions, I'll escort you back to your car."

"We're good," Greg says, capping his pen.

"You know how to reach me, if anything should come up in your transcription." He doesn't offer his hand in farewell, but stands sentinel in the middle of the parking lot as they drive away.

"As if he wants to make sure we leave," Greg says, watching in the rearview mirror. He swears. "What a nut job that one is. Makes great copy, though."

"Yeah," Julian mumbles. He intends to go home, process the photographs, and try to forget about Abram's Covenant. Those things he perceived about her, Ada, they cannot be right. He's having some sort of midlife crisis at thirty-eight. Mitchell's fear, however. It was genuine. And, for some reason, Julian believes it has something to do with him.

CHAPTER SEVENTEEN

He doesn't help the student choose her photos, but she thinks he does, thanking him as he comments on her composition and guides her to answer her own questions. She says, "I think you're right," each time she makes a decision, even though he offers no suggestions. He supposes she'd like to tell her professor, "Julian Goetz told me these were the best ones," as if somehow it will influence her grade.

It might. Who knows?

Hortense works with another student on the opposite side of the room. M&H Gallery hosts at least two students at a time, often three or four, depending on the size of the projects. The kid is another photographer, wearing his best pants and shoes, arriving at the gallery six minutes after the girl and still fourteen minutes early. He was clearly disappointed Julian had already been nabbed by his classmate and he had Hortense to assist him. His bowtie askew and his Donegal tweed ivy cap on the floor, he slaps the photos on the wall, one after the other, asking, "Straight?" and moving to the next before Hortense responds. His display is finished before the girl has half her pictures chosen. Julian goes to him, shakes his hand, and compliments one of his better shots. The kid beams, plucks at his tie, and launches into a monologue on lens angle and exposure, and why he chose this particular crevice to immortalize on paper and not another, more jagged one just inches above it. "You can see the corner here. The morning's condensation looked like diamonds in the sun's first light, but I don't want to explore only the beautiful things—"

"Mr. Goetz?" The girl. Oh, what's her name? Emily. That's it. "I'm sorry to interrupt but I'd really like your professional opinion on a few of my other selections and I have to be to class in"—she looks at her watch—"less than an hour."

"Of course, Emily, of course." He shakes the guy's hand again and says he hopes to be at the opening, if he's in town. The kid swipes his hat off the ground and smacks it against his palm several times before jamming it down over his hair. He glares at Emily through his bangs, forced over his eyes by the brim of the cap, and she returns a satisfied smirk of her own with raised eyebrows and a shimmy of her head. He disappears without thanking Hortense, his Army surplus messenger bag slung across his bony, sullen shoulders.

Hortense snorts.

Emily hangs her remaining photos, bumping against Julian too many times for coincidence, and then thanks him profusely before saying, "I hope I'll see you again, Mr. Goetz. At the opening."

He almost responds, *Please, call me Julian,* a habit more than anything meaningful, but stops short because to this girl it will have some meaning beyond the polite words of a thirty-eight-year-old who doesn't want to feel like someone's grandfather. She uses her movements as pheromones, her words sticky with pink and carmine and violet. He nods, steps backward. "Like I told your friend—"

"Oh, he's not a friend. Just some wannabe hipster from photog 403. So immature." She glances at her wrist again. "Well, I'm off. Class, you know. And then work. At Coffeehaus. I'm there pretty much every afternoon."

The girl flips her hair, a shoulder-length mane of frizz and crinkle that's more poodle tail than Pantene commercial, moving in one solid poof instead of a long, healthy swing. Julian holds his breath until she's safely through the door, than exhales. "Whoa."

Laughing, Hortense says, "I haven't seen it that bad before."

"I'm old enough to be her father," he says.

"Only if you had a kid at sixteen."

He shakes his head. "What happened here? I'm sure girls weren't like that when we were in college."

"Okay, Mr. Oblivious. You think that." Hortense crouches beneath Emily's display, collecting scraps of the backing paper the girl peeled from the adhesive strips she used to mount her photos on the wall, then tossed on the floor.

"I would have noticed."

"Maybe. If you saw it through your viewfinder."

Her words have a serried edge to them, little puppy fangs biting into his ankles. He kneels to help her but she keeps her head down and back toward him. He reaches the opposite way, fingertips on the slick paper rectangles, sliding them close enough for him to grab and crumple into his holding fist. Then footsteps, and Mark stands above both of them, a framed print in one hand and an invoice in the other. "Hey hon, can you tell me what color mat this lady wanted?"

Hortense stretches to a stand, takes the paper. Glances at it. "This is your writing."

"I know." Mark grins, looking like the goofy, big-eared kid Julian roomed with freshman year, the one with the AC/DC poster above his bed and the mini-fridge full of blueberry Yoplait and pepperoni logs. "I can't read it."

"Hunter and navy, double matted."

"Thanks." He kisses her cheek. "Lunch after this?"

"Sure."

"How about you, J?"

"Uh, yeah, okay." Julian brushes the dust from his knees. "I have something to tell you both, then."

"What?" Hortense asks.

"It can wait for lunch."

"I don't think so," Mark says. "You look like someone kicked it. Is everything all right?"

"Oh, yeah. It's fine. Nothing serious like that."

"Then what?" Mark asks. "Come on, J. Something's up."

The papers in Julian's palm poke him. He squeezes them tighter. "I met someone."

Mark drops the frame he holds, glass shattering across the floor. Hortense jumps back as the shards pounce at her ankles.

"Man, I'm sorry. You just shocked the living crud outta me." Mark holds his hands out in a stop motion. "Stay here. I'll get a broom. And don't say a single thing until I get back."

He strides into the framing room, leaving Julian and Hortense facing each other in a confetti of glass, and then calls from behind the other side of the wall, "Hon, where's that broom?"

"Upstairs," Hortense says, nowhere near loud enough for her husband to hear.

Mark peeks his head out. "Hon? Broom?"

"It's upstairs."

"Right. Back in a sec. And I mean it. Nothing."

Julian waits beneath the scurrying footfalls of his one best friend, staring at his other, Hortense willowy and perfect in slim, to-the-knee azure shorts and capped-sleeve blush blouse. And the shoes. Julian hasn't seen her wear the same pair twice. Today's offering is woven pink wedges with dried, grassy heels. Her face is blank, her posture skewed over one hip, still as nightshade. He closes one eye as if he has his Nikon, narrows his vision as if fidgeting with the zoom, and sees it.

He wanted to be in love with her when he was twenty, when he prayed and prayed, and the Lord told him no. He went to her and told her, and she squinted at him as if blinded by the news. For all his talk of skipping Saturday

night parties in order to get up for church Sunday morning, of his Thursday night campus Bible study and his grace
before cafeteria meals and drive-thru burritos, she never
took his faith seriously. People pray on Sunday and live on
Monday. She never knew anyone who pursued God like
Julian; he had a lover and there was no room for her in his
bed. Julian watched his gentle and oh-so-intimate confession sting her, rubbing alcohol in the scrape of rejection,
and she said to him, "There is no God," retreating behind
the safety of her dormitory door.

Two weeks later Mark told Julian he and Hortense were
dating. "It just sorta happened. You cool with it?"

"Yeah, I'm cool," he had said, and was, and jealous all at
once. Eventually his bruising faded as the Comforter cradled his heart with tenderness, soothing it with the balm of
promise. *Something better is yet to come.*

He still doesn't know what Hortense told Mark about
them, and in his mind the connection is so loose it falls away
if he focuses too much on it, like brushing too close to ash.
Them, if it existed at all, is too small for notice on eternity's
timeline, a stray pen dot mistaken for a star.

Julian's love for Hortense is that of one friend for
another, a deep, abiding, sacrificial friendship, but no more.
He can think her beautiful and not move beyond that, and
he believed her feelings to be the same. Now, however, in
his monocular vision, he sees she's still in love with him.
Not in an everyday, all-consuming romance sort of way.
It's a battered suitcase, once used when youth and adven-
ture were paramount, stickered with progressive slogans

and imagined causes, and stored on the upmost closet shelf once twenty turned to graduation turned to settling down, and it became clear no one would be traveling with it again. But it was there, behind the extra blankets, the shoe box of keepsakes, the heating pad. Most days she never saw it, didn't remember it. But occasionally, when packing away her winter sweaters at the beginning of May or tucking a surprise gift up there for safekeeping, she glimpses it. She doesn't take it down and open it. In fact, she tucks more stuff in front of it—bedsheets and last year's jeans she's yet to donate, and the waffle iron she'll never use, and dust. But she won't get rid of it. She needs it there, just in case.

For all her talk of finding a woman for him, the blind dates and teasing and sisterly concern for him being single, Hortense wants him alone. Not because she loves Mark any less, or has any expectation of being with Julian, but because she's claimed an identity around the fact she's the only woman with which Julian has been in love. It's hers. He's hers.

And now he's not.

Mark stumbles down the stairs, flies into the gallery, broom and dustpan in opposite hands, his awkward wings. "You haven't told her yet, right?"

"No," Julian says.

Sweeping the glass into the corner, Mark props the broom against the wall, bristles guarding his pile, dustpan clipped to the handle. "Okay, spill," he says, looping his arm around Hortense's waist. She doesn't soften into him.

"Well," Julian says, all jitters, smearing his face with his hands, oil from his nose greasing his fingertips. He puffs the air from his lungs, lips flopping. They will think he's insane. "Her name is Ada. And I, ah . . ." He sucks breath through his teeth. "I don't know. That's really it."

"J, come on. Where'd you meet? How long have you been seeing her? We need details."

"Um. I can't say we're together, actually. We only met a few weeks ago when I was in Massachusetts with Greg Eisen."

"The cult story?" Mark asks.

"Well. Yeah."

"Are you telling us she's in this cult?"

"I guess."

"Have you totally lost it?"

"Maybe," Julian says. "No. I don't know. It's something."

Mark scratches between his eyebrows, glee replaced with confused disappointment. Hortense bleeds relief. She's not been replaced. To her, Julian's new love is nothing more than a phantom. She shakes her head. "This is your stupid messiah complex talking."

"No."

"Fine, Julian. You don't have to admit it, but everyone else sees. Legless veterans, Palestinian students, widowed hoarders. You swoop in and have to fix all their problems. This woman is just another somebody to save, your good deed for the month."

Julian bites down, hard, until he thinks his molars might burst like hard candies with liquid centers, spilling his frustration at her. His anger. "You wouldn't understand."

"You're right. I don't read crazy."

"I'll see you both later."

Mark grabs at his shoulder. "J—"

He shakes his head. "Just later."

It's warm outside, the sounds of almost summer bouncing down the sidewalks, children on playgrounds, the noxious scent of road workers tamping hot tar into potholes. He walks toward home, having known his friends would respond the way they did yet still awash with disillusionment.

Hortense is right. He does have a propensity to meddle in the misfortunes of others with hopes of making a difference. Not because he thinks himself some sort of Christ figure, but because of guilt. Photography is his passion, the thing he is created to do. And yet on some level, he hates that he enjoys it so much, that he excels. Pictures don't better lives or save souls. They're only images on paper, a bit of death, the moment captured past and gone.

God knows he's tried to leave it behind. He's fasted from his camera, forty days and forty nights of pleading, *Take this cup away*, and then mortification he'd even think of uttering his Lord's words in the same context of his own struggle. He seeks out ways to help those who do the real work of God, offering his services for free. He considers seminary, long-term missions, adoption, anything that will make a tangible difference. He finds ways to do penance. It's why he's still in his college city of Trent, one of the many hardscrabble urban areas in the Capital District, when he could have a studio in Manhattan or LA, staying to *give back*—sounds good for interviews but in all honesty it's a pithy way of saying he doesn't deserve to move away. His offerings are in secret, his left hand unaware of his right hand's actions. But his mind knows. None of it enough to change the fact he's successful and renowned for *taking pictures.*

Ada Mitchell is different. She has to be. He'll drive back to Abram's Covenant. He'll sit beneath her tree and wait for her to come. If she doesn't, he'll know he was wrong about her. He'll return to being a prize in Hortense's hidden suitcase. He'll squeeze every drop of singleness from life and drink it. He'll cover his guilt with more work and more giving and more sacrifice, despite understanding it's all dross to be consumed by fire one day, his only hope his obedience will mean something when the Master returns and it's time to present his talents. How many he'll have, he doesn't know.

CHAPTER EIGHTEEN

I t decides to rain the day Julian travels to the Berkshires
again, stodgy gray droplets, plump as grapes, tumbling
from the gray sky. He adjusts the intermittent wipers as
he drives, reducing the frequency to avoid the squawking
of too-dry glass, increasing it when trucks splash through
puddles from the pavement. He never turns them on full,
though, even when the drops become thin, silver needles of
water, insistent in their attempts to drill through the glass.
He hates the lull of the constant, steady *woosh*-*WOOSH*
woosh-*WOOSH*. The delay surprises him—he's never quite
sure when the wipers will spring up again—and keeps him
from falling asleep at the wheel.

May weather is notorious for its unpredictability in the
northeast. One day it mimics summer, the next autumn,
forcing the humans at its mercy to be prepared with umbrel-
las and jackets and sandals and sunglasses. Sometimes
winter boots; it's been known to spit snow a time or two

as late as Mother's Day. He doesn't expect Ada to visit her tree today, but the Lord of Creation controls the rain, and perhaps this is his way of telling Julian he misheard and there is no wife in his future, at least not one from Abram's Covenant. Julian planned his trip for today, and God knew it. If he wanted the weather to be lovely enough for a picnic beneath that tree, he would have made it so.

Julian should have stayed home.

He drives only out of a sense of obedience. And because he needs to know if he's gone a bit, as Hortense would say, *crazy in the cabeza.*

It's been almost a week since he's spoken to either her or Mark, not since the argument in the gallery. When this excursion fails, he'll go home to them with his tail between his legs and they'll lick his wounds with the encouraging *other fish in the sea* and not mean any of it, and watch him closely for other signs of increased religious delusions.

If.

If it fails.

He's moved beyond doubt into utter disbelief all on his own.

He drifts off the exit, the tightly wound bundle of trepidation unraveling, stretching wide and releasing its more potent cousin—dread—and the hollow in his gut grows, devouring the sensations around his middle until he's half convinced he's gone invisible between his diaphragm and pelvic bone. He sneaks his fingers from the steering wheel and wipes them across his abdomen, to be certain he is still in one piece.

Her tree is ahead. The car bumps onto the shoulder of

the road, and he parks, headlights off, engine off. The windows fog, glass spider webs trapping his breath. He wipes the driver's side with his sleeve. The digital numbers on his dashboard clock reorient. 9:03.

She's not there.

"Get it together, Julian," he says, warm embarrassment pooling first in his head, filling his arteries, trickling through his vascular system until he begins sweating despite the still moon-cool air; he tugs his favorite cable-knit sweater over his head, the one he's been wearing since college, with holes in the armpits and stretched two sizes larger than new, and wipes his face on it.

Suddenly he's unsure which he fears more, having mistaken the Spirit's voice for his own, or not being able to have what he believed he heard in those whispers.

He isn't lonely. Friends, colleagues, clients. Family and neighbors. Strangers. Enough people walk through his days to satisfy the basic, human need of connection. Sometimes there's so much crowding he pushes through the arms and legs and demands and conversations, and closes it all behind his studio door. *Click.* Silence. He fits with Mark and Hortense in a shared story, instant commonality begetting closeness. He has a church home in which to wrestle with the so-called bigger things. None of these, though, is a wife. He's not been someone who has been on his knees pleading for his missing rib. In fact, he's prided himself in his satisfaction with singleness. *This is how it's done. This is a life devoted to God and the things he's given over to me. It is possible, and satisfying, and perfect.*

Except it isn't.

He's Paul, not Aquila. He's Julian Goetz, gifted in singleness, running the race alone. Even at night, he doesn't huddle on one side of the mattress, stroking the empty place on the other, wondering if it will be filled. He sprawls in the center, a snow angel on its stomach, drooling in the crack between the two pillows. But possibility breeds clarity and he realizes he won't ask for his Priscilla because he doesn't want to be told no. To him, to be denied a wife is the same as being told he can't succeed at being married.

He's not failed at anything before.

She's not coming.

Julian fiddles with the radio, bypassing his usual Christian station and settling on ESPN. The talk show hosts argue over baseball. Seven weeks into the season and no surprises; they manufacture news and make stats and scores take on an importance undeserved. It's only a game. And yet, his father—athlete and rabid sports enthusiast—told Julian the same. *It's only pictures.*

He shakes his head. One disappointment is enough for any day.

The diner is a stone's throw ahead. Julian decides to eat his sorrow's weight in humble bumble pie. He feels beneath his seat for an umbrella and, finding none, shrugs and thinks he'll walk anyway. His car will be fine on the side of the road. He wants the gloom of rain upon him for longer than the few seconds from parking lot to door.

He steps onto the pavement at the same moment he sees her, moving toward the tree with much less determination than last time. Her stride is looser, more timid. She approaches the oak's trunk and rests her forehead on it. Julian doesn't move, or reach for his camera. He waits for her to notice him, and she does, lengthening her neck and turning first her face, and then her entire body, toward his Jeep.

The drizzle transitions to mist, millions of precipitate particles suspended in the air, compacted tightly together, body parting the sponginess as he approaches her. Dozens of sticky burrs hitch a ride on his jeans, and the tall, soggy grasses whip his shoes. Her arms, wrapped snuggly around her rib cage, straighten, hands migrating down her sides and settling on her hips, a protective X created, breasts pressed into her biceps, forearms crossed at her navel.

"Ada," he says, stopping two yardstick lengths away.

"What are you doing here?"

She's not shocked to see him, but more quietly awed, as if his appearance isn't unexpected and yet amazing nonetheless. Like the birth of a baby. Yes, that's it. There's no surprise that the baby will come, and soon, and yet the mother cradles the new life, knowing how all the pieces work from conception to final push into the world, and still there is nothing but wonderment.

"I came for you," Julian tells her.

"Why?"

He hesitates. "You'll think I'm crazy if I say."

She draws her arms back up her torso, hugging her shoulders. The rain begins again, *rat-tat-tat* on the oak leaves, the top of his head. "You're my Boaz."

Her proclamation startles Julian. "How do you—"

"I've dreamed about you every night since we first met."

"God is speaking to you, too, then?"

Ada lowers her eyes. "I'm no prophet."

Lightning claws at the horizon, and the sky coughs one thunderclap, then another. It pours, a torrent of sea in the firmament. The waters above come down from heaven. Julian grabs Ada's hand, cold, frail, and tows her behind him as he runs to the Jeep. He closes her into the passenger seat, climbs behind the steering wheel, and turns on the heat. It blows in their faces; he switches to the floor vents.

Ada shivers. He bunches his sweater, stretching the collar wide. "Here," he says, and she bends forward to receive it over her head, struggles into the sleeves, and tugs the waistband down. They sit wordlessly, both knowing an invisible line has been crossed. She's in a heathen's car. She's been touched by him. She can't go back.

"I have this," she says finally, reaching down the neck of her shirt and removing an envelope. He takes it. Opens it. Her birth certificate. "It's the only thing that shows I'm me."

"Are you certain you want to leave?"

She nods. So does he.

* * *

They drive to Vermont because Julian has done his research. No waiting period. No identification. No residency restrictions. They can walk into the first town hall they find, pay for a marriage license, and skip over to the justice of the peace for the civil service. No muss, no fuss.

Ada talks, first about her dreams, each one a variation of the same: she goes to the tree and he waits for her there. In several versions he proposed, down on one knee. Once she found him asleep in wildflowers. Once they raced away by moonlight, on foot, with dogs and men pursuing. She ignored the dreams at first; they leave her waking warm and disappointed and wanting. They must be from her own depraved mind, or sent by the adversary. She's unsure which is the worse of the two possibilities.

"But four nights ago I had one where we met again, and I showed you a paper, and you said, 'How did you know to get this?' And when I looked down I saw *Certificate of Birth*. And when I woke there were numbers, written in fire. I rubbed and rubbed my eyes but they didn't go away. Only faded. Like when you write across the sky with sparklers, you can still see where the tails have been?"

Julian nods. "Yeah."

"It was early, still dark, on a morning my father had planned to go out of town to meet another prophet. My brother was supposed to be in charge, looking over us, but he was still sleeping. I tried to go back to sleep but the numbers burned behind my eyelids. I knew what they were for. I got out of bed and as quiet as I could, snuck down from the loft and into my parents' bedroom. My mother was snoring. It struck me as so funny, I had had to cover my mouth to keep from laughing out loud.

"The safe was under his desk. He locks all his prophetic

journals in there, to protect them. Only he knows the combination, he says. I got down in front of it as low as I could, scared because I couldn't see my mother to know if she woke; she shifted and rolled over in the bed, so she was breathing softly now, and my heart was beating in my ears, and I could only hear that and not her. But the numbers were still there. I'm not certain I could see them anymore, but the impression in my head was so bright, it's like they were still shining in front of me. I don't think I'll ever forget. Thirteen. Twelve. Twenty-nine. Fifteen. I twisted the safe dial, somehow knowing which way to turn and when to pass zero twice, and there was a click and it opened. It was full of notebooks and I was so tempted to look and read, but I knew time was running out, my pulse racing like a stopwatch. There was an orangey envelope tucked along the side, a big one, and I unwrapped the string tying it closed, and found a bunch of white envelopes with names on them. I grabbed mine, stuck it in my shirt, tried to position everything as I found it, and got out of the room. I heard someone getting up, so I opened a Bible and sat at the kitchen table, and pretended to read as my brother came downstairs. He looked at me and said, 'You're up early,' and I shrugged and told him I couldn't sleep, and he said he was hungry so I got up and cooked him breakfast, and by the time I was done everyone was awake and that was that.

"I kept the envelope with me. And the next three times I went to the tree looking for you I refused to be discouraged. The numbers were real. I knew your coming would be real too. And then it was."

He wants to take her hand, but she keeps them hidden in the sleeves of his sweater. They drive in silence now, Julian in prayer, Ada sinking deeper within herself.

When he turns into the parking lot of the Bennington Town Offices, she is half the size she was when they left her tree two hours ago. A dark sedan passes behind the Jeep, bass roaring, hip-hop squeezing through the closed windows. Two women walking by shout expletives at the driver for spraying puddled water unto their shoes. Ada bites the skin from her lip.

Julian's romantic notions drain away, and he begins comprehending the effects of the way she's lived for so long. She's a hatchling, fallen from the nest to the rocks below. How can she not be injured?

"Ada, listen to me. We don't have to do this today. You can stay with me anyway."

"Not married?"

"Yes, but not like that. You'd have your own room."

"I can't do that."

"I can find a place for you, then. I have friends who would let you live with them, for a while, until you were . . . ready."

"You don't want to marry me."

"No, Ada. I do. Of course I do. What I don't want is for you to feel pressured into it. Like you have to, and you don't have any other choices. You do. No one is forcing you to go through with . . . well . . . anything."

She pulls another piece of skin from her lips, with her fingers this time, a long, whitish flake. "I'm ready," she whispers.

He opens the car door for her, and they go into the building, a columned New England home converted into the local government headquarters. The floors squeak as they walk down a musty hallway to the third room on the left. He holds her arm, just above the elbow, and feels her trembling.

They must look quite the pair, rumpled clothes stiff with dried thunderstorms, wind-tossed hair, muddy shoes. Her in a frumpy skirt and too-large sweater, despite it now being afternoon and warm enough for short sleeves. Him with field grass woven into the laces of his sneakers, a blob of ketchup on his pants, dripped from the Whopper he grabbed a half hour ago. Ada ate nothing, though he offered to take her anywhere she'd like for lunch.

The clerk records the necessary information—he learns Ada is twenty-five years old—and processes their marriage license, handing Julian a list of a dozen justices of the peace in town. Her eyes flicker between him and Ada, and when she asks, "Are you okay, miss?" Ada nods and steps closer to him. Back in the car Julian calls down the list until he finds someone to perform the ceremony. Fifteen minutes later they stand in the justice's home office, their shoes left on the front doormat, their feet sinking into the plush pomegranate-colored carpet. The whole ordeal takes less time than a dental appointment. No exchange of rings. No "You may kiss the bride." The justice seems unfazed, signing here and there, and wishing them well. "The Sox are playing," he tells them as he ushers them from his house. "If they were winning, I wouldn't have answered my phone when you called."

And, like that, they're married.

The drive home is another ninety minutes. Julian tries to engage Ada in conversation, and she answers his questions but not much more. Her posture tightens as the rural landscapes turn decidedly urban. He steers down the tight alleyway leading to his driveway, parks the Jeep, and says, "Well, this is it."

They enter through the back door, and once into the living room Julian bumbles through a tour of the downstairs, pointing here and there while Ada makes no eye contact, hands clasped at her waist. Then the same upstairs, motioning toward rooms and closets while she twists the hem of his sweater. And then he's done talking about the brownstone and they stand with their backs against opposite walls of the hallway, neither sure what comes next. Finally Julian offers to make her some food. "You have to be hungry. You haven't eaten all day."

She shakes her head and asks if she can bathe, and perhaps wash her clothes so she'll have something clean to wear tomorrow.

"I'll throw them in the laundry for you. Just leave them outside the door. I'll get something for you to put on for tonight too."

"I can take care of it."

"I've lived alone for the past twenty years. I promise you, I can work a washer."

Hesitating, she bobs her head up and down. Swallows. "Okay."

He gives her towels. "I'll be back for your clothes in a few minutes."

She closes the bathroom door. He waits in the bedroom until the water has been running a good five minutes and then peeks into the hallway; her skirt, shirt, tights, and his sweater are folded and waiting for him on the floor. He exchanges the pile for a pair of flannel pajamas and takes them downstairs to the stackable washer and dryer hidden in the other bathroom's closet. After adding a few of his own things to the mix, he pours in too much powdered detergent and sets the cycle to gentle. Then he rinses off in the small corner shower, runs through the house clutching a towel at his waist, and throws on clean jeans and a shirt, thinking Ada will be more comfortable with him fully dressed.

He doesn't know what this evening will bring.

God, what have I gotten myself into?

More waiting. He reads. He prays. He lies on the bed with his forearms across his eyes, listening to the shower. Eventually, the water stops.

Ten minutes. Twenty. Still no Ada.

He knocks on the bathroom door. "Ada? You okay?"

When she doesn't answer, he tries the knob. Unlocked. He opens it only enough to peer within and sees her, undressed, cutting her hair with his nail scissors. She notices him and drops to the tile floor, breasts against her knees, arms around her legs, her remaining hair fanning over her in cover.

"I'm sorry. I didn't—" He shuts the door.

He's suddenly and completely overwhelmed. What can he do for this girl, this stranger, now his wife, cowering beneath the pedestal sink like a feral Lady Godiva? When imagining the possibilities, he'd never moved past the romantic, the love-at-first-sight fantasies, the tingling notion that what God has joined, no man can pull asunder. He never considered the years of spiritual abuse Ada suffered in Abram's Covenant, and perhaps other abuses as well. He didn't think about the difficulties she would have adjusting to life outside the only community she knew.

What does he do now?

Help her.

How?

Silence.

Julian can't imagine anything helpful at the moment, except perhaps a different pair of scissors. He takes the pair from his studio table and knocks again at the bathroom door. Again, Ada says nothing so he goes in to her, drapes her in a towel, and helps her to her feet as she shudders with tears.

"Julian, I'm so sorry. I should have—"

"Shh," he says, touching a finger to her lips. "You'll never get the back straight. Let me help."

Ada nods and gives him the scissors.

"These wouldn't cut dental floss," he tells her, dropping them in the tub. "I have better."

When he was a child, his mother cut his hair to save money. His and Sophie's, always the same day, Saturday after bath so they'd be presentable for mass the next morning. She made him sit on the toilet and he'd wiggle and fidget, and she'd smack him with whatever was handy—the tube of toothpaste, the paperback novel she was reading, sometimes the handle of the plunger—telling him he'd better keep still or else. One time the *or else* was her cutting the tip of his ear. He bled and sobbed, and his mother doused the wound with alcohol and said, "Stop being a baby." On other occasions the *or else* was less painful—crooked bangs, pronounced cowlicks, a scratch at the back of his neck, not from the scissors but her fingernails; she kept them long and polished like Barbra Streisand.

He folds a towel on the closed toilet lid, easing Ada onto it. She crosses her legs; her feet are purple and goose bumps sprout on her skin. He turns on the hot tap in the tub and shuts the door.

In the medicine cabinet there's a comb he never uses. He eases it through Ada's hair, teeth tangling in the snarls. With one hand he holds the hair above the knot, protecting her scalp from the tugging. With the other he hacks at the tangles until they loosen. "How short?" he asks.

"You decide."

"No. This is all you."

Shaking, she touches her shoulder. "Here?"

So Julian smoothes her hair and does his best to cut in a straight line, stretching the ends to be certain they are even, kneeling to see his handiwork up close. He finishes, dusting the stray stubble from her back and face, wiping the steam from the mirror so she can see.

"Do you like it?" he asks, standing behind her, cradling her thin frame against him. She's all bones, her pointy places digging into his own. She doesn't seem to notice, and he carries her to the dark bedroom. She hides beneath her towel while he finds more pajamas, the bottoms and top unmatched, and waits in the hallway for her to dress. "I'm done," she calls, and she's still on the bed, her skin as white as the plaster walls, toes curled under. He sits beside her.

"I don't know what to do," she tells him. "I wasn't supposed to marry. My father told me my spirit was too rebellious, and that I was to stay with him and my mother because he was the only one who could ensure my obedience, and I would care for them when they got old. I had resigned myself to it."

"Ada."

"No one was allowed to talk about any of . . . it . . . with me. I mean, I heard a little here and there, listening to my sisters when they were being . . . too open. But I don't—" She begins to cry.

He draws her into him, her head on his chest, and lies back on the pillows. Her body resists at first, and then follows, and he twines his fingers in freshly cut hair. Julian wakes in the night to find Ada has crept closer, her arm over his stomach, hand buried under his waist. He doesn't want to move and risk waking her, but he's cold, so he manages to hook his toes in the blanket folded at the bottom of his mattress. Bending his knee, he pulls it high enough to grab with the hand not pinned beneath her, unfolds it, and covers them both.

CHAPTER NINETEEN

It's more difficult than he thought, though he had no sense to think anything prior to stealing Ada away from her family. She's been born into this new world naked and innocent, and like a newborn all the lights are too bright and the air too cold and the blankets too scratchy. She can do very little without him. Yes, she knows how to work the kitchen stove and count money and scrub the floor. But she can't write a check or use an ATM machine. She doesn't know how to pay for groceries at the store. She needs to be taught how to use a computer and cell phone. She can't drive or use public transportation.

And she won't leave the house without him. Ever.

He cancels almost all his jobs and appearances, rescheduling what he can for the new year, refunding deposits, issuing sincere apologies. He says his wife cannot be left alone, which is true, and leaves the reasons unspoken. The people on the other side of the phone fill in the blanks with terrible illnesses or a disfiguring accident and Julian lets them.

He had imagined them traveling together, her learning how to identify lenses or set props at photo shoots. He imagined a partner, but he's a parent. He takes her shopping for clothes; she circles the racks, touching each garment, never pulling anything from the hanger. He plucks an armload of skirts and blouses and t-shirts, and encourages her toward the changing room. "I don't need to try anything on," she says. "You tell me what you like and I'll take those things." She'll wear what he says, eat what he says, spend her time in the way he picks for them. He explains these are her decisions to make. She can't function without someone granting her permission. She's incapable of disagreeing with him, of saying no. He has to read every quiver, every flicker of the eyebrow, each swallow. He notes her response time. How many seconds between question and affirmative answer mean she doesn't want to do what he's suggested but she's agreeing to it anyway? Even when he orchestrates situations for her to object, she cannot. She doesn't eat tomatoes; she picked them from the first salad they ate together, and each one since. He makes them grilled cheese for lunch and asks, "Tomato on that?"

"If you want," she says.

He leaves the tomato off hers, of course. She bites into the sandwich with trepidation. Tasting only cheese, bread, and butter, she looks up at him with confusion and relief. And delight. He sees it in her stooped-shoulder smile, the one she gives when she's ashamed of her happiness because she thinks she doesn't deserve it. "No tomato."

"You don't like it."

"I never told you that."

He kisses the tip of her nose. "You didn't have to."

By evening's end, he's exhausted from all the maneuvering, a constant chess game he needs to lose, but his opponent keeps stumbling her pieces into check.

The two things fueling his hope are the bitty glimpses of the Ada he met at the store that day—the clever, lively one who flustered him in the first moments they met—and his certainty of God's hand in all of this. He remembers the story of the safe, Ada's dreams, and holds onto them. He writes the combination on his arm in black Sharpie. *13-12-29-15.* She notices, splays the fingers of her right hand and touches each number with one, applies pressure one tip at a time as if the ink marks are buttons.

"I love you," he says, and he can only describe it as a supernatural love, sown in him by Christ himself because he has no other reason to feel so deeply for a woman he's known so short a period of time.

Ada turns her head away. Julian has only a disoriented sense of her opinion of him. She doesn't say she loves him, and that's fine; she came because God called her, and he understands if it is too soon for her to love a stranger in this strange land. He lives with the certainty she will come to feel for him all the things a wife feels for her husband—good and bad. He has time.

What he lacks is patience.

He's restless, not working, repeating the same routine each day. He swells with untaken photographs. Some days he goes from window to window, capturing the outside world on the camera's memory card. He shoots random items in the house. He comes up behind Ada and takes pictures of the nape of her neck as she washes the breakfast plates.

"Don't do that," she tells him.

He touches her instead, in the identical place, where her up-pinned hair reveals a fuzzy point of stray strands.

"Julian."

"We have a dishwasher."

"I don't like it."

He doesn't ask if she means the machine, or his touch, but goes and sits behind the closed door of his studio until she finishes, holding the silent camera in his hands.

It's so easy to believe oneself sanctified when single.

Finally, selfishly, he calls Hortense. He hasn't seen her or Mark since the day in the gallery when he told them about Ada—nearly two months ago—though they've incessantly asked when they can meet his new bride. He wants to have a barbeque. "Invite people," he tells her. "But not too many. I don't want Ada overwhelmed." He needs the outside world to come to him, doesn't care who it may be as long as Mark and Hortense are part of it. They are his only friends. He has hundreds, thousands perhaps, of acquaintances. Any of them he can call if he needs a favor—a ride to the airport, a couple weeks of collecting his mail, a few pulled strings for a dinner reservation. But only the two of them does he trust with his innermost workings. For as much as he confides to God, sometimes he needs to share with flesh and blood, not only Spirit.

He tells Ada about the cookout. She nods. Then he tells her about Hortense. "She's the most beautiful woman you'll ever see," and he's been watching his wife closely enough to recognize the twinge of jealousy she blinks from her vision. "And she has no hands."

So they come, clamoring through the brownstone with twelve-packs and hot dogs and quinoa salad, the women drinking wine coolers on the patio while Mark pounds horseshoe posts into the ground. Ada watches from the pic-nic table, overwhelmed, body rigid. She answers questions with yes or no, or "Julian can tell you," until the sparse con-versation directed her way dries up completely. He lights the grill, and then goes to her, cups his hands around her upper arms, claiming her. She relaxes slightly.

"I'm going to get the burger meat from the kitchen," he says into her ear. She nods, and he thinks she'll follow him, but doesn't, and once inside he realizes it's because he didn't instruct her to do so. Hortense, however, does fol-low him, tweezing a carrot stick from the vegetable platter on the counter. She swoops it through the ranch dressing and chomps. "It's not what you thought," she says, mouth full.

She's pert and self-satisfied, drawn to her full height, breasts forward, smudge of dip at the corner of her mouth. Julian points to the identical spot on his own lip, and she licks the stain away, no embarrassment whatsoever.

"And you're happy about that?" he asks.

"Happy? No. But come on, Julian. You can't seriously be that blind."

He can say nothing to make her understand. So he says, "I love her, okay?"

She closes her eyes. Nods. "Okay." And with all the determination that has always been Hortense, she marches outside to the patio, parks herself on the picnic bench beside Ada, and says, "Hey, Julian said you grew up on an organic farm. I'm having the darndest time with my tomatoes. I have a couple of those ones you keep in pots, you know? The leaves are turning yellow and falling off. Any ideas?"

Ada hesitates. "Are you watering them?"

"It may not look like I have a green thumb," Hortense says, laughing, "but since I don't have any thumbs, period, that's not a good indicator. Water, yes. I can handle that. Beyond water? You got me."

Julian watches, leaning against the frame of the open sliding glass door, as Ada smiles, and then hides it behind her hand. "Without seeing them, I would have to guess they're root bound."

"Well, maybe you and Julian can come by tomorrow, and you can take a look."

"Okay."

"J-man. Hurry up with those burgers," Mark calls. "We're starving."

"I thought you were drinking your dinner tonight," Julian shouts back, lifting the lid of the grill and dropping the patties on the hot racks. The meat sizzles. He adds hot dogs and looks back at Ada. The conversation wraps around her as the women share gardening failures; she's within it, even though she doesn't speak.

Julian meets Hortense's gaze. Their silent exchange is imperceptible to everyone else. *Thank you. You're welcome. And it won't be spoken of again.*

Later, after people have gone, he and Ada lie atop the gray cotton sheets, a box fan in one window, cooling the humid July night, which has settled in their bedroom. She looks as though she wears the moon, in his white t-shirt and her own white underpants. He wears white, too, boring boxer shorts and nothing else, sweat dampening the hair beneath his arms. He hates the feeling, raises his arms over his head so the breeze from the fan will dry him.

His knees are bent. Hers too. Twin mountains in the semi-darkness, facing opposite directions—his feet point to the bedroom door, hers toward the closet. On their backs, both staring at the ceiling, his ear against her jawbone, and vice versa. She turns her head first, tilts her mouth toward his, stretches her neck so she can kiss him.

CHAPTER TWENTY

I t's the only appearance he couldn't postpone or cancel, an event at MOCA in Los Angeles, for which he was hired eighteen months in advance. He worries about leaving Ada, but she assures him she'll be perfectly fine for the three nights he's away.

"Are you sure? Hortense said she'd come stay with you. Or you can go there."

"Julian. Just go."

"I'll be back for your birthday."

"I know."

"Promise me you'll get in touch with Mark or Hortense if you need anything. Anything."

"I promise."

So he goes.

He calls each evening—evening for him, bedtime for her—but they don't speak long because of the time difference. Instead Ada tucks the phone next to her pillow and falls asleep, and he listens to her breathing change, and he leaves his phone on as well, on his chest, and wakes in the mornings with it having shut off sometime in the night.

On the morning of her twenty-sixth birthday, he takes a cab to the airport, checks into his flight, bumps through security, and boards his plane without incident. During his layover in Cleveland, he eats two Egg McMuffin meals and a couple of extra hash browns. He arrives at his gate to find it overflowing with passengers, so he tucks himself at the end of a row of seats, leans his forehead against the window, and watches coverall-clad mechanics on the tarmac scurrying back and forth under the belly of the airplane. He digs his camera from the satchel at his feet and shoots.

"My son loves photography," a voice says.

Julian looks down into the face of a woman, perhaps midforties, in a brazen white coat. He squints to make out her features, but they are swallowed by the echo of whiteness he sees around her, snow blindness, halos of glare. He averts his eyes. "How old is he?"

"Fifteen," she says. "Are you a professional?"

"Yes," he says. "Is your son with you?"

"No." Something shades her response. He tries again to see her face beyond her coat, wishes he could stare through his viewfinder. Instead he crosses his arm over his chest, his chin wedged in the crook of his elbow, blocking the brightness. Her face is clearer, and there it is. Shame.

"It is a school day," he says.

She nods. "Do you want to see some of his pictures? I

mean, would you mind looking? I think he's good, but I'm his mom."

"Yes, sure. Of course."

Everyone has a book idea to pitch to a published author, a song to play for the uncle in Nashville, a portfolio for the photographer. He's seen everything from scrapbooks to iPhone galleries, scrolling through, searching for the smallest, most hidden compliment he can offer with truth. But he always says yes, because no one said yes to him. His mother died when he was nine. His father thought taking pictures was for homosexuals and liberals, especially when his sensitive son had no interest in pummeling others on a football field. So Officer George Goetz, third-generation German-American, lover of whiskey, fighter of local crime with the local sheriff's department, purveyor of sorrow and gambling debt, made certain his pansy son had plenty of pummeling at home. His sister, older by eight years, was already out of the house, at first in college, then traveling, then marriage. Even if she wanted to protect him—which he believes she did—Sophie kept running so her grief wouldn't catch her. When she finally popped her head back into his life, he was sixteen and mostly out of the house as well, crashing on friends' sofas on weekends—proper spend-the-nights—and climbing into their bedroom windows after parents were asleep on weekdays. By the time he'd been accepted into the college photography program, his size-thirty-waist jeans wouldn't stay on his hips without a belt and since he couldn't afford a meal plan, he'd join whatever student activities boasted food. One Thursday night he showed up at an Intervarsity Christian Fellowship meeting and found much more than pizza. Finally someone said yes to him.

Jesus.

The woman glows now, lugging her oversized fuchsia purse onto her lap, pawing through it. "Oh, here it is." She hands him a dollar store photo album, floppy floral cover, ten thin sheath pages.

He looks. The boy is learning, yes; only taking pictures maybe three years at most. But he's past the trying-too-hard stage, the odd-angle stage, the blurry-weird-lighting-is-cool stage. This kid understands composition, probably naturally. But more so, he peers over the edge of the photograph to discover all that is behind it.

He's good.

And Julian recognizes so much of his own teenage fumblings in these ten plastic-laminated images, printed at home and cut unevenly to size with wobbly scissors, and given as some sort of homemade gift, tied with leftover Christmas ribbon.

"What's your son's name?"

"Evan."

"You tell Evan he needs to listen to his mother. He has talent." He finds a business card in the front flap of his camera bag. "Have him get in touch with me. I'm serious."

She glances at the card. "Thank you, Mr. Goetz. He'll be so pleased. After he gets over the fact I showed his pictures to some stranger at the airport. He made me promise these were for my eyes only." She tucks the photo book back into her purse, with more care than she yanked it out. Sticks his card in her coat pocket. "He's my heart. Both of them."

In the din of the waiting area, a blurry voice rattles in the public address system. Several names. He picks out his own. "Excuse me," he tells the woman, and twists through the crowd to the airline counter, where he learns the flight has been overbooked, and due to issues with his reservation, there is no seat for him.

"No, it can't be. I've had these tickets for months."

"Sir, I realize how inconvenient this must be for you."

"I don't think you do."

"The next available flight is the nine fifteen to Albany, New York. We're also giving you a three-hundred-dollar travel voucher and coupons for a free meal and drink at the—"

Julian holds up his hand. "Just do whatever."

He calls Ada. "My flight's overbooked. Why in the world airlines do that, I don't know."

"What does that mean?" she asks.

"I've been bumped to the nine-fifteen flight."

"Oh. It's alright."

He'd made reservations tonight for her birthday. He wants the day to be special. She's twenty-six and never has had any recognition of her value. The cult didn't celebrate birthdays. No one in that place was significant, except the prophet. Julian angers thinking of Abram Mitchell, his scrawny face and limbs, though for as sticky as Julian's memory is, he cannot bring Mitchell into focus. He pictures him as one of those lanky aliens, the stretched humanoid frame and soulless, unblinking serpent eyes.

"No, it's not." He sighs. "Look, just let me—I'll call you back."

Does he pray? His jaw clenches. It has always been his personal philosophy to avoid prayer for matters of inconvenience—parking places close to the grocery store in rainstorms, slow traffic while late to appointments, sold-out events, ill-timed sinus infections. He's seen so many worse things through his lens. Children have died of starvation in his arms. Men with war wounds bled at his feet, blackening the dust. Women wailing in the streets as lost loved ones were carried past. No, this doesn't deserve a prayer.

But perhaps the persistent window treatment? He approaches the airline desk again. "Please, it's my wife's birthday. It's very important I get home this afternoon. Could you ask one more time if anyone would be willing to trade seats with me?"

"Sir, I've announced it three times already."

"I know. I know. Just once more. Please."

The attendant makes his plea over the loudspeaker. He waits. The woman in the white coat approaches. "I'll switch flights," she says.

"Thank you, thank you," Julian says. He offers his hand. "Honestly. I cannot thank you enough."

"It's my pleasure," the woman says. She offers her hand. "Katherine Walker."

"Mr. Goetz," the attendant interrupts. "You need to board now."

"Yes, wonderful. Thank you."

The woman says, "Tell your wife happy birthday."

"She's *my* heart," he tells her. Katherine.

She nods. Understands.

"I'll be waiting to hear from Evan," he calls as he backs toward the gate. Hands the waiting attendant his boarding pass. His neck flushes with happiness and he cannot stop grinning.

He's the last one into the plane; the attendant locks the door as he steps on. One seat, the middle, between two businessmen three-quarters of the way to the back. Julian jams his carry-on in the overhead compartment and waits while the outside man stands and steps into the aisle. He twists into the row, falling heavily between the armrests. The other man stares out the window. Julian stuffs his camera bag under the seat in front of him, buckles his belt.

Before powering off his phone, he texts Ada: I'LL BE HOME IN TIME. BE READY TO PARTY.

PART THREE

EVAN

CHAPTER TWENTY-ONE

ey, Evan. Hey. Wait up."

Evan stops in the stream of teenagers; they bump around him, textbooks and elbows and sneakers, as if the hallways of high school are a rock tumbler, and he thinks, *I'll have no edges left by graduation. Evan Smooth. That's me.* Then Grace hooks her arm through his and pulls him from the bodies and against the lockers, which are painted that peculiar blue only found in schools and stadiums, too vibrant to be royal, too bruised to be aqua. She snaps a sheet of paper open with a flick of her wrist. "They've released some of the names of the Flight 207 victims."

"So?"

"That photographer you like is on there."

"Let me see that," Evan says, snatching the list from his friend. He drops his binder and copy of *Brave New World* onto his feet and holds the paper with both hands, as if it will keep him from falling. The names are in alphabetical order; his eyes dive into them, catching the eighth one. Goetz, Julian. "Maybe it's someone with the same name."

Grace shakes her head, silky hair dancing, and he gets a rare glimpse of her ears. She wears her hair parted in the center, straight over her cheeks, only the center third of her face visible. "It's him."

"How do you know?"

"I saw the story. It's online, all over."

He bangs his head softly against the locker behind him. He's been avoiding the crash news altogether; it only reminds him of how close his mother came to getting on the flight. "I don't look at that stuff."

"I get it," Grace says. She leans back onto the adjacent locker.

Their arms touch.

He's known Grace since they were in diapers, their mothers best friends and partners in the real estate business. Maybe he'd have a crush on her if she wasn't four inches taller than him. His father insists Evan has one good growth spurt left, but his cardiologist told him not to get his hopes up; he may be five-and-a-half feet tall forever. It isn't only the height difference. She knows so many of his most personal secrets. How he wet the bed until he was nine. How he still can't watch *Toy Story* because it reminds him of the time he was in the hospital after his fifth heart surgery and the little girl in the room next to him died while his mother kept turning up the volume of that stupid movie to distract him from the frantic code team rushing past his door. Or how he isn't circumcised. "Oh, we never had it done when he was a baby because of everything else," his mother told Miss Robin while he and Grace played Nintendo in the next room. They were eleven years old. "Now he says he doesn't want to. Will tried to convince him, but I guess he's been through enough so I suppose he can do something about it on his own when he's an adult, when some girl gets a look at him and comments." The women titter. Evan's face burned and he ran the two blocks home and didn't look at Grace until school began a month and a half later. Grace told his mother he felt sick and didn't want to puke in a strange bathroom. Katherine showed up at the house a half hour later, tucked him into bed, and brought him chicken broth and saltines to settle his belly.

Grace never mentioned the conversation to Evan.

"You think she saw him?" Grace wants to know.

"I don't think I could ask." He's done what he can to help her forget. Putting on the funny if the situation calls for funny, keeping all his interactions with his mom buoyant, trying not to act fifteen more than necessary, doing chores without being asked multiple times in increasing volume and sharpness. If it's working, he'd hate to see what she'd be like if he back talked and failed chemistry and left his dirty socks all over the house. "She's not herself."

"She's depressed. She looked death in the eye and now she's reevaluating her suburban soccer mom existence. It's to be expected."

"Did you get that from *Oprah* magazine or something?"

Grace shrugs. "I need something to read on the toilet."

"Too much information," Evan says, wiping his hand through the air.

The bell rings. Students scatter, ducking into doorways, sprinting down the hall. Grace pokes him in the ribs and says, "Bus?"

"Yeah," he tells her, and she disappears too.

Only his binder is on the floor next to him; Huxley has been kicked away by some oversized jock foot. He finds it in a puddle beneath the water fountain, wipes it on his jeans, and heads to gym.

* * *

The other boys run the cross-country trail. Evan walks the track. He's medically excused from anything high intensity. He can usually manage baseball, as long as he doesn't hit more than a single, which never happens unless there's a throwing error to first, and even then he simply stands on the bag while the ball is found in long grass against the chain-link fence surrounding the field. He also participates in the archery unit, ballroom dancing, and Ping-Pong. Otherwise, he walks the track, or the perimeter of the gymnasium on the days it's too cold for outside, dodging misplaced jump shots or avoiding the occasional wayward hockey puck.

His teeth are fuzzy from lunch and because he forgot to brush them before school; he runs his tongue around his mouth, last night's plaque scaly at the gum line. He polishes them with the cuff of his sweatshirt and returns his hands to his pockets, shuffles along, thinking of Julian Goetz and washed with a strange, in-between feeling. Not grief; he'd have to know a person for that depth of melancholy. But more than hearing about a random celebrity to which he had no connection, other than recognizing the name. It's a bee sting—sharp, sudden pain that fades to a mild throbbing for several hours, a bit of swelling brought down by ice, a bitty red welt for a day or two, and then it's forgotten until everyone is around the dinner table sharing stories of past insect bites.

Three years ago, his parents bought him and his brother digital cameras for Christmas, and subscriptions to several photography magazines. Bryce took a few pictures of the family around the tree, holding up their new sweaters and matching coffee mugs. Evan fell in love with the images he saw through the viewfinder. Everything seemed sturdier, sharper, more real. He borrowed every book on photography in his town's meager library. He tried techniques he read about in the magazines, joining photography club and entering whatever contests for which he was eligible—from county fairs to national calls for entries. And, in the pages of *American Photo*, he met Julian Goetz.

It was an interview and a dozen photos, each one lighting places in Evan he didn't know existed—thin, underdeveloped corners of mercy. Evan dares to close his eyes as he walks, trusting his feet on the rubberized surface, so he can see those images again, calling them each to memory until he wobbles with his self-imposed blindness, stops, blinks, and continues his slow circling around the track.

How will he stop himself from asking his mother about Goetz? For the past eighteen months, he's kept an eye on the photographer's itinerary, hoping for a lecture at one of the not-too-far state universities or a gallery show in New York City. But Goetz's appearance calendar had been mostly silent, nothing close enough for him to attend and then, nothing at all for the last six months due to his new marriage.

He doubts she noticed Goetz. She's not a people watcher, an observer of detail. He can almost guarantee she sat herself in one of those uncomfortable plastic airport chairs and only paid attention to whatever real estate magazines she brought with her, or fiddled with her cell phone. She's like Bryce, self-sequestered from those around her unless it's business or family. Strangers waiting for a plane? No chance of interaction whatsoever.

A herd of boys runs from the trees, finishing the cross-country trail. He attaches himself to the tail end of the line, follows them into the locker room, and changes into his jeans without showering. Thank goodness for ninth-period gym.

On the bus, Grace sits next to the window, her French horn beside her, saving a place for him. She moves it to the floor, propping her feet on it, knees against the seat back in front of her. She huffs on the glass, smeared with the handprints of dozens of other students, and draws faces in the condensation. This one with oversized ears. That one with rabbit teeth and a curl of hair in the center of its forehead. She rubs her palm through them and begins again. Hearts this time. "There's a memorial service. It's open to the public."

"I can't ask anyone to take me," Evan says.

"I checked Greyhound. Forty-six dollars, round trip. You can walk from the depot to the church." She blows on the window, filling in her doodles. "I'll go with you. We'll be back by like, eight or nine."

He shakes his head. "Thanks, though."

Grace twiddles with the handle of her horn case. "Whatev."

His stop comes first, and he waves as the bus passes, but she ignores him. He's not bothered by it; her moodiness goes as quickly as it comes and tomorrow it will be as if this hiccup between them never happened. Evan doesn't know what caused Grace to turn inward this time, but blames it on being a girl. He can't think of any other reason for it.

No one is home yet. Bryce has basketball practice and the parents are still at work. Evan kicks off his sneakers inside the back door and snags a two-pack of Ring Dings on the way past the pantry. In his bedroom, he drops his coat and backpack to the floor. He finds last year's May/June issue of *American Photo*, in the bottom desk drawer, and it falls open to the interview, to the page with the highlighted passage, because he's turned to it so many times before.

Why am I a photographer? I ask myself that every single day. There's always a moment, usually in those dead spaces when the mundane takes over—I'm driving through the McDonald's window for a double cheeseburger, buying toothpaste, staring out at the potholed street while drinking coffee, wasting too much time clicking around the Internet—when the sheer absurdity of what I do for a living punches me in the face. I don't perform delicate, life-saving surgeries on vulnerable infants. I don't rescue people from burning buildings. I don't even do simple, useful services like changing the worn-out brakes on someone's car or unplugging backed-up pipes. I take pictures. So what? Any three-year-old with his mother's cell phone can do that.

Then I remember it is my God who gave me the desire and ability to do what I do. I take these photos so others can see *imago dei* in humanity. We must look deeply because we've forgotten it's there. Some will never see it; they've lost it to the Fall. But for those who retain the ability to recognize God With Us, either by the Spirit or because he has graciously allowed it, I give them a window through my camera. I don't capture landscapes or weddings or toddlers on Santa's lap. My photographs— I hope—bring the viewer to the doorstep of the divine, stirring them not only to compassion but to action.

"Then the King will say to those on his right, 'Come, you who are blessed by my Father; take your inheritance, the kingdom prepared for you since the creation of the world. For I was hungry and you gave me something to eat, I was thirsty and you gave me something to drink, I was a stranger and you invited me in, I needed clothes and you clothed me, I was sick and you looked after me, I was in prison and you came to visit me.'

"Then the righteous will answer him, 'Lord, when did we see you hungry and feed you, or thirsty and give you something to drink? When did we see you a stranger and invite you in, or needing clothes and clothe you? When did we see you sick or in prison and go to visit you?'

"The King will reply, 'Truly I tell you, whatever you did for one of the least of these brothers and sisters of mine, you did for me.'"

This is why I take pictures, so the housewife in farm country who's never set foot outside a fifty-mile radius can see the hungry and thirsty in sub-Saharan Africa, or Flint, Michigan. Or the night-shift cashier at the Sunoco, working his way through community college, can see an overflowing hospital in Calcutta. We're all of us too busy and too focused on our own needs to look up and notice the desperation of others. Or the laughter. If someone looks at one of my photographs and his heart is awakened by what is framed there—grief, loss, joy, poverty, peace, illness, ignorance, fortitude, grace—then perhaps he'll be moved to respond when he comes face-to-face with those same things when passing his neighbor on the sidewalk in front of his own home.

Evan finds Grace's number on the contacts page of his cell phone and touches the green receiver icon to dial her. "What you'd forget? The Spanish homework?" she asks.

"Still up for a funeral?"

"Does that mean we're skipping school?"

"Uh, yeah."

"Epic."

CHAPTER TWENTY-TWO

They go to homeroom so they'll be counted in the morning attendance, avoiding a phone call home by the office secretary asking their folks to please call the school if they're home sick. The question is phrased so politely—*This is Mrs. Spelling at Roosevelt High. I'm just wondering if Evan will be in to school today. Please call me as soon as possible and let me know.*—but it's only a ploy to identify students who are skipping and parents who are unaware. When the first-period bell rings, they stuff their coats into their backpacks and walk to the gymnasium, across it, and out the side door because it's closest to the road and on the windowless side of the building. Evan zips on his jacket as soon as they're out of eyeshot, the brisk November wind passing straight through his skin, but Grace is content to fight the gooseflesh and pretend she's not cold in the slightest.

Neither wore black. Evan owned one pair of black slacks, last worn in June for his choir concert, and when he uncrumpled them from the back corner of his closet, they had grown a pelt of dust and were three inches too short. Grace's mother hated black and she didn't want a lecture about turning Goth, which she endures any time she dresses in anything her mother disapproves of, despite Grace repeatedly saying her style choices slant Emo and not gothic whatsoever. So Evan wears his everyday clothes—nondescript jeans, though he chose his darkest wash ones, plain gray shirt, and his Nikes. Grace's flamingo pink denim pants are bunched around brown-and-yellow plaid Converse high-tops, and her white hooded sweatshirt is decaled with glittery hearts and skulls.

"Irish Larry's is three miles from here," Grace says. "That okay?"

"Perfect," Evan says, though he feels like he's running to keep steady with Grace's long-legged stride. Their small town has no real bus station, but Greyhound stops twice a day at a local diner, leaving this morning at nine. At the high school, homeroom begins at 7:40 and they were on their way twelve minutes after that, which is plenty of time for most people to walk three miles, but not someone with half a functioning heart.

He can't hide his wheezing from her, and she slows down, glancing at her watch every few seconds. "We'll make it," he says, urging his feet to move faster, toes catching the pavement because his oxygen-depleted limbs are stubborn and clumsy and disobedient. Grace checks the street and when the next car approaches, she waves at it to stop. It does, easing onto the shoulder in front of them, hazard lights blinking.

"Are you crazy?" Evan asks. "They might know us."

"Who in this town doesn't?" She runs ahead, sticks her head through the open passenger-side window, and then waves at him to come on while climbing into the car.

Great.

Evan does, indeed, know the driver, a friend of a friend of Grace's stepbrother. He smokes cloves and doesn't ask questions, and Grace gives him ten dollars when he drops them in front of the diner.

They don't talk much on the ride to Trent. Grace knows him well enough to leave him be, twisting buds into her ears and switching on her iPod. He stares out the window, eventually nodding off, waking when the bus stops for a toll, Grace's head on his shoulder. He lets her sleep until they're at the depot, and then blows her bangs from her forehead. Her brows pull together and she opens her eyes, poking the corners on either side of her nose with two fingers, flicking away the sleep, and then straightening. "Sorry, I was totally out."

"I've heard you snore before."

She elbows him. "Jerk."

Neither is comfortable in the city, everything concrete and tall and unfamiliar. They walk close to one another, bodies bumping. Evan doesn't make eye contact with the passersby; Grace jerks her chin at them with a quiet, "Hey." Some nod back. Some smile. Others glare, or Evan thinks they do from what he can glean in his periphery.

Two blocks over, two blocks down, then another three blocks. The service has already started when they arrive, the church offering standing room only, so they slip off to the side and lean against one of the open window ledges. All the bodies absorb the voices of those who speak; Evan understands little of what's said. But he recognizes the photographs, shown one by one as a woman sings something he's heard before, accompanied by a lone cellist.

"What's this song?"

"'Fire and Rain.' James Taylor."

"The guy you like."

"Hey. He's my Julian Goetz."

"Don't even."

Grace tugs the zipper cord on his backpack, still strapped over his shoulders. "Camera?" she asks, knowing the pocket he keeps it in.

He shakes his head. "Not here."

The crowd sways like reeds as the memorial ends, tilting toward the family as it moves up the center aisle.

"Hurry," he tells Grace, tugging her sleeve. He must see them, shoves through the mob, saying, "Excuse me, excuse me," despite his rudeness, and manages to worm to the edging as the family passes. Later he won't remember any of the faces except one. The hollow one. Julian's wife.

Death carves the insides out of people.

He can't forget the first time he saw it. He was twelve and at Children's for his biannual checkup, between his echocardiogram and lab work, the nurse telling him and his mother to have lunch and report to phlebotomy in ninety minutes. Evan convinced his mother to buy him pizza, and ice cream, and a root beer, which wasn't difficult; at the hospital, he got whatever he wanted. When they finished, with nearly an hour left before his blood draws, they crossed the street to a local bakery and bought all the remaining donuts, not quite four dozen, and toted them to the sixth floor—cardiology—for the Ronald McDonald family lounge.

Sugar is the currency of survival in hospitals. Parents live from Coke to Coke, from late night trips to the vending machine for a Hershey's to a cardboard box of Corn Pops from the cabinet of the nutrition room. How many times had his mother sent up a generic sigh of thanksgiving for the restocked basket of goodies in the lounge, donated by someone who understood a baggie of fruit gummies could take the edge off utter exhaustion, and free for the taking? So she and Evan left the donuts on the community food table with a sign—Help Yourself!—though no instruction was necessary, and when they stepped back out into the corridor, a young woman streaked by, wailing, followed by another woman in a silk blouse, and two male nurses.

"Mom?" Evan asked.

"Shh. Let's go," she said, nudging him beneath her arm and hustling him in the opposite direction. He looked back to see the sobbing woman collapsed on the floor, and the professional woman on her knees beside her, whispering in her ear.

"Mom?" he repeated. "What—"

"Her baby died," Katherine said.

And after his blood was taken and the needle prick covered with a Snoopy Band-Aid, and after the doctor proclaimed his heart looked as perfect as it possibly could look and he didn't need to come back for another six months, Evan and his mother waited at the elevator. Next to them, in a wheelchair, sat the crying woman. Her flannel pajama bottoms were ripped at one knee. Her t-shirt stretched over her still-protruding belly. She wore Tweety Bird slippers, and hugged her overnight bag as if her dead child rested in it. She wasn't crying anymore. And when Evan looked into her face, he saw two empty sockets and cavernous darkness descending into her soul.

Hollow.

For the first time, he considered why he had lived and this baby died. Why any one individual was allowed to stay on this earth, and another carried away. Who chose? Some white-bearded guy in the clouds named God? Fate? Happenstance? His family went to church sometimes, and he knew about Jesus and heaven and Christmas, though Easter confused him because there were too many days around it when different stuff happened. But the minister didn't ever talk about the dying part, except to say perhaps God needed another angel.

He didn't buy that. Maybe he would if he still believed in Santa and the Easter Bunny, but not in sixth grade. He tried to talk to his mother about it, but she had shushed him and told him not to be negative. "Just be thankful you're here."

"Come on," he tells Grace, and shrinks into the crowd, mourners parting around him as he plants his feet and allows them to brush by.

"What are you doing?"

"Nothing." Minutes later the pack of strangers has loosened, and Evan moves in the opposite direction, toward the far door, and breaks out of the church into the street.

"The reception," Grace says.

"I want to go back."

"The bus doesn't leave until five."

Evan shrugs. "We can wait at the depot."

He expects Grace to argue but she trudges back the way they came, and he jogs a handful of steps to catch her. She reaches for his hand, holds it, and it's awkward because of their height difference—his arm in front of hers, shoulder twisted and wrist bent upward to meet her fingers—and because the more he thinks about how clammy his palm is, the wetter it becomes. Grace doesn't look at him; her fingernails prick his knuckles. He feels more like a child being led than a boy holding hands with a pretty girl.

They kill time at the bus station, watching daytime television, the sets mounted at the ceilings so they crane their necks to see *Judge Judy* and the *Rachael Ray Show*. Evan wants to take some pictures but is afraid—perhaps unreasonably, perhaps not—he'll be knifed by one of the several tattooed men who look like they could star in those street gang movie clips his English teacher made the class watch after they read *The Outsiders*. Grace buys a deck of playing cards from the snack store and they play war, and then eat Fritos and drink Mountain Dew while trying to solve the half-filled crossword puzzles abandoned around the depot, and then take turns playing Angry Birds on Grace's phone until boarding the bus. And in the darkness, with Grace's chatter and the buzzing of the highway in his ears, he's faced with the question again. Why did Julian Goetz die and his mother live? Still without answer, but left with all the hollowed-out people—he stumbles over them all the time, in shopping malls and at garage sales and once while waiting in line for the Avalanche at Six Flags—and a longing he doesn't understand, one to fill them back up again.

He needs a reason.

He thinks, if he could have asked Julian Goetz, he'd know.

CHAPTER TWENTY-THREE

Y ou see Seth today?" he asks Grace, passing her in the corridor. The sea of students washes him toward social studies and her toward art. She shakes her head and waves her phone. "I'll text him," she calls, and then is carried away, out of sight.

He's tired today, sluggish, one of those times something feels off and he knows he's not ticking quite as he should. His throat itches and pressure builds behind the bridge of his nose, so he expects it's only a cold coming on. He doesn't dare tell anyone; it's a sure trip to Children's for half a dozen tests and probably an overnight stay. No thanks. He puts his head down on his desk while the teacher prattles on about the Indian caste system, comparing it to the hierarchy of high school. His ear against the composite top, he hears the scrawling pens of the note takers vibrating down the metal legs of their desks, through the floor, and up his.

"Mr. Walker, am I boring you?"

He sits up. "No, Ms. Picardi."

"Good. I hoped not. Though I suppose I'll be certain when I see the results of your test Friday."

She continues to mark the blackboard, drawing two pyramids, chalk squeaking when she tips it at the wrong angle. The first she labels with *Brahman* at the pinnacle, then *Kshatriya*, *Yaishya*, *Sudra*, and untouchables. She instructs the class to draw their own triangle and fill in the blanks with the so-called castes they experience at school. "Jocks, cheerleaders, geeks and nerds, Goths, student council, the smart kids, the drama club, however you see the social stratification of public education working out in real life. Don't put your names on them. You'll be handing them in at the end of class and we'll discuss them tomorrow."

Evan flips open his spiral notebook, finds a clean page, and sketches his triangle. The pen feels weighted in his hand, swollen. He clenches his fingers, tightening them to claws, and then rotates his wrists, popping them. He doesn't care about classifying the sophomore cliques. Perhaps he'll write that on his paper. *I will not participate in this assignment because it perpetuates the idea that some people are better than others.* Obviously, that's Ms. Picardi's point, and they'll talk about why his classmates decided to order certain groups the way they did. If he comes to school tomorrow. His throat aches when he swallows and his eyes feel gritty when he blinks. When the bell rings, he'll walk out of class without handing in the assignment.

Class ends. Scratching of chairs, snapping binders, and papery rufflings surround him. Evan slips his book atop his folder and mixes with the other students. "Evan, don't sneak out yet," the teacher says, and he waits for her to give him a once-over. "You really look like you're not feeling well. Can I write you a pass to the nurse?"

He shakes his head. "I'm good."

"Are you sure?" And the unspoken, *I'm worried it's your heart.*

"It's just a cold. Really."

Two periods later, in lunch, he regrets not taking that pass. The babble of cafeteria noise tires him, and it's too much effort to talk above it. He opens the bag of Doritos and eats one, holding the chip by its tip because he hates the feel of the cheese powder on his fingers. He sips his Arnold Palmer. Outside, snow falls in tiny, salty flakes. "Maybe we won't have school tomorrow," he mumbles.

"What?" Andrew shouts.

"Nothing. Never mind."

"Mr. Greene said he thinks we won't have school tomorrow," Andrew says.

"Dude, watch this," Clayton says, stuffing the turkey from his sandwich into the top of his milk carton. He turns it on its side, hammers the bottom of the container with the side of his fist. The turkey shoots out, down the table, landing in front of two freshman girls. They stare at him, disgusted, and then move down several seats, leaving the pale, slimy meat stuck to the tabletop.

"Nice," Andrew says, raising his arm for a high five.

Clayton slaps the offered hand. "And that's how we impress the ladies," he says, laughing.

Evan supports his chin with his hand, elbow on the lunch table, food ignored. He stares out the window, toward the playground. This building previously housed all students, from kindergarten to graduation, but as the district grew a new facility was built for the younger grades and the high school stayed here. The playground, after years of neglect, has disintegrated. As pieces broke down, they were removed, not replaced. There are supports without teeter-totters and half the swings have fallen off, monkey ladders with no crossbars and stairs missing from the slide.

Someone sits on the last swing, swaying into view and then disappearing. Evan sees only the sleeve of a jacket but recognizes the bright yellow and neon green stripe. He calls it the parakeet jacket, made specifically for the ski slopes, but Seth wears it daily, his lift pass fastened to the zipper.

Leaving his lunch, Evan asks the monitor if he may use the restroom. The lady smiles and gives him a pass. Instead, he hurries around the corner and pushes through the double doors closest to the playground. The snow bites his face. He huddles against the brick wall and calls, "Seth."

His friend doesn't turn his head. "I knew you'd see me. You notice everything, don't you?"

"What's going on? Why are you out here?"

"My parents are getting divorced."

Evan sniffles; he wipes his nose with the cuff of his shirt. "I'm sorry."

"I always thought my mother was the problem. I figured if anyone would mess up their marriage, it would be her.

Nope. Not her. My dad. He couldn't keep his pants on, so Mom kicked him out."

"Wha—"

"An affair, Evan. My father is having an affair." Seth leans back in the swing, opens his mouth wide to catch the snow on his waiting tongue. "Well, he was. I guess it's over now, but my mom doesn't care about a little thing like timing. I don't think I blame her."

He wants to be supportive of his friend, to say the right things, but all he can think about at the moment is how the cold gnaws at his bones. His fevers begin in his eyes, his back, and both those places burn. "Hey, come on. Let's go inside. You can talk to Mrs. Wright. I'll go with you."

"You'll go with me? You're gonna need her as much as me."

"I don't get you."

Seth drags his feet in the patchy gravel covering, heels cutting two trenches in the accumulating snow. "It was your mother. The one my dad was sleeping with."

"No. How do you—I mean, that can't—"

"Yup."

Evan shivers against the wall, searching for warmth, finding none. He stuffs his hands in his back jeans pockets and leans on them, arms tucked behind his back as well. His teeth won't stop shaking. "No," he says again.

"You know why she wasn't on that plane? Your mom, I mean. Because she wanted another night with my father. They were both in Cleveland. Together." Seth snickers. "Like together, together."

The bell rings. Evan yanks open the door, runs down the corridor, sneakers cheeping and sliding from their wet soles. He nearly falls once, crashing into a group of three kids who shove him upright and then shove him again, against a recycling can, for good measure. It tips over, sticky aluminum cans and plastic juice bottles clattering across the floor. "Spaz," one of them says, and another barks at him, and they all laugh. Evan ducks into the boys' restroom and locks the stall, breath puffing, esophagus thickening with the threat of tears. He waits for the second bell, and then a few more minutes, and goes to his locker for his coat and backpack. He takes no books. He simply leaves.

He can't go home. He can't stay outside, wandering the snowy streets. He needs someplace warm and private, where he can think, where no one knows him or will notice him, or will think it funny some kid is out alone in the middle of a school day. Grace's house isn't far from here. They always leave the garage door open—Grace broke the key off in the lock years ago and it hasn't been repaired—and the door into the mudroom. And Aunt Robin is probably at work.

There are no cars in the driveway. He lifts the garage door, turning the knob with one hand and yanking the bottom-most handle with the other. The door groans, tenses, and then relents, and he slips beneath before it crashes back down. He sneaks into the laundry area. What to do now? He doesn't know. Suddenly he feels incapable of making decisions. He slumps over the washing machine, still so cold. He checks the dryer; it's full of towels. He starts it, high heat, and then tiptoes into the kitchen, to the cabinet where Aunt Robin keeps her Tylenol. He licks his finger and fishes inside the bottle; a capsule adheres to his wet skin. He does it again, sucks the two pills into his mouth and cups his hand beneath the faucet, filling it with water. Drinks. Swallows.

He can go lie on the couch, and if Aunt Robin finds him, tell her he was sick at school and couldn't make it all the way home so he came here. She won't care. Instead he limps back to the mudroom, opens the dryer, and buries his face in the warm, floral-scented towels. He rolls one for a pillow and shakes the wrinkles from two more, and then climbs atop the laundry machine. He curls his body to fit, covering with the towels, the dryer top radiating heat, his terry cloth blankets losing it almost as fast. And he bangs his fists against the shiny white metal, hammering down blows while he shouts terrible, angry things toward his mother. He regrets his words and savors them all at once. When the pain in his knuckles finally catches up with his emotional anguish, he strokes the dent he made, the indentation fist-sized, heart-sized, and uncomfortably noticeable.

He doesn't consider his parents perfect. Seriously, he's fifteen. It's a total bummer they won't let him have a smartphone with texting and data plan. The one he uses has a screen half the size of a business card and no keyboard; he can't play games or take pictures, or get online. They're overprotective, and when he protests, "You let Bryce do that at my age," they wave him off with a, "That's different," and all three know what different means. But they're cool about having his friends over—in fact, they want them there—buying plenty of teenage boy food and shuttling the pubescent, long-legged, and long-nosed creatures home at all hours of the day and night. They support his love of photography, attending the annual photo club's show with too many black-and-white self-portraits shot at odd angles and streaky, ill-focused objects someone thought looked awesome rather than inept, all mounted on faded construction paper around the gymnasium. They rarely fight, and while he has noticed his mother's and father's paths intersect less than they used to, that's common for busy families. Isn't it? They go to church together, sometimes. He also knows they get along better than most of his friends' parents, who scream and swear at one another, storm out of rooms, work long hours to avoid interaction, and live vicariously through children and hobbies. Evan thought they were happy. He never believed either capable of an affair. Cheating is something only bad people do, the worst people; even when shown on television as the romantic, only-way-to-be-together situation, it always ends badly. Some jilted wife goes insane and tries to kill the mistress. Some kid runs away and turns to a life of drugs or prostitution—or both—in a cry of pain and a way to get revenge upon the offending parent. One of the lovers discovers he has a brain tumor. Blackmail letters arrive from a mysterious stranger. And inevitably, the offended spouses discover the affair.

Yes, they always find out.

His mother. No. Selfish people have affairs. His mother

is one of the least selfish people he knows. When he thanks her for bringing to school his forgotten gym shorts or staying up late to help with the essay he waited until the last minute to finish, she says, "I'm a mom. That's what mothers do." But sleeping with his Boy Scout leader? Evan can't wrap his mind around it all. What will his father say? What will happen to his family?

He's known real heartache in his young life. This feels nothing like those times, deeper and more piercing and unidentifiable. And pervasive, radiating from his chest and weighing down his body on a cellular level. All he can do is run conversation after confrontation through his mind, playing his mother's responses, rewinding their expressions, watching it again as he tweaks his dialogue and writes her contrition. He does this until he falls asleep, exhausted from his imaginary interactions. When he wakes, the tiny laundry room is suffocatingly hot, and voices murmur on the other side of the door. As quietly as possible, he hops off the machines and hides the dent beneath hastily folded towels. Then he escapes through the garage, unseen.

The snow falls with a fury matching his own. Evan plows through it, almost jogging, focused on getting home. His chest burns. He rests, panting, head dipped down. His kneecaps shift beneath his hands. Then he's moving again, his open coat behind him like a cape. His house is ahead, front lights on, windows bright. All three cars are parked in the driveway. He bursts through the door, startling his parents and brother. "I walked home," he says.

"Why didn't you call?" his mother asks. She tries to

remove his hat. Evan twitches from her reach. "I would have come to get—"

"Mr. Bailey, Mom?"

"Evan."

"Seth told me. He heard his parents arguing. About you. About what you and Mr. Bailey . . . did."

His father comes behind his mother, threads his arm around her waist, protecting her. Choosing her. "Not now," he says.

"Holy crap," Bryce says.

His father glares at his brother, and then back to Evan. "That's enough, both of you."

"They're getting divorced, Mom."

"I said that's enough," his father shouts.

"You know about this?" Evan rips off his hat and straightens as tall as he can, still eight inches shorter than Will. "How can you both just stand there and—"

He doesn't see the blow coming, but feels it, thick and meaty against his ear and jaw and cheekbone. He trips over his feet, flails, grabs the pan from the stove; it flips, spewing vegetables onto his jeans, the floor. Evan regains his balance, stares at his father with nostrils flapping, his hands cupped to his face.

"Go to your room," Will says.

He does, slipping on the greasy linoleum, catching the doorjamb to keep from falling, and then takes the stairs two at a time to his bedroom. Slams the door, barricading it with his body, arms and legs spread-eagle. His breath rattles in his throat. Moments later, he hears Bryce's door swing shut. He squishes his cheek up and down, as if it has bones to break, but finds only soft tissue and fire. Turning the lock in his doorknob, he flops on his unmade bed and stares at one of his three framed Julian Goetz photos, *Still Life with Invisible Hands, Number 7*.

He knows the story behind it. For his senior project in college, Goetz showed a series of nineteen pictures, everyday objects engaged in their tasks. Eggs in a cast-iron skillet, sizzling on a 1950s stove top. Dishes in a sink, tap water disappearing into the foam. A paintbrush dancing over a wall, a line of gray trailing behind. A crisp man's shirt on an ironing board. And number seven, a smiling glass Kool-Aid pitcher suspended in the air, pouring liquid over ice in a waiting glass.

The brilliance of the series, though, is how the photographs are staged. The eggs are being flipped, the dishes washed, the shirt ironed, and each task is performed by a pair of arms without hands. And the arms aren't simply pinching a spatula between them, or draping a rag over the handless wrist. No, in each picture the arms are positioned as if the hands exist, and the props—iron, pitcher, paintbrush, dirty ice cream bowl—are held in place by the invisible.

He doesn't know how Goetz pulled it off; had he not read the explanation of the series claiming otherwise, Evan would have simply thought the scenes were photographed in their entirety and the hands digitally removed. Goetz insisted that wasn't the case, but didn't reveal the secrets behind the pictures. He did, however, disclose his reasoning for the name:

Yes, I know they aren't still lifes in the strictest sense—there's more motion than the technique usually allows, though you will notice I pulled visually and conceptually from traditional works like Diego Velasquez's *Old Woman Cooking Eggs* and Joachim Beuckelaer's *Four Elements* series. The focus here is twofold, however. Yes, there are the inanimate objects, mundane objects no less. Things we encounter on a daily basis while engaged in our so-called normal activities. Our "regular" living. That is to say, nothing special. So what is the point, then? People make grand pleas for *carpe diem*, and often that is just a code word for backpacking across Europe or learning to skydive or buying the expensive car you always dreamed of. Is being alive not enough? Is it not *still life* if you're making fried eggs for your kids' breakfast? What if the tasks are being performed by someone with no hands? Does it make them more fantastic? More worthy? Do we think, "Yes, it's just washing dishes, but, wow, she doesn't have hands so, you know, that's pretty amazing." How do we perceive all those in-between moments when we're alive but engaged in something we esteem so little? Why are some labors acceptable for certain people, but beneath or above others, and how do we make those value judgments? These are some of the questions I'm trying to explore with these photos.

Evan coughs, his throat raw, the illness he forgot about in his anger roaring again in the silence of his bedroom. He expected his mother to come to him by now, to apologize or explain. He still wants her, even though nothing she says can make things better. Those times in the hospital, she made no promises other than *I will stay with you, no matter what*. Through chest tubes, puddles of blood-spiked vomit like coffee grounds, those first torturous steps after surgery, headaches, fevers, sleeplessness, constipation, she stayed. Sometimes in the bed beside him, often in a chair, him in her lap, or with her head on his mattress, holding his hand. She was his constant. Even as he grew and separated, he still knew she would be there for him if he needed her. Now, he wasn't sure. She went to see her lover—the word explodes in his head—leaving her family and lying about it. She's only alive because she chose him, chose to stay an extra day with him. That, and because she overheard some man asking if he could please make it home for his wife's birthday.

And Julian Goetz was on the same plane.

Evan throws his legs off the side of his bed, standing, the sudden movement curling his vision at the edges. He sways, sits until the vasovagal response passes, and then is at his desk, shaking *People* from old homework and PSAT practice handouts. Something Grace said when she gave him the magazine. "I guess someone won't ever be able to celebrate her birthday again." He didn't understand, but stuffed the comment away with the glossy pages, deep into his backpack, and then purposely buried on his desk. He couldn't look at the photos for fear of seeing his mother's face in every one of them. But now he flips the pages, the back of his hand held against his forehead, blocking the images. He skims the captions until he reads this one:

A love note, written by Goetz to his new wife, Ada. He was traveling home for her birthday from a shoot in Los Angeles.

No. It can't be.

His mother gave her seat to Julian Goetz.

CHAPTER TWENTY-FOUR

He shakes the contents of his backpack onto the bed—pencils, folders, his biology binder, a crushed notice about holiday break—and crams clothes into it, random articles he grabs from the floor without thought to cleanliness. Dashing across the hallway, to the bathroom, he collects his toothbrush and medication. *What else do I need?* Money. He has his wallet, the credit card his father gave him—"For real emergencies, Evan. And being hungry isn't an emergency."—and four dollars. It'll have to do, for now.

He listens, hears nothing. He can be down the stairs and out the front door before anyone notices, but where's the drama in that? Instead he opens his window, climbs on the roof of the front porch, and jumps down. He stumbles, snow attacking him, sneaking up his pants and down his collar, and he thinks, *I should have put my boots on, at the very least.*

No going back now.

It's six o'clock, but dark. His breath is loud in his ears, magnified by the ski cap he wears, insulated, scratchy, the way it sounds in his underwater dreams. His thoughts are red, incoherent, a swirl of mist and hormones and upheaval.

He needs to speak with Ada Goetz.

Balling his hands into the sleeve of his coat, he walks with head down, and ten minutes later enters the first Cumberland Farms he comes across, the signs announcing today as FREE COFFEE day, any size. He half fills the largest Styrofoam cup, and then adds caramel creamer to the top rim. Dumps a little out in the garbage can so the lid will fit without overflow. Then he holds the cup up to the clerk, offering a toast to small blessings. "Do you have a pay phone here?"

The clerk snickers. "For reals?"

"I need to make a call."

"Why?"

"Taxi."

Evan decides this is an emergency. He'll take a cab to Trent and pay by credit card. His father can ground him when the statement comes.

The clerk, about twenty, ears gauged but otherwise quite boring looking with his short, lawyer hair and Cumby's polo shirt, squinches his face. "Aren't you Howie's kid sister's boyfriend?"

"We're just friends," Evan says.

"Yeah, right." The clerk offers his cell phone. "Here."

"Um, phone book?"

"Duh, Internet?" The guy mumbles something else, snatches the phone back, and fiddles with the screen. It rings, the image of a face flashing, and he answers it. "Your ears burning, dude? I was just talking about you . . . your sister's boyfriend is here . . . I don't know. That skinny, blond kid she's always with . . . dude, that explains some stuff, he's trying to get a cab to come get him . . . yeah, hold it." He tosses the phone at Evan. "Your lady wants you."

"Hello?" Evan asks.

"Your parents are flipping out, Evan," Grace says. "They've called me, like, eight times already. What is going on?"

"I can't explain now."

"At least come hide here. Howard can come get you."

"That will last until, oh, I don't know, your mom sees me?"

"Well, then at least tell me why you need a taxi?"

"Grace."

"Tell me or I'll call your parents and let them know where you are."

Evan sighs. "I need to get to Trent."

"What?" she shouts, and he holds the phone from his ear. "And you're taking a cab? Do you know how much that will cost?"

"No."

His response silences her, and then she says, "Don't move. I'll call you back."

She doesn't call, but shows up twenty minutes later while he hides behind the snack racks, making himself small each time the door opens, string of sleigh bells jingling in announcement. Fortunately, with the snow, the only people coming in are the few whose tanks are too low to make it home from work without pumping a couple bucks of gas, and those desperate for cigarettes. When Grace sees him peering out from behind the Funyuns, she grabs his arm and drags him outside, into the backseat of her stepbrother's car.

"Evan." She says it as if she's his mother.

"What are you doing here?"

"Well, we told my mom we were going out looking for you. But really I'm saving your butt."

"I don't need your help."

"Right. Because taking a cab in the middle of the night to some city you've been to once is a great idea. Do you know how much it will cost? Like six hundred dollars."

"It's not even seven. And how would you know?"

"You can figure out the fare online. You don't have that kind of money."

"Dad's emergency credit card." Howard steers the car onto the highway. "Where are we going?"

"There is a Greyhound that leaves from the Bayton station at quarter to eight. It will put you in Trent just after eleven, if the roads aren't too bad." She looks at him. "Are you sure you don't want to do this in the morning?"

He shakes his head.

"I didn't think so. You have that look."

"What look?"

"Your stubborn one." She takes his hand onto her lap,

pinches the tip of each finger. "You can't tell me what's going on?"

"Not yet."

"Well, then at least say thank you."

"Thank you," Evan says, obliging.

"You're welcome." She pries open his fingers and matches her palm to his.

The snow continues, flapping toward the windshield like a swarm of frozen, white-winged moths. Howard changes lanes, moving from behind a plow. The adrenaline dissipates, lulled away by time and mile markers. Evan's head throbs, deep inside, at the ends of his ear canals. He should have waited. Julian Goetz's wife won't let some strange teenager into her home at midnight, not if she has any sense at all. And yet, he can't not go. He's pulled by an invisible cord radiating from his solar plexus, tugging, tugging, urging him to look this woman in the face and beg forgiveness for his mother's sins.

The tire of the car catches the rut on the shoulder as Howard pulls off the exit, the grooves intended as a safety, a way to wake sleeping drivers should they drift off the pavement. He sees the bus station, lit like Christmas, like hope, glass and neon and fluorescent bulbs attracting those beginning their travels, repelling those at journey's end. Grace presses money into his hand. "A loan, you hear me?"

Evan counts it. One hundred dollars. "Where did—I can't—"

"Birthday money. And yeah, you can. You'll be able to

pay me back when you turn sixteen next month. It's a gold mine, really."

"Grace," he begins.

"Yeah, yeah, and all that. Just go."

He kisses her cheek, dry and soft the way he imagines it, her skin yielding to the pressure of his lips.

"Hurry up, Romeo," Howard says. "Bus leaves in five."

Evan stuffs the cash in his jeans and hooks his backpack over his arm, rushes into the tiny bus station, and buys his ticket without wait; there's no line at the window. He settles onto the Greyhound, in the same seat he occupied when he and Grace went to the memorial. No one sits in her place.

CHAPTER TWENTY-FIVE

He's surprised to find Julian Goetz's address listed—the terminating bus station has a pay phone and phone book—since Evan imagines him a celebrity. But he supposes the photographer isn't the kind of celebrity people go searching for, not like rock stars or supermodels or athletes. Two taxis wait outside the depot, and he pays the fare to Goetz's apartment because he doesn't know where it is, is too tired to read a map or walk or come up with some other plan to get there. It isn't far and costs twenty-seven dollars. The cabbie doesn't wait.

Evan rings the doorbell of the brownstone, hands in his jacket pockets, less for warmth and more to have some way to keep from fidgeting, from picking the scabs from his knuckles. He bounces to stay warm and then rings the bell again.

No answer.

Again, he realizes he didn't plan well. It's nearly midnight, temperatures hovering a few degrees above freezing. The snow has stopped, for now, but his feet are soaked and his nose drips despite all his sniffling, and he's a skinny white kid in a city where he knows no one. He passed an all-night laundry a few blocks back, already filled with people and with a few dryers spinning. He couldn't find his way back to the bus station if he wanted to.

Why didn't he listen to Grace and leave in the morning?

"Dumb, dumb, dumb," he mutters.

He pushes the letter slot open and peers in, spots a scattering of envelopes on the floor, a few catalogs and magazines. A postcard. The home is dark, except for a small nightlight plugged into a low outlet near the foot of the stairs.

"Dude's dead, man," Evan hears, and quickly stands. A kid in jeans and a black ski cap rolls a snowball in his bare hands. He nods back across the street. "My ma saw you from the window. Told me to go tell you how it is."

"I was looking for his wife."

"Nobody ain't seen her in days. She ain't dead in there, though." He rolls his hand toward his wrist and holds it there, as if it's crippled, and flails his arms in big, awkward circles. "The horses lady checked it all out. Told my ma to call if we seen her."

Evan doesn't know if he's confused from cold and hunger and illness, or because he can't understand how this kid speaks.

"Horses? I'm not—"

"See where that plow just turned up the hill? That's

Burnett. Go up there something like a mile and find the purple building. Big ol' plum right there touching the street. Probably look black in this light. Some picture something place. You'll find her." He waggles both his wrist bones toward Evan, hands tucked down, arms stiff as a black-and-white movie's Frankenstein monster. Then the kid skids across the slushy street and into his apartment building.

Evan has no choice but to walk. He stays in the street, most vehicles safely tucked away due to the storm and the time, following the salty tracks of the plow. If a car happens to come up behind him, he jumps onto the curb, where feet have trampled a thin path through the snow, but most of the sidewalk is still piled high with the stuff. Had he worn over-the-calf socks, he would have tucked his jeans into them by now, to keep the crystalline white shards from sneaking up there and stinging his legs. But, again, anger doesn't make for the best premeditation and his socks are the ankle kind, his favorite kind, offering no warmth beneath his wet pants.

He huddles deeper into his coat. No longer behind the tall downtown buildings, the wind cuts over him, burning his face and slinking down his collar. Finally he sees the place the kid told him of, set at an accidental angle, one corner of brick so close to the street a car parked at the curb can smash the passenger-side door into it, if someone opens too quickly. Evan doesn't see a light, but some of the windows shimmer warmly, as if lamps may burn in the belly of the building and spill light outward. He hopes that's the case, anyway.

He knocks, at first with his knuckles on the glass front door, the gold lettering advertising hours of business long ended. He rotates his hand, pounding now with the side of his fist, then an open palm. *Let someone be here.* And there is, a dark-haired woman in leggings and an oversized brown cardigan, sleeves flopping over her hands.

"What's going on?" she calls. "Are you hurt?"

"No. Please. Someone sent me here from Julian Goetz's building."

The woman crosses to the door, pushes her face to the glass so she can see Evan more clearly. Swears softly and then twists the deadbolt between her two covered hands. She turns the knob the same way. "It's after midnight."

"I know. I'm sorry." Evan steps inside, shivering.

She swears again. "I thought my husband was being mugged, or worse." She looks at him with a lopsided, alien gaze, one eye soft with oil, lashes short and clean, the other shadowed with lines and smears of peacock colors and lengtheners. "You're not from around here."

"I came from Wynson. It's about, well, a lot of miles north. I need to—" As he speaks, the woman raises her arms, shakes them so the cuffs of her sweater fall back over her wrists. She has no hands; she uses the stubbed ends of her arms to bunch the sleeves over her elbows. "No. Way. It's you. *Still Life with Invisible Hands.*"

For a second, there's no response from the woman, and then she laughs. "Seriously, kid?"

"I can't believe it. I mean, I have number seven framed in my room."

"Now I know you're harmless." She jerks her head toward the open door behind a narrow Scandinavian-styled table. "Come on."

They pass through a framing workshop, and then up the enclosed stairway to an apartment, into an open, eat-in kitchen where Evan can see straight through to the living room and the television, tuned to some home decorating show. The woman motions to the mat and says, "Shoes."

Evan wriggles his sneakers from his feet, like loosening teeth, and then peels back his socks, exposing white, puckered skin. He rummages around his backpack, finds a dry pair and puts them on, rubbing his hands over the cotton to warm his toes. He removes his coat and zips a sweatshirt over the one he wears already, keeps his hat on. "I'm Evan." He coughs. His throat burns like road rash.

"Hortense. Sit. You want hot chocolate?"

He nods. "Thanks."

She moves through the kitchen, hooking the teakettle over one wrist, bumping up the faucet with the other, turning knobs, opening drawers. She slips a packet of cocoa mix across the table to him, and a spoon. "I'd make it up for you, but I'm not sure you'd want me ripping it open with my teeth."

"It's fine. I mean, either way. I mean, I don't—"

"I know what you mean." She pours the water into a mug and brings it to him. "Food too?"

He didn't have lunch or dinner today. "Uh, no, I'm good."

Hortense sits in the chair next to him. "Look, kid—"

"Evan."

"Evan. Tell me what's going on."

"I need to talk to Julian Goetz's wife. It's important."

"You run away?"

"No."

She lifts an eyebrow.

"Not exactly," he says.

She stares.

"Sorta."

Nodding, Hortense sighs and drums lightly on the table with her wrist bones. "Okay, k—Evan. How old are you?"

"Fifteen," and when she gives him the one-eyebrow look again, he says, "Really. I'm just small."

"Yeah," she says, touching the nape of her neck with the ends of both arms, arching her spine and rolling her head backwards. "Drink your cocoa."

She leaves the table, and he dumps the chocolate powder into the mug, stirs, picking up the miniscule marshmallows that fell onto the table and tossing them into his mouth instead of the water. They crunch, flattening into his molars; he scoops them out with the tip of his tongue and swallows.

Hortense returns, both eyes bare and matching, her face flushed, the tips of hair around her ears damp. She squats, clatters in a low cabinet, removing a canary-yellow pot, which she fills with water and sets on a burner to boil. She manages to pry open a box of capellini and slide it into the pot. When the pasta bends, she presses it beneath the water with a plastic ladle, drops on a lid.

"I don't know where Ada is," she says finally. "I haven't heard from her in a couple weeks."

"I really, really need to talk to her."

"Want to tell me what about?"

Evan seals his mouth in a lipless crease.

"Right. Well, then, you can stay here tonight and we'll figure this out in the morning."

"You're not going to call the police on me, are you?"

"No. Not yet." She stirs the pasta, lifting a tangle of limp strands from the water. Then she turns off the stove top and spills the pot's contents into a waiting colander, positioned already in the sink. He's transfixed on her arms, absorbed at her movements, so like all others who have made this meal before her and yet entirely unfamiliar.

She uses her knees as a vice, tightening them around a jar of marinara, and screws off the lid. She doesn't bother to heat the sauce, cold from the refrigerator, swirling it into the nests of angel hair she already scooped onto two plates. She gives the first dish to Evan. "I know you're hungry."

She joins him with her own portion, her fork held in place in the center of her plate with one wrist, and she uses her other to spin the utensil, a dancer pirouetting with its partner. He can hardly keep his own pasta on the tines, always a sloppy twister, his fine motor skills underdeveloped from his time in the hospital; years of occupational therapy made it possible for him to button his own shirt and write half-legibly. Food falls into his lap, staining his sweatshirt. Hortense pushes back from the table, reaches for the drawer she minutes ago took the flat-ware from. She catches something red between her elbows and drops it in front of him.

A battery-operated noodle-twirling fork.

"Push the button on the side," Hortense says. "You need it more than I do."

He does. The head turns around and around, whirring like a dentist's drill. "Um. Wow."

Hortense laughs. "The person who bought it for me thought they were being helpful."

Evan thinks of the dozens of stuffed animals he'd received, most in the first seven, eight years of his life, each with some sort of heart-themed focus—hearts sewn onto the chest, buttoned into the chest, with Band-Aids, zipper scars opening to hearts or half-hearts, leftover Valentine bears with heart-shaped noses or paws, hearts clutched by a kitten or puppy or bunny rabbit and some-times with added sutures by the giver. His mother bagged most of them for donation so some child in the cardiac unit at Children's could add another heart animal to her own overabundant collection. As a toddler he cared noth-ing for the gifts, but as he grew he learned to do as his mother did, smile and thank the giver, despite growing disappointment at his mountain of plush and puzzles and coloring books—sedentary things—while his brother unwrapped the rowdy toys. One Christmas, Aunt Jennifer gave Bryce fifty dollars for new sneakers while Katherine was instructed to use Evan's money for something that wouldn't make him stop breathing. His aunt must have forgotten most nine-year-olds could read; Evan found the card in his mother's purse while searching for gum.

Well-meaning was a phrase he heard over and over, and he believed it. "People want to do something. They can't fix it, but want to show they care. So they give out of their helplessness." Which is why he came home with piles of handmade pillowcases, and blankets, and crochet slippers after each hospital stay, his mother said. Which is why she gave money to Mended Little Hearts and organized bowl-a-thons for other sick children. She felt the same helplessness.

Everyone does.

He picks up the mechanical fork, presses the button, overfills the tines with pasta, and sticks it in his mouth.

CHAPTER TWENTY-SIX

Evan wakes and hears the low murmurs of the strangers on the other side of the wall, the voices warm and buzzing, a comfort to know he's not alone in this unfamiliar place. Soothing, like air conditioners and running showers and vacuums. For so long noises scared him. How many flat, heavy cakes did his family eat because he cowered at even the idea of his mother running the electric mixer? His parents blamed the hospital, the constant beeping and whooshing, and waited patiently for him to outgrow his fear. He doesn't remember when white noise switched from foe to friend; like so many other aspects of growing up, one day the world turns upside down.

He yawns, stretches his arms above his head, the blankets slipping to his waist. His scars greet him as he looks down, one flat, whitish line from manubrium sterni to xiphoid process, and eight puckered stars. He has another thin scratch of a scar under his right armpit extending onto his back, which is barely noticeable now, and most days he pays no attention to any of them; even though he sees them, they don't register as anything other than a normal part of his body. He doesn't stare in the mirror and think, *Oh, those are scars from my multiple open-heart surgeries for a fatal-unless-corrected and still-most-likely-life-shortening heart defect.* In fact, he rarely remembers it at all. He takes his pills and wheezes with excessive exertion and checks his oxygen saturations at least weekly, but it's become his life. What he does. What is necessary. The reasons behind it don't matter much.

It's on his mind now because of Hortense. She has no scar tissue or other markings at her wrists, and along with what appear to be underdeveloped fingers on the end of one arm, he figures her deformity is from birth, not man-made. The people at home know about his heart because he's lived in that small town his entire life. He's the boy with half a heart, though fame has lessened over the years. Most think he's cured and no longer haunted by death. If he moves somewhere tomorrow, he can hide it all. Avoid public showers and throw a swim shirt on with his trunks and no one is any the wiser. Hortense doesn't have that option. She can only keep her *hands* in her pockets for so long.

Adultery is a defect too. He doesn't know yet which kind it will be for his mother, his family. One that is intensely worrisome and pressing while it's fresh, and then slowly fades into the background as other louder, more worrisome things overshadow it? Or one that will always be seen, a scarlet *A* sewn onto every article of clothing his family owns?

He hates he has to consider the options at all.

What was she thinking?

He dresses and folds the blanket to the top of the bed, beneath the pillow, and strips the sheets. Those he balls up and carries down to the kitchen where Hortense sits at the table, sipping coffee with a light-haired man. "You didn't have to do that," she says, coming to take the linens from him and dropping them in the corner. "This is my husband, Mark. Mark, Evan."

"You want breakfast?" Mark asks. He lifts the domed pot lid from atop a plate of French toast and bacon. Evan serves himself several strips of the crispy, fried pork. *The heart patient diet*, Bryce teased each time Evan ate his favorite food.

Hortense folds a napkin next to his plate. "How did you sleep?"

"Okay," he says. "I think. I don't remember. I was really tired."

"I bet," Hortense says.

Mark pours orange juice, so gelatinous with pulp Evan bites through it at the rim of the glass and then swallows down the hairy, citrus drink. Two iPads flicker on the table, one screen trampled with fingerprints, the other smudged with whorlless blots. A news site is up on one, a Google search on the other. Paranoia gnaws at Evan's ears; they were looking for information about him.

"Mark and I were talking about . . . everything,"

Hortense says, and Evan snaps his eyes back to his plate where he splinters an extra-crispy slice of bacon by folding it in half, and in half, and in half again. "We thought you might like to talk with Julian's pastor."

"Does he know where Mrs. Goetz is?"

"No. But maybe he could help in, well, other ways."

Evan nods. Yes, it's right, a baby bear kind of idea, and he's Goldilocks. It fits. It's what to do in this situation, like porridge that's perfect in temperature, warming his insides in all the necessary places.

"Good. I'll give him a call and bring the car around. You finish up and meet me downstairs in the gallery."

Hortense closes the door to a room on the other side of the kitchen, and when Evan lifts his plate and glass, Mark waves them back to the table. "Just leave it."

"You sure?"

"Dishwasher's full anyway. I'll take care of everything."

"Well, okay. Thanks. I'm gonna get my bag."

Mark nods, face in his tablet. Then suddenly he says, "Hey. Do you really have Julian's *Still Life* seven in your bedroom?"

"Yeah."

"When Hortense told me, I nearly split a rib. We haven't thought of those photos in years." His words aren't directed at Evan, but somewhere to the right of him, over his shoulder, a memory hovering in the corner. Mark shakes his head, wistful smile creasing the skin around his lips. "That shoot . . . man, we were dumb kids then. Julian would roll in his grave if he knew people were still looking at those."

"I think they're amazing."

"That's 'cause you're not much younger than we were. You'll grow out of it, with any luck." And his smile dies. "Get your stuff."

Evan slings his backpack over one shoulder and hurries out of the apartment, head down, hood up, hoping the combination of posture and clothing has rendered him invisible. In the gallery he waits for Hortense while looking at the art on the walls. On one side, watercolors featuring sleek lines and translucent bubbles. On the other, a photo collection called In the Cemetery. Plenty of rusty fence finials, off-center cracks in hundred-year-old headstones, footprints in mud, and butterflies.

"We can't all be Julian Goetz." Hortense stands behind him, so much taller, her sadness dripping on him, a light, drizzling rain of loss.

"What is this?"

"Projects, from the college."

"Is that what you do here?"

"Some. We give space to students who need to show for their classes. Some local artists too. Mark and I have the frame shop, you saw, and then we also have our own photography business. Weddings, location portraiture, special events now and then. Sometimes one or both of us will take a few shots for the local paper, if they're short a freelancer."

"Do you do shows too?"

Hortense loops her chunky scarf around her neck, burying her chin and lower lip. Then she holds the door open for him. "We can't all be Julian Goetz." Her voice changes;

the sadness still there, but layered with something else. Regret, perhaps. Discouragement. Envy. Evan can't decide. Big feelings? Yeah, he has those, testosterone driven and loud as the garbage trucks outside his window at five in the morning. But he hasn't lived enough in the gray areas of emotion to recognize the subtle whispers.

In the car, the vents blow air as warm as breath and it's like falling asleep beside his father, when he was young, and Will would exhale in his ear, against his neck, blowing his hair across his forehead until it tickled. Evan would scrunch his nose and try not to wiggle, pretending his dad was a sleeping giant who would devour him if he stirred, but soon couldn't help but move to scratch his face. And his father would wake and tell Evan to quit moving or he'd have to go back to his own bed.

Hortense steers down the steep hill and through one-way streets and traffic lights to a misplaced wood-sided building in the midst of brick and brownstone. A vinyl banner strung above the chrome blue doors reads, Holy Zion. All Are Welcome. She parks at the curb in front, leaves the car to idle, and jerks her head toward the church. "Well, come on."

A compact, springy man in his shirtsleeves and tie meets them on the sidewalk. He hugs Hortense quickly and then offers his hand to Evan. "I'm Pastor Ray White."

"Evan."

"Pleased to meet you, Evan. Why don't we get ourselves inside. I'm freezing."

"Wait," Hortense says. She manipulates the button of

her crochet purse through the fastener and loops her wrist through the handle of a flat plastic bag, no larger than a paperback. "Here. If you need us, just call."

Evan folds the bag into his coat pocket, and she returns to her car, driving away without looking back. He follows Pastor Ray into his study, a glossy paneled room off the church's main office. The secretary, a woman round with extra joy and extra weight, smiles so wide her cheeks bury her eyes. "Welcome to Holy Zion." She draws out the first vowel in each word. *Hoooooly Ziiiiiion*. Like a game show host.

"Evan, this is my wife, Shanelle."

"Don't look so scared, child. You ain't heading into the lion's den." She laughs, the hundreds of tiny braids in her hair quivering. "You want a pop?"

"She means soda," Pastor Ray says. "She can't help it. She's from Detroit."

"Um, okay."

Evan sits in one of the oak chairs at the table in the pastoral study. Ray takes the fetched ginger ale from Shanelle and closes the door. He opens the can. "Want a cup?"

"No. This is fine."

The pastor joins him at the table. "Well, Evan. I'm just going to start. Mrs. Travers—Hortense—said you were looking for Ada Goetz, and you were far from home. That's all I know so far. Want to fill in the rest?"

He sniffles, glances around the room for a tissue. There are none. He sticks his hands in his pockets and digs out a crumpled paper towel from yesterday, stiff with dried mucous. He uses it anyway, finding a clean corner. "I don't know what to say."

"Just start. Anywhere."

He takes a deep breath through his one unclogged nostril. "My mother killed Julian Goetz."

"Now, Evan—"

"She was the one who gave up her seat for him. He wanted to get home for his wife's birthday. And she—my mom, that is—wanted to stay one more night in Cleveland because . . ."

"Because?"

"Because that's where she was meeting the guy she was having an affair with." His words rush together, as if the quicker he says them, the less they'll hurt. It doesn't work.

"Okay." The pastor closes his eyes and nods once, slowly. "Okay. I'm going to drive you home."

"What? No, you can't. I have to—"

"Evan, I'm sure your folks are worried sick about you. Let's get you home and then figure this out."

So Evan goes because now that his anger is a dull throb rather than the repeated stabbing of last night, he knows the pastor is right. He no longer wants his parents suffering with uncertainty, expending energy on unanswered phone calls and missing person reports. And he can't camp out on the Goetzes' front stairs indefinitely.

Pastor Ray doesn't try to force conversation on him, and Evan spends most of the trip doing what he does best, playing out scenes in his head, perfecting the dialogue, changing the blocking, the timing of entrances and exits, until he's constructed the perfect fantasy for his current situations. He talks to Ada Goetz, his parents, Seth, even Julian Goetz; in that one, he stops the photographer from getting on his flight and he lives, forever indebted to the teenager who saved his life. He suddenly wishes all living took place behind his eyes, where he can be God. He wonders if the real God does such things, intervening, rewinding, changing outcomes, making all *right*, and the people on earth have no idea they're being manipulated, like playthings, living each interaction over and over until he's satisfied with the outcome.

And sometimes those outcomes are death.

It surmounts him, a crushing desire for God, for him to be real and good and at work in some way Evan doesn't understand but will eventually make sense. Julian Goetz believed, or so it seemed from the interviews he gave. And yet his belief didn't keep Flight 207 in the air. While his mother—well, she didn't let a small thing like the Ten Commandments influence her actions, but the cosmic Rubik's Cube shuffled her off the plane and into the safe arms of Mr. Bailey. Evan stumbles around this theological house of mirrors, lost, deformed, and pounding the glass, begging to be let out.

He's gone to church as long as he can remember, more when he was younger and their lives were less busy. He was confirmed last year; that's what is done in ninth grade. Sometimes he went to youth group, if Seth planned on being there. But he doesn't *know* God, not in the way the kids talk of it, who go to *that crazy Baptist place*, as his father calls it, whose congregants tape cartoon booklets about Jesus to their Halloween candy and whose pastor preaches the possibility of dinosaurs still alive in the Amazon. He can tell the flannelgraph highlights of the Bible—Noah's Ark, David and Goliath, wee Zacchaeus—and pretty much agrees with everything from the pulpit, which is a weekly Mr. Rogers-esque *love your neighbor, love yourself* message.

He isn't going to pray over his lunch in the school cafeteria.

"I don't understand God," he says.

"You and me both."

"What good is being a pastor, then?"

"Do you believe in God, Evan?" Ray asks. He opens the plastic nub on his coffee cup lid and sips. Winces. "Oh, that's still hot."

Even unscrews the cap to his own drink, a Dr Pepper, and it hisses at him. "I want to," he says, "but when I try to make sense of it all, it's like one big mud puddle. I mean, I was born with . . . a bad heart. Lots of babies with the same problem I have, they don't make it. I don't know which is better, thinking it's all random, like luck, like survival of the fittest. Or thinking there's some big plan. One seems so, well, depressing I guess. Desperate. And the other just feels like a whole lot of pressure. If there is a plan, I better figure out what it is, and I better be able to live up to it."

"I can give you platitudes. Tell you God loves us and wants our best. Tell you we'll understand when we get to heaven and are able to ask him, face-to-face. I can toss out verses about comfort and trust and hope until the cows come home. I can tell you about the deep, philosophical discussions we had in seminary, with words like *predestination* and *omnipotence* and *Arminianism*. But in the end, honestly, I struggle with it all too." The man puckers his lips, swishing his jaw left and right. And then he sniffs. Blinks. Sniffles again. "There's a drug dealer three doors down from my church, selling crack to kids, getting them hooked. Prostituting his girlfriend and his nineteen-year-old niece. And he's walking around, fine and dandy, doing his thing. And then there's Julian Goetz. One of the best men I've known. And he's dead."

"There has to be a reason."

"Oh, yes, there's a reason. There are a million reasons. But none of them matter one single iota unless you can fall on Jesus, wrap your arms around his neck, and weep."

"I don't know what that means."

"It means—" The pastor's words crack with phlegm and tears. He coughs. "It means hope isn't an explanation. It's a person."

Evan keeps silent, more confused than minutes ago and too exhausted to ask another question, or two, or ten. But also something else. A Goldilocks answer.

Just right.

And then they're in his town. On his street. Before Pastor Ray shuts off the engine, his mother is out the door, running coatless with mismatched shoes down the icy steps of the front porch, slipping, flailing, catching her balance, and then she's in front of him. "Evan!" she shouts, drawing him into her body, embracing him. She threads her fingers into his hair, tugs his head back so he's looking her in the face. "Oh, thank God you're safe."

His father's arm cocoons both of them. He cries, too, something Evan can't recall happening before. Will looks toward Pastor Ray and says, "Thank you, Mr. . . . ?"

"Ray White. Pastor of Holy Zion Community Church down in Trent."

"Trent?" his mother says, pushing Evan back by the shoulders. "Why in the world were you there? You could have been mugged—"

"Mom."

"—or worse. That city is dangerous, Evan. It's—"

"Mom!"

Katherine stops, and he continues, "I'm really tired and really not feeling all that great. Can we talk about it later?"

She nods. "Let's get you inside."

"Mr. and Mrs. Walker, a moment?" Pastor Ray shifts from hip to hip, blows on his bare hands. "I was wondering if you would allow me to speak with you for a bit. I'd like to help. Evan told me a little about your situation—"

His father inhales sharply, filling himself, suddenly taller and more resolute. "There is no situation."

"I understand the delicacy—"

"Mr. White, I thank you for bringing my son home," Will says. "Now get the hell out of my driveway."

Pastor Ray nods, touches the brim of his hat. Evan tries to tell him with his eyes, *It's okay*, but is unsure at his success. The man drives away and his parents coax him into the house, up the stairs, tucking him into his bed with more hugs and hair smoothing, but without questions, and they linger at his door while he turns over, closing his eyes, wishing sleep to come to him rather than having to go search for it. Finally they close him in his room, alone, and in his head he conjures an image of Jesus, the one hanging in the church nursery, a long-haired, white-robed, smiling Jesus with a blue-eyed toddler on his lap. And Evan pictures himself hiding in the dark folds of his tunic, and finds rest.

PART FOUR

CHROMA

CHAPTER TWENTY-SEVEN

She is in awe of the Internet, where anyone and any-thing can be found. Julian had shown her how to navigate a search engine the first week they were mar-ried, but she didn't use it much of her own volition. Only when Julian asked for her help did she slip her finger over the rectangular sensor, navigating the teeny arrow to the compass icon and pressing down. Then she would type his request in the blank space and hit the return button. They were simple questions—*Could you check what time TD Bank closes today? What's the name of that deli on 4th Street? I can't remember. Has the new Hondros book been released yet?*—he could find the answers easier than she, but he had wanted her to become familiar with the com-puter and its capabilities. The past few days, by herself in a motel outside Erie, Pennsylvania, she immersed herself in the online web of information using one of the two com-puters in the closet-sized, complimentary business center or her cell phone. One click leads to another to another, always more and different beyond the last page she reads. She learns about Julian, the awards he won, the work he did, his life before they met. She types his name beside the magnifying glass and is rewarded with two hundred and seventy thousand results.

She knows so little of him, and he must have believed there would always be more time.

She misses him.

It's been two months since Bowen and Wright rang Julian's doorbell. News of the wreckage is still reported, not daily, but once or twice a week. The last bodies have been identified, the black boxes recovered. Pieces of metal and glass continue to be salvaged. Lawyers collect families for the impending court battle, while the airline frantically attempts to woo the same loved ones with large settlement amounts.

The public loses interest in pain, moving on to the next sensation, leaving those who mourn behind. For those only watching the crash on the television, life continues forward. People have short attention spans, or perhaps they become overwhelmed by one tragedy after another, one more request to give, one more photo of someone else's devastation, one more mess to clean up when they have plenty of their own, thank you very much. There is only so much emotional energy to spare. Those within the tsunami of loss have one focus; they are trapped in that one, terrible moment forever. It fades, yes, like the newspaper clippings from the event, the print lighter, the page more brittle each time they flip through to read it again. But it doesn't matter how pale and distant the words become; they were memorized a long time ago, imprinted on the soul. That's Ada, in the fading, the pain and immediacy of it all bleached slightly by the light, but still very much there.

There are times now when it doesn't hurt—minutes, even hours. However, the longer she goes without thinking of Julian, about what she's lost, the more violently it pounces on her when she does remember, the famished attack of a grief unfed. It's in those moments when she wonders if what her father said is true, if she killed Julian by choosing to run away with him and abandon the way of the righteous.

She's here in town to see Sergeant First Class Terrance Brimworthy, the soldier in the photograph she pulled from the wall when she left the brownstone. It took her less than an hour to identify him from the picture, to locate him, and to phone his home, asking if she could visit. He agreed once she told him who she was—Julian Goetz's widow. He seemed anxious to meet her.

The cell phone rings. She reads the screen. Hortense. Again. She keeps calling. Ada keeps ignoring. She texts every few days to say she's fine and not to worry. Hortense wants her to come back for Christmas.

Ada has never had a Christmas. Too pagan, her father said. Too Roman. A foothold for *ha-satan*.

She won't this year, either.

Time to go. It hasn't snowed in days, so the plowed mounds at the side of the street are dingy with soot and gravel. The computerized navigator directs her to a trailer park, rows of aluminum houses on wheels, some with built-on front porches, or sheds, or carports. Terrance Brimworthy lives at number fourteen, strands of colored Christmas lights wrapped around the three tree trunks in his yard and the eaves of his home. Ada knocks on the door and a woman answers, waving her inside and then hurrying to pluck a wailing infant from the high chair. "I'm Sara. Terry will be out in a minute."

From the hallway, Terrance lumbers into the living room, prosthetic feet poking from the bottoms of his running pants, and shakes Ada's hand. "Sit, sit," he says, and she settles into a pink-and-yellow chintz armchair, decidedly out of place with the overstuffed brown sofa and recliner, the trampled beige carpet, the orangish wood dining set. He plops onto the couch, Sara beside him, the baby rubbing its face into her shirt. She dangles a bottle above the little one's mouth, and the child opens and gulps toward it like a fish; Ada can't tell if it's a boy or girl.

Terrance is rounder in the stomach and face than six years ago, his hair longer and his neck tattooed with NO FEAR in bruised lettering. But his eyes boast the same deep, shaded circles beneath them and his nose is identical to the high-bridged, aquiline one captured in Julian's photo. She holds the picture out to him.

"I don't smoke anymore," he says. "That habit stayed over there, where you couldn't tell the difference between ash and sand."

"Afghanistan."

"Yeah." He pulls the loose skin at his jawline. "I'm sorry for your loss."

"Thank you."

The infant bleats, kicking its legs and arching its back before pushing the rubber nipple from its mouth. "Hush, Mirabelle," Sara says, laying her belly-down on the couch. She pats the baby's diapered bottom.

"How old?" Ada asks.

"Almost ten months. She's a peanut, like her mama. Not me," Terrance says. "You got any?"

Ada shakes her head.

"How long were you and Goetz married?"

"Five months."

"That's rough." His fingers find Sara's, and they shift into one another in the glow of the Christmas lights, skin pink, and then green, and then aqua and gold as the colors oscillate on the plastic pre-lit tree.

"Can you . . . tell me something about him?"

"Oh, sure, yeah. He was quiet, you know. Over there, I barely noticed him. I can't remember him taking my picture that day. He didn't pester us or anything. Just did his job, I suppose. And I can't say I took much notice when he was gone, either. One day I looked up and realized the dude with the camera wasn't the same one as before. That one after him, he liked to gab, who-yeah.

"I don't remember much about the explosion. Some routine day and bam, IED goes boom while we're making the rounds. I woke up in Landstuhl with my legs blown off and biggest cow pie of a headache ever. They sent me back to the States and I was a mess. Depressed. Angry. Just one big blob of pity and sh—well you know. Always been—what's they say?—the glass empty kind. I saw all those other amputees at Walter Reed, the ones who were fighters, with their positive rah-rah, we can do it attitudes, and I wanted nothing more than to break their faces." He swears, absent-mindedly drumming his metal legs. "And to die. I wanted to die.

"So I wake up from a nap one afternoon and some guy is sitting by my bed. I don't know who he is, but sometimes the local churches send their people to visit the patients who don't got family around. But I wanted no part of their charity and told the guy to f—to go away. He just asked if I remembered him, and when I said no he told me he was Julian Goetz. The name sounded familiar and he told me like I should know, but I didn't and I said nothing 'cause I didn't want anyone to know my memory was screwed up too. The guy just sat while I ignored him, then told me he'd be back. I didn't think I'd see him again but the next week there he was. And then the next week. He would read to me from his Bible, not the pansy garbage but all this stuff about battles and warriors. Gave me some Twix bars and I couldn't figure how he knew they were my faves, and when I asked him, he told me 'bout some poker game over there in the desert, where I won the pot and there were some Twix in there, and I said how much I liked them. Don't know how or why in blue blazes he remembered that.

"My folks are dead so I didn't have anyone 'cept a dead-beat brother who I hadn't seen in years and couldn't tell you where he is now. Probably prison. There was no Sara and Miri, then. Goetz told me his parents were gone too. He had a sister. They were close. He tried to find my brother for me. No dice."

Ada shifts in the chair, uncrossing her legs at the knees because her foot begins to throb, then lacing her ankles because it's what she's been trained to do. The warm scent of simmering tomatoes grows with the temperature in the trailer, and something else, a perfumed smell, spicy and flowery. She doesn't know what it is or where it comes from, but it makes her nervous, along with the woven, feathered circles hanging in all the windows, the paintings of wolves and eagles on the walls, the purple streaks in Sara's hair. Her apprehension isn't based in fear, but unfamiliarity. She's not been around people she doesn't know in alien surroundings, not without Julian. She also knows what her father would say of those like Terrance and Sara, with children born out of wedlock and Native American spiritualism and odd smells and alcohol. Ada doesn't know if she'll be completely free of Abram Mitchell's voice in her head, ever. At least while Julian lived, he spoke louder and more lovingly, and covered over the years of the community's teachings.

"Babe, get me a Coke, will ya?" Terrance asks.

Sara moves gingerly as to not wake the baby, places a pillow on Mirabelle's back. "So she think I'm still here," she explains. "Want a soda too?"

Ada shakes her head.

"Anything? Water? Bud Light?"

"We have Bud?" Terrance asks. "You didn't tell me that."

"Picked it up yesterday when we were in Walmart."

"Get me one of those instead."

Terrance watches his fiancée reach deep into the refrigerator to find beer, eyes soft upon her. Sara opens it and takes a sip, stirs the pot of sauce on the stove. "Bring that here. I got no spit, darling," he says, snapping his fingers. "Can't finish telling Ada my story with this dry mouth." So she does, and sits again, close to Terrance, the baby's toes twitching against her thigh.

"I was in that hospital for three months," Terrance says, after swishing a mouthful of beer. "Julian was there to see me every single week until discharge. Friends ain't the right word for us, but we were something, whatever it was. I didn't find out until he died that he lived in New York. I figured he must have had a place in DC, since he came so often to visit. He emailed every little bit or so, to make sure I hadn't offed myself, I think. When I told him Sara and me got engaged, he said he'd take our wedding pictures. Now we got no one."

Sara elbows him in the ribs. "Don't say it like that."

"She knows what I mean." Terrance shrugs, holding his hand out to her. "You know what I mean. Just that who could we possibly get, after him?"

Ada nods. She understands.

Who, possibly, after him?

"When is the wedding?"

"June," Sara says. "Hopefully Miri will be walking well enough that she can be the flower girl."

"She'll walk better than me, sure as eggs is eggs." Terrance laughs. "I barely had coordination when I had two feet."

"Just stop." Sara turns toward Ada. "We've been taking ballroom lessons, for our first dance as husband and wife together. He's good as anyone else in the class."

They're in love, these two.

"Can I take your picture?" Ada asks. The words startle her. She doesn't know where they come from, hadn't thought them before they hatched from her lips. But the request pleases Terrance and he says, "Heck, yeah," before she can apologize for her rude request. She sways to her feet, wrapping her jacket over her shoulders, and tells them the camera is in the car and she'll be back in a minute.

Evening divides the sun, bottom half smeared red atop the horizon, raspberry jam on bread, top half subdued by the late winter hour. She unlocks the trunk and reaches for Julian's camera bag, a spare one he left in the Jeep, just in case. Unzips it. The camera is smaller than his Nikon, the one he had on the plane with him. A Canon. She turns it on and nothing happens. Of course the battery is dead. She knows he keeps others, though, and finds three more in the front right pocket, the same place he kept them in his everyday bag. Her mouth folds with a sad smile. Creature of habit; she has this much about him.

She blows on her hands to warm them, opens the door on the bottom of the camera and slips the new battery in. Spins the wheel to on. This time it powers up with an electronic sigh, a few dolphin-like clicks and whistles, a sly wink from the bitty green light on its backside. Despite the camera's sleek design, it feels blocky in her hands, angular and ill-fitting; she's a toddler trying to jam a rhombus into the circle hole of her shape-sorting toy. She takes it back to the trailer where Terrance and Sara wait, the baby awake, chewing on her fists.

"Where you want us?" Terrance asks.

"There, I guess. Where you are."

She doesn't know what she's doing, having used a camera only once before, Julian's camera, heavy and mysterious in her hands, tapping the shutter release a few times before passing it back to him. She didn't even look through the viewfinder, though she could see what she was shooting on the back screen. She does the same now, centering the family in the window—Terrance laughing, Sara grimacing as Mirabelle pulls her hair with spit-covered fingers—and capturing the image with a press of the button. She does this two more times, before Sara says, "What if Terry holds the other picture?"

Ada shrugs, shakes her head. "I don't know what you mean."

"A picture of the guy holding the picture he's in." She laughs. "It will be cool. Ya know?"

So Terrance holds Julian's photo, a shield in front of his chest, and then his girlfriend and the baby join him, all three of them partially protected by the image of a soldier with bandaged hands, on his smoke break in Afghanistan. And Ada captures the moment within the memory of the camera.

CHAPTER TWENTY-EIGHT

Evan feels more displaced than ever, trapped in a transparent corridor between the way his life used to be and the way it is now; he can see both playing out but no matter how frantically he pounds the glass, no one acknowledges him. At home, he and Bryce occupy their own small corners while their parents are loud and clumsy in their attempts at marriage. In school, the students pass him in the halls, making obscene gestures or tossing out snide comments about his mother. The girls whisper. The guys make grunting sounds. Small school, small town, and a very angry soon-to-be ex-wife who isn't shy about sharing her story with every bank teller and Avon associate she knows. There are no secrets here.

Evan's friends have stayed with him, with as much emotional support as fifteen-year-olds can muster and not without the occasional joke at his expense, which he can forgive. He buys lunch today, chicken patty and tater tots, which the lunch ladies call *rounds*. "You want rounds with that?" Of course he does; they're the only thing worth eating, and he gets an extra, *à la carte* helping in one of those red-and-white paper hotdog holders. An apple. Chocolate milk. He'll get an ice cream from the machine, probably Nutty Buddy, or a Neapolitan sandwich if the cones are sold out. And an iced tea, since no eight-ounce carton of anything is enough for a high school sophomore. He slides his Styrofoam tray onto the table and sits between Andrew and Clayton, his sentinels, as one fills his cheeks with potato rounds, like a squirrel, and makes little chirping sounds, and the other frantically copies someone's math homework.

And he thinks, *what's the point of all this?*

In that moment, something snaps in Evan, so loud in his soul he's sure everyone in the cafeteria hears it. No one looks his way. But he picks up his tray and, one part of his mind screaming, *you've lost it Evan, you've gone crazybrains*, he manages to get over to *that* table, where the First Baptist kids eat lunch—girls in long skirts, boys in button-downs and the kind of creased, shiny pants most teens only wear if forced by a parent—with their Bibles open.

"Hey," he says. "Can I sit?"

They stare at him, all seven of them, faces various shades of dumbfounded, until one boy says, "Uh, yeah, I guess."

"Cool. Thanks."

No one knows why he's joined them, not the Baptist kids—also known as the Fundie Dundies—nor Evan's friends, who he sees making faces and waving and mimicking gunshots to the head three tables away. Nor Evan, who felt the same pull in his gut he felt the night he tried to find Ada Goetz, and feels it still, knotting his feet so he can't leave. If he wanted religion, he only needed to wait until school ended and he could have called Pastor Ray from the anonymity of his own bedroom. He is already on the fringe of social suicide given the now very public affair of his mother and Seth's father. This move puts the coffin in the ground, and there is no lack of people to shovel dirt over him.

The Fundie Dundies (*stop calling them that*, Evan tells himself, but each time he looks up at them he hears Andrew singing *fundie dundie fundie dundie fundie dundie* in the voice of Scooby Doo) glance at one another, and at him, and then at the pages of their Bibles. The first boy who spoke, Evan doesn't know his name because he's a senior, says, "We're doing our study now."

"Are you talking about Jesus?"

"We're in Philippians," a girl says.

Evan shrugs. "Is that about Jesus?"

Someone snorts, and the girl rolls her eyes. "No."

"The whole Bible is about Jesus, in a way," the first boy says. "But this part isn't about him in the way I think you mean. Nate, share with—" He snaps his fingers twice and opens his hand toward Evan.

"Evan."

"I'm David. Okay, then, Stephanie, you're reading still. Verse seven. Why don't you go through twelve."

The eye-roll girl begins. "'But what things were gain to me, those I counted loss for Christ. Yea doubtless, and I count all things *but* loss for the excellency of the knowledge of Christ Jesus my Lord: for whom I have suffered the loss of all things, and do count them *but* dung, that I may win Christ, and be found in him, not having mine own righteousness, which is of the law, but that which is through the faith of Christ, the righteousness which is of God by faith: that I may know him, and the power of his resurrection, and the fellowship of his sufferings, being made conformable unto his death; if by any means I might attain unto the resurrection of the dead. Not as though I had already attained, either were already perfect: but I follow after, if that I may apprehend that for which also I am apprehended of Christ Jesus.'"

Evan understands none of it. He hears the words, and as individual dictation entries he could define them, but all together it's a mass of children's play slime, formless, dripping from his hands. Except for the word *dung*, which surely can't mean what he thinks it does.

David bites his lip, and says, "Hold on a sec." Then he opens his eReader tablet and swipes the screen. "Maybe this will help, Evan."

He reads aloud. "'I thought things like that were for my benefit. But now I consider them to be nothing because of Christ—'"

"David," Stephanie says.

He reads louder, holding his palm up to stop her. "'Even more, I consider everything to be nothing compared to knowing Christ Jesus my Lord. To know him is the best thing of all. Because of him I have lost everything. But I consider all of it to be garbage so I can get to know

Christ. I want to be joined to him. For me, being right with God does not come from the law. It comes because I believe in Christ. It comes from God. It is received by faith. I want to know Christ better. I want to know the power that raised him from the dead. I want to share in his sufferings. I want to become like him by sharing in his death. Then by God's grace I will rise from the dead. I have not yet received all of those things. I have not yet been made perfect. But I move on to take hold of what Christ Jesus took hold of me for.'"

Take hold? Is that the same thing Pastor Ray meant when he spoke of wrapping our arms around Jesus's neck? He wants to ask but the bell rings, and students spring up like jack-in-the-boxes, tossing apple cores and milk cartons in enormous gray trash cans before scurrying from the room. Andrew waits for him at the door, flapping at him to *come, come, come,* but Evan ignores him.

"Evan," David says, holding one of those shiny little brochures at him, "you're welcome to come to church Sunday. Time and place is on the back."

Shaking his head, disappointed, Evan says, "Thanks anyway."

He starts down the hallway, to biology, when he hears, "Evan, wait."

David again, with that colored paper. "I wrote my phone number and email down, in case you want to talk about what we read today. Or anything, really."

Evan squints at the tract, slick and dark like the catfish in the lake where his family camps; he was finned by one when he was younger, Bryce daring him to pick the writhing thing up from the dock and not telling him how painful it was to be pricked by the spines on its fins. His brother and another teenaged friend from the campsite adjacent to the Walkers laughed as Evan screamed and dropped the fish, and then started crying. "Don't be a baby," Bryce told him, nudging the disgruntled catfish back into the water with his toe. Evan ran back to the camp and his father soaked his hand in hot water, removing the barb protruding from the wound with tweezers. "It was on the beach," Evan had lied to Will, protecting his brother. "I wanted to throw it back in."

With Evan's hesitation, David laughs a little and tears a page from the spiral notebook in his pile of books and binders and folders, which he balances on one arm while scribbling on the paper. He holds the pen between his lips and folds the paper in an uneven rectangle, hands it to Evan. "Email and phone number," he says, mumbling around the pen.

"Thanks." Evan takes it, stuffs it in his back pocket.

"Tomorrow at lunch?"

Evan flicks his top teeth over his bottom lip. "I don't know."

"Well, you know where to find us." David transfers his stack of books beneath his arm and ducks into a classroom not far from where Evan stands, his palm throbbing with the memory of the catfish sting.

* * *

He's on the bus before Grace, and she sprawls next to him in the seat, legs so long in her skinny jeans, her blond hair dyed a purple-red, the color of grapes and already beginning to wash out at the ends. "How was lunch today?" she asks.

"Fine," he says.

"Evan."

"What?"

"Don't snap at me."

"Then don't ask questions you already know the answer to. You and Andrew have tech together."

"Okay, so yeah, he told me you totally lost it and actually went over and sat with the Fundies. What the heck, Evan?"

"What do you care where I sit?"

"Because I'm your friend, and if you hadn't realized already, your social standing is precarious as it is."

Evan snorts and stares out the window.

"Look, okay." Grace lowers her voice. "Lots of people turn to religious stuff in the hard times. I know my mom was at mass every single day at seven in the morning after my dad ran off with the step-witch. But you know what? Things got better and she got over it. She married Dennis and we're back to hitting church only on Christmas Eve, if we're not too busy last-minute shopping. It's all good."

"You can't stand Dennis."

"I never said that."

"Sure, Grace. Whatever."

"Evan, look at me," she says, and when he doesn't, she yanks his hair, twisting his head around.

He shoves her hand away. "Knock it off."

"No, I will not. You need to listen to me. Just hold on. By next September, no one will care about your mom and Mr. Bailey. Either they'll just forget, or some other scandal will take its place."

"Thanks for the expert advice."

"I'm your friend, Evan, which is more than I can say for that bunch of Bible-thumping weirdos. They don't care about you. They just want a notch on their soul-saving belts."

He moves his backpack from his lap and stuffs it between them, crosses his arms, and slumps low in the seat. They're both silent the remaining ride, and when the school bus slows in front of his house, Evan is sure to whack Grace with his bag as he steps over her.

The house is empty, and while lately he wants it this way—he doesn't have to worry about butting up against an argument or an awkward hush—today he wishes for fullness. Tucking a bag of potato chips beneath his arm, he fills a plastic cup—the largest in the cabinet, a souvenir from Six Flags, $10.95 with dollar refills all day, the bendy straw and lid lost, the image of the Boomerang coaster peeling from the dishwasher—with generic lemon-lime soda. In his room, he dumps his books onto his bed and stares at them, devouring the chips and wishing he'd brought the entire bottle of Twist-Up to his room. All the grease and carbonation bloats his stomach but his limbs and head remain disembodied, helium balloons pinned to his torso, ready to escape into the sky if released. He's angry with Grace. Even though her father left, she and her mother were the offended party and the ones garnering sympathy. If Evan's father had left his mother, and he'd gone to live with him instead of her—like Seth's situation in reverse—people would feel bad for him too. But because his family is intact, at least for the moment, he's seen as *aiding and abetting* in some unspoken code of infidelity conduct and consequences. Someone should write a handbook; at least then he'd have a firm understanding of the etiquette of this situation.

He's never felt so alone.

Footsteps pounding the stairs, striding with purpose down the hall. Bryce. Evan jumps off his bed and follows, stands in the doorway of his brother's room as Bryce rummages through his closet, tossing a clean shirt and pair of jeans on his perfectly made bed. His entire room is straight and ordered, without a single rumpled pair of gym shorts on the floor or drawer peeking open. Even his video game consoles are arranged in the cubbies of the television stand, the controllers wrapped in their cords and tucked in orange canvas storage cubes.

"Bryce?"

"Hey."

"Where you going?"

"Nick's, probably."

"No practice tonight?"

He shakes his head. "Never the Thursday before a game."

He's so tall, Evan thinks, watching him fold his outfit, smoothing them before slipping them into his backpack.

If it was Evan, he'd cram everything into the front pocket after picking the clothes off the floor, denim legs half-inside out, socks mismatched. Bryce also seems thinner, his face lengthened by the stress and loss of appetite, the bluish smudges beneath his eyes, perpetually there due to his dairy allergy and a refusal to drink the almond milk their mother buys for him, are darker than usual.

"Scootch," he says, meeting Evan in the doorway.

"Can't you stay?"

"Sorry, Ev. On your own tonight."

"Every night."

Bryce looks down on him—everyone looks down on him—takes his fist and bops him twice on the top of the head with the fleshy side of his oversized hand. Both his hands and feet are larger than his body needs and somewhat comical to see, especially in the summer when he wears swim trunks and nothing else, his thin body beaded with chlorinated water, his hands and feet human flippers.

He had resented Evan for the longest time, at least Evan thinks he did. There was this sickly baby occasionally showing up in Bryce's life, home for a week, a month, rarely longer, in between hospital stays. And while it kept his mother away, he had his father and his canned ravioli for dinner and all the television he wanted to watch when the babysitters came over, and nothing was all that disruptive. Then Evan was home more, crying, needing the care of both parents, Bryce dragged along to waiting rooms in various doctor's offices, trips to the playground pushed off because his brother had speech therapy or another respiratory infection. Sometimes, Evan remembers, Bryce would pinch him when their mother wasn't looking, push him over, turn the lights off and close him into a dark bedroom. At some point, Evan was well enough for Bryce to become indifferent to him. Bryce was old enough to take his bicycle to friends' houses and go to Boy Scouts on his own, and he didn't need to see Evan at all most days, except at the dinner table and when they did things together as family. And that's how their relationship stayed, not close, not hostile, simply two boys with little in common, born to the same two people and sharing the same space.

Emotions are not Bryce's strength, but Evan must give off enough neediness for the older boy to feel it, because Evan sees him soften, and he hangs his pack on the back of his desk chair and asks, "Madden or Reach?"

"Reach, definitely," Evan says. "Let's blow stuff up."

CHAPTER TWENTY-NINE

They go to counseling, and it's hard. Brutal. They stride into their first session with all the optimism of newly-weds, and leave razed by their own words—about one another, about self—and the observations of the therapist. The next time, Katherine sits in her car waiting for Will to join her from work, devouring packages of Fun-Sized Snickers, crumpling the wrappers in her fist until no more will fit, and then cramming them in the crack between the seats. She leans back in the seat, closes her eyes, and basks in the tingling sugar euphoria, hoping it will last long enough to anesthetize the next fifty-five minutes of pain.

The struggle helps, in messy ways. Time with Will at home is louder, more vulnerable. The blending of their long, too-separate lives stings like water washing over exposed nerves in their molars, the absolutely necessary thing bringing pain as well as survival. They subsist out in the open now, speaking their thoughts, giving up their hiding spots.

They are clamoring children, noisy and messy and exploring what it means to be in relationship with one another again, mopping up all the spilled emotions before falling into bed, exhausted.

At least they fall into bed together.

Bryce still isn't talking to her, other than the obligatory answers to her questions. His silent treatment angers Will, but Katherine tells her husband to let him be angry. He has that right.

"We should tell them both about what I did," Will says. "You're not the only one at fault here. They can hate both of us."

"No, don't," she says. "They need someone safe they can go to, if they need to talk."

"You're safe."

"Not to them. Not right now." Katherine sighs. "I'll take one for the team."

"You shouldn't have to. And what if they find out later?"

"I don't know. I've never been through this before." And she goes to him, and burrows into that place where his bicep and side come together, her nose tickled by the hair on his arm. He flattens his lips against the top of her head, blowing onto her scalp. She wants his warmth.

With Evan, the distance continues as well. Not so much anger but introspection keeps them apart; she doesn't know exactly what's going on in his head, but it consumes him much of the time. He's polite toward her, coming home from school, taking out the garbage, and asking what, if anything, he can do for her before shutting the door to his bedroom. He comes down for dinner, which is more than Bryce does; her older son either eats once everyone else is in bed, or he comes back to the house after eating elsewhere. They've not spoken about Evan's overnight runaway to Trent. He asks about her day, but cares nothing for the answer; it's habit, muscle memory of the tongue. She can't *read* him, though, and that is most concerning to her. This is a kid who is incapable of camouflaging any thought or feeling, or so she thought. He's become a leaf-litter mantid, a tawny frogmouth, blending his inner workings so perfectly with his surroundings, someone might believe he is empty.

She knows better.

She heats a plate of Bagel Bites in the microwave, tries to open the two-liter of Coke so she can bring Evan a glass with the snack. Someone—Bryce—overtightened the cap and she can't get it off. She searches the dish-towel drawer, beneath them, where she keeps the rubber gripper. Not there. *Boys.* Checks the storage bag and food wrap and flatware drawer. Nothing. Junk drawer next. She shovels through and finds it. The business card. Julian Goetz. 3741 4th Street. Trent, NY.

Of course.

She carries the pizzas upstairs with an empty plastic cup and the entire bottle of soda. Bangs on the bottom of Evan's bedroom door with her foot. "Brought you a snack," she says when he opens.

"Thanks," he says, taking them, setting them on top of his dresser.

Katherine waits, and when Evan doesn't invite her in, she asks, and he shrugs and uses a single finger to push the door; it creeps open, loses momentum, and stops. She steps inside and looks around at laundry strewn over every surface. "Clean much?"

He shrugs again.

Three framed photographs hang on his walls. One is a smiling pitcher suspended in the air by an arm without a hand, pouring liquid in a glass. The second is of an elevated train dripping with graffiti, faces peering from the windows. Next to it, a portrait of a soldier with bandaged hands, smoking a cigarette. She doesn't understand the pitcher photo, but the other two stir her. This Julian Goetz, his images—it makes little sense. She's seen plenty of train pictures, of soldier pictures. But these, it's as though Goetz lifted a tiny corner of universe and she peeks inside, but her head blocks the light from above so there are only shadows and half-certainties, and a choice: dance in the vague impressions or go deeper to unearth why she responds to the images in these ways.

"These are . . . his," she says.

"Yeah." Evan points. "*Still Life with Invisible Hands, Number 7.* He took that one in college. That one of the train is from a series he did on transportation and poverty. And the soldier, that's a Pulitzer winner. He's the only person ever to win five times."

"We got you that one."

"Last Christmas."

"I didn't pay much attention to it, just sent your Amazon

link to your dad. He bought. I wrapped." She sits on his bed, mattress exposed, fitted sheet twisted in the center with the rest of the blankets. "I didn't put it together."

"You had . . . other things on your mind," Evan says, flicking tiny, diced pepperoni from the cheese topping.

She shakes off his bitter words. "I met him. That day. Spoke to him." He rolls only his eyes toward her, but the rest of him stiffens. "He had his camera out. I told him my son liked photography. I showed him the album you gave me—"

"Mom, you promised—"

"—and he said it was good, Evan. You were good." She holds the business card out for him to take. He does. "He wanted you to get in touch with him."

Evan reads the card, presses it between his hands, a bookmark, the place where all things changed. "I went to see his wife. When I left that night . . . after."

"And you told her?"

"Nothing. She wasn't home." Now he looks at her with the forthright eyes of a man; her baby gone. "I wanted to apologize."

Katherine grimaces. "It's not your apology to make."

Slumping, backbone compressed, shrinking, his body regains the childlike posture his eyes outgrew. He opens his hands partially, cupping them, as if expecting the business card within to have metamorphosed to some sort of winged creature and flutter away. The card stays put. He buries it in the top drawer of his dresser, in the folds of the undershirts Katherine buys for him but he never wears. "I have to ask you something, Mom," he says, back toward her. "I need you to answer. Please."

She's been waiting for him to ask—both the boys, really—about her affair, preparing responses to every question she imagines possible. *No, it's not about you, or your brother, or your father. This was about me. My brokenness. Yes, I still love all of you. If I could do it again, I'd choose differently. No, I wasn't thinking about Susanna and Seth. Yes, it was selfish.* And on and on and on. She promised herself she'd be truthful. No more lies.

"Do I need to sit down?"

"You're already sitting."

"Well, then. Go ahead."

"Why do you think some people live and others die?"

Confused by his unexpected words, Katherine stutters, "W-why?"

"You said you'd answer."

"Do you mean everyone in the world, or Julian Goetz?"

"Everyone. Him." Evan turns now. "Me."

"Oh, Evan—"

"Please. Just answer."

He's asked before, and each time she put him off— changed the subject, distracted him, offered a Popsicle— because it isn't something she wants to think about anymore. When he was born, an infant, a toddler, the question stalked her. There was no algorithm to predict which babies would live to see their first birthdays, which children would have complication-free surgeries and leave the hospital in less than a week. She overheard conversations—everyone walked the corridors with phones pressed to their sweaty ears, explaining the most recent treatment plan to someone on the other end of the line, back home, sleeping in their own bed with their own healthy kids in the next room—a mother or father weeping because minutes earlier they'd been told there was nothing else medicine could do for the small piece of their own soul hooked to a dozen tubes and wires in ICU incubator number six.

Katherine attended the support group meetings and received the daily emails as parents sought stories of experience from the ones who had been through it already. And at least twice a week, someone would announce her baby's death—a baby with the same heart defect as Evan.

She's ashamed to admit it now, but she held her son so loosely those first years. Yes, she did what was necessary to meet his needs, to comfort him, to make sure he took his medication and made it to appointments. She slept next to him, her hand on his chest or back so she would know he was still breathing, not trusting in her constant state of exhaustion that she'd hear the monitor *ding, ding, ding.* She'd slept through other notifications, the pump announcing the end of a feeding, the oximeter warning his saturation level had dipped below 70 percent. Still, she built a wall—or she told herself she had—because she'd seen too many grieving parents, too many babies whose condition improved so much doctors encouraged optimism, and then who were taken off life support three days later.

She didn't want to know the soul-grinding agony of loss.

As Evan's health improved and with the immediacy of

his illness behind their family, Katherine allowed herself to grow more furiously in love with her child each day. She watched him learn to tie his shoes when he was eight, and celebrated. Instead of scolding him for dragging a chair into the kitchen to stand on so he could reach the freezer and sneak the Thin Mints she stashed there, she poured them both glasses of milk and joined him in a feast of thanksgiving; two years prior he would have been too weak to push the chair away from the table. She had patience with him because in every moment of frustration she remembered, *He could not be here.* That patience eventually found its way into her relationship with Bryce as well; she understood how tenuous life's hold truly is.

How can she tell Evan she doesn't care why some live and some die? He didn't die. She still has him. That's enough.

"I don't know. Honestly," she says.

He unscrews the cap from the soda without effort, drinks from the bottle. "I'll finish it."

"Okay, then. I'm going to cook something up for me and your dad. You're probably good with the pizzas."

"Yeah," he says.

And as she leaves, her foot tangled in a pair of jeans on the floor, she kicks them back into the room and hears, "Mom?"

"Mmm?"

"You and Dad are gonna be okay. Right?"

She nods. "It's getting better. It will be better," she says, closing the door. And she wonders if Evan has thought *better* would be if she'd never offered Julian Goetz her seat.

CHAPTER THIRTY

Two days later Ada eats dinner from a vending machine at a rest area off the New Jersey Turnpike, all the food places dark and locked with metal gates. It's Christmas Eve. She drops her coins into the slot and buys D4 and A7—a package of Chuckles and a bag of potato sticks. Then she pays two dollars for a bottle of water.

Another hotel, a Marriott this time. She likes the solitude of the rooms, the luxury of someone else cleaning and bringing towels. She hates the king-sized beds. She gets lost in them, crawling in on one side and waking on the other, traveling the expanse in her dreams. Now she knows to ask for a double bed instead. If not, two double beds.

A complimentary bag of popcorn hides between the single-serve coffee packages and the napkins. She sticks it in the microwave and washes her face while it *tings* and *tangs* for two-and-three-quarter minutes.

She props the pillows around, four of them, all tucked

so tightly into their cases she thinks of them as mini marshmallows. She's finding she has her own names for many things now. Flipping through the channels, she bypasses all the Christmas movies. If she learned about the holiday wholly from television, she'd think it was about fat men in red, flying reindeer, and desperate attempts to secure a boyfriend before the clock struck midnight. Instead, she falls asleep to people renovating their kitchen, and then wakes with a fireplace scene flickering on the screen, an elevator's rendition of "Jingle Bells" playing.

Christmas Day. Hortense calls. She ignores it, again. She's beginning to hate pity.

Her stomach grumbles. She dresses in layers—two pairs of tights and knee socks beneath her skirt, a t-shirt, turtleneck, and sweater on top. The sweater is gray, cable knit, and she saw it in the store only the other day and bought it because it reminded her of Julian's sweater, the one with which he dried the rain from her on their wedding day, the one he wore when he left for California two days before he died. She imagines he wore it home, too, was wearing it when the plane dove into the river.

She checks the vending machine. A half-dozen selections are empty, leaving spaces, missing snack teeth. She can't eat junk all day. Twenty-five years she went without eating any sort of packaged food and now she lives on it. Passing the lobby desk, she nods at the attendant, a young woman with a Santa's hat pinned to her crinkly hair. "It's cold out there," she says. "Drive safe and Merry Christmas."

Ada pulls into a shopping plaza first, the one with the

grocery store across the street from the hotel. Everything closed. She finally finds an open gas station with a convenience mart. Inside, the revolving warming displays—usually filled with foil-wrapped egg, cheese, and ham biscuits or sausage bagels—are empty, as are the pastry trays and the rolling hot dog griddle. She buys several sleeves of the bite-sized powdered Softee donuts, a box of cherry Pop Tarts, several bags of salty chips and pretzels, and a few frozen burritos. And apple juice. She pays too much for all her booty and, staring through the windshield of the Jeep, wonders, *Where to next?*

Home.

She doesn't know what the word means anymore. Not Abram's Covenant. And not the brownstone. She straddles two worlds, but can't tell which of these worlds is on either side of the cavern. She can only stare down into the darkness of grief, dropping pebble after pebble, listening for some indication of the distance to the bottom, and hearing nothing.

Limitless grief. Yes. Each time she thinks it's stabilized and she can't sink deeper, something happens—a news story about a new piece of evidence in the Flight 207 crash, a commercial advertising Julian's brand of deodorant, the sound of church bells like on the day of the funeral—and she's sucked down toward an abyss out of which she fears she won't ever be able to crawl.

So she drives.

An envelope on the passenger seat. On it, her handwriting and an address. She will go by the house today, to make sure she can find it for her appointment in two days. It keeps her out of the hotel, for a while.

The trip is twenty-five minutes, with little traffic. A car here, a minivan there. Most people are home, exerting all willpower to fashion this day as the only perfect one of the year. They've not yet changed from their pajamas and packed into the car, each kid dragging his new favorite possession, parents frantic to get to the grandparents' house on time.

She's here, without the help of a computerized voice. A yellowed, nondescript ranch-style house with a FOR SALE sign in the yard, the only home on the street without some sort of light, either porch or window or stringed bulbs. Ada parks at the curb, stands at the mailbox, her booted toes crunching the frosted grass. There's little snow on the ground, short frozen mounds along driveways and at roadsides, places where it had been piled a bit higher from plows and snow blowers and shovels. Otherwise, a brownish Christmas.

A woman approaches, fur hat perched on her head, holding the leash of a wiry dog wearing a red reindeer sweater, several metal tags jingling on its collar. "Are you lost, dear?" she asks, frigid words puffing from her mouth.

"I'm just looking."

"My mama's place. Passed six months ago. Cute little house. Would be lying if I didn't tell you it needed some updating. The realtor is on vacation 'til after New Year's, but if you give the number a call, I know she's got someone checking her messages to get back to folks, and to show houses while she's gone."

"Joy Robinson?"

"The one and only. Who's asking?"

"I'm Ada Goetz."

"We're not supposed to meet 'til Thursday."

"I know. I wanted to make sure I wouldn't get lost."

The woman cocks her head. The dog does the same. "Okay, come on now. Let's go."

"Pardon?"

"You can walk along with me while Loretta Lynn here does her business, or you can take your car and drive 'round to my place. Turn right, then right again. It's number five, right behind here, actually. My backyard touches this one."

Ada watches the woman waddle past, the dog obediently by her feet, jangling and wagging as they turn the corner, and then gets in the Jeep. She doesn't have to follow, can simply drive back the way she came, with her donuts and burritos, and snuggle into the bed in the motel room. But the woman told her to come, and she still is unable to disobey a perceived order. So she turns the key and shifts into drive with her foot on the brake, checking the mirrors like Julian taught her, looking over her shoulder and into the blind spot. One of the first things Julian did was bring her to the middle school parking lot and tell her to get into the driver's seat. She did. And he explained how the pedals and the shifter worked, but she had watched men drive her entire life and knew those things already. A few husbands or fathers did let their women—daughters, mostly—start vehicles on cold days or drive the tractor to the fields, especially the couple of families that had no sons, but her father would never allow such a thing. It felt rebellious to shift the Jeep from *P* to *D*, to remove her foot from the brake and creep forward. She drove figure eights around the lampposts and parallel parked between a school bus and a trash Dumpster. And after she passed her driver's test, Julian took her into the country, to a long stretch of rutted farm road, and they rolled their windows down and she watched the speedometer quiver at eighty while the wind tickled her exposed neck. She felt uncaged, as if anything was possible to her now, and she could escape the boogeyman pursuing her. Then Julian yelled, "Slow down!" and she skidded to a stop as a stream of cattle flooded the road in front of them and then behind them, meandering from one pasture to another. The cows bumped their noses against the glass, licking and mooing, jostling the car as Julian snapped their pictures, and he and Ada laughed themselves to tears at the absurdity of it all.

So she turns right, and right again, parking in front of number five and waiting for Joy to come around the corner with her dog, and when she does a plastic bundle swings in her hand. The woman waves her from the Jeep, and Ada responds, more dutiful than the terrier on the leash. Joy drops her plastic bag into the garbage bin beside her garage, waits for Ada to catch up. "It's a bit chaotic in there, I warn you," she says. "Grandkids are clamoring to open presents."

The home, a split-level, is narrow and decorated in mauve and blue. Geese dance around the wallpaper. Almost every inch of wall is covered with dried floral wreaths, knick-knack shelves full of bear figurines waving American flags and wooden angels with Spanish moss for hair, and folk art prints of milk cans and covered bridges. "Okie-dokie. Mimi's back."

Everyone in the living room turns, the children's cheers cut short by the sight of Ada. The adults' smiles falter, and they shoot confused glances at one another. Joy says, "Oh, that's enough of that. I've not gone off my rocker. This is Ada Goetz. She's the wife of that fella Julian who took Grandma Nona's picture." She starts pointing. "That's my daughter Nona-Anne, yep, named after my mama, and her husband Roger. Those two belong to them, Sam and Lila, in the striped jammies. Then that's Pansy and her husband Graham, and the wonder boys Brian, Cody, and baby Ian. And this is my own better half, Vinny."

The man in the chair stands up and gives Ada a sturdy hug, surprising her. He pulls away and pats her cheek. "Welcome, welcome. Of course. Forgive our rudeness. *My* better half forgot to tell us you were coming."

"We ate our breakfast, but there's plenty left," Joy says. "Brian, start pulling those presents out from under the tree. Let's see what Santa brought."

The kids whoop and dash across the room, the oldest boy reading names and directing them where to pile the gifts. Joy removes her coat and hat, draping them over the banister, and shoos Ada into the kitchen. Pans of casseroles and cinnamon rolls clutter the counter. "Help yourself," Joy says, thrusting a plate toward her. Ada hasn't seen home-cooked food in almost two weeks; she takes a bit of everything, pours a glass of orange juice, and settles into a chair at the dining room table, adjacent to the living room where the family now waits, each person with their own tower of wrapped boxes and gift bags.

Vinny snaps pictures on a digital camera so small it's lost in his fat hands. Joy whoops and encourages, "Another! Open another," as her grandchildren tear the paper from their presents and hold them up briefly for everyone to see before tossing them aside for the next. The parents untwist ties and cut tape to free toys from their packaging, and the electronic blips and flashes add to the holiday cacophony.

So much joy.

It was not like this in Ada's childhood. There were times of laughter and fun, hayrides and weddings and Thanksgiving. But she never abandoned herself to them because an undercurrent of foreboding remained, always, and she knew at any moment things could change. Someone might suddenly break a rule, spoken or unspoken, and discipline would fall upon him. A word from God might come to her father, and all would stop. Often these times would come while everyone gathered outdoors, and it didn't matter if little children shivered as the sun dimmed and night came and they had no jackets, or the rain pelted them and they sank ankle-deep into the mud. They stayed until the prophet exhausted his given message, heaping coals upon their heads for hours and hours, until he was certain all had been properly communicated.

And there was always, at the very least, one person forced out of the celebration, watching, outside the community due to some not-yet-repented behavior. That is, her father had not granted them restoration.

More than once it had been her.

A peppermint-scented sleepiness comes over the house. One of the little boys naps beneath the tree, clutching a brand-new Tonka dump truck. Vinny and his son-in-law assemble a track for the race car set. Pansy nurses the baby and talks quietly to Nona-Anne. And Joy ambles through it all, stuffing wads of paper and bows into a black plastic bag. She ties it and plops her gnomish body into the chair next to Ada. "You're free for seconds," she says, nodding to the plate.

Ada shakes her head.

"Well, then, we might as well do what we were gonna do Thursday."

"Oh, no. I can't intrude any more on your holiday."

"Please, please, intrude. To me, Christmas is one of the most boring days of the year. Once you get the presents opened, what's there to do?" She waves her hands. "Ah. The men will take the kids to the movies this afternoon and my girls and I will make dinner, but until then, it's like snoozeville."

"My wife doesn't know how to relax," Vinny adds.

"All truth there. I hate being idle. Gotta be doing and moving and keeping busy." She winks at Ada. "So if you don't talk to me, I'm going to start scrubbing my bathroom tile. And on Christmas. *Tsk, tsk.* Save me, Ada Goetz."

"Well," Ada says, smiling a little, "I don't really know what to ask. I just wanted to know about the photo."

"Hold it right there." Joy pops up from the table, disappears for a few minutes, and then returns with a loose-leaf binder and a magazine. "Julian sent these to us. All the pictures he took that day, and then this, when the story appeared. The *New York Times Magazine*. Who would of thunk it?"

Ada flips the pages of the binder, dozens of black-and-white photographs in transparent page protectors. Many feature a woman who looks like Joy, all roundness in every part of her, from cheeks to nose to belly, floundering in a house filled floor to ceiling with, well, everything. Boxes of clothing, newspapers, small appliances, shoes, baskets, artificial flowers, empty pet carriers. Hundreds of lamp shades. Bags of old-fashioned golf club sets. Then images of others—Joy, Vinny, children, and grandchildren—with the woman, sorting, packing, cleaning, crying.

"Your mother?" Ada points.

Joy nods. "Sweetest lady in the universe. After my daddy died, she started collecting things. Going to auctions. Said she might start bringing things to the flea market over there on Route 70. My brother and I, we thought, 'Good, something for her to do.' Daddy was sick a long time and she took care of him day and night, never wanted a break, though we asked her.

"We didn't know how much stuff she had. She kept it in one back room, then another. Doors were closed. There was no reason for us to look in there. Then more things, in the hallway, in the living room. She said it was tempo-rary while she was waiting for space to open at the market. Then it took over. Once it was in, we couldn't get her to let go of it.

"That day," Joy taps the photos, "we were clearing everything out. We told her if she didn't let us, we'd have to put her in a nursing home. She was out by the mailbox, just crying, and your husband drove by and stopped, and asked if she was okay. I looked out the window and my mama is clinging to some strange man, and I charged out there, ready to tongue-lash the blue blazes out of him, but I got close and saw this expression on his face. Like compassion, but, oh, I don't know how to describe it but to say it was deeper than that.

"He introduced himself and asked if he could take some pictures, and I asked my brother and we agreed. And he took these, but except for a few I don't know that I saw him all that much with the camera to his face. He rolled up his sleeves and helped us pack and organize. The next day he came back early and set up the garage sale with us, brought lunch back to us, and then came back again to move all the leftovers onto the Goodwill truck. Three days this stranger stayed around.

"And my mama loved him. He reminded her of my daddy."

"Was she able to stay, in the house, I mean?"

"Funny you should ask that. Yes, she was. I think it broke her heart, though, watching her things carried off by greedy neighbors who argued to pay a quarter less. She didn't go out much and went downhill pretty fast. Here," Joy says, tapping her temple. "I was there, checking in on her every day, but she needed 'round-the-clock care and the good Lord knew we couldn't pay for it. My brother and I were starting to look at options, and then we find an envelope in the mail. From Mr. Julian Goetz. Truth be told, I didn't remember who that was. But Mama heard the name and says, 'It's that nice man with the camera.'

"There was a check for twenty-five thousand dollars and a note telling us he won some contest with his pictures of our family. And he wanted us to have the prize money to use for Mama's care. I nearly fainted dead right there. I had prayers answered before, but never like this, let me tell you. So we were able to hire a live-in for my mama until she went to be with Jesus eight months later. At home. In her own bed. The one she shared with my daddy."

Ada doesn't tell her the Pulitzer Prize pays less than half that. Ten thousand dollars. She touches another photo, the one of Nona in a chair, surrounded by her things, eyes vacant, old skin brittle with loss. "This is the one that hung in Julian's hallway."

"The cover of the magazine," Joy says, flipping it to expose the matching image, a game of Memory. Then she turns to the next photo, the same woman in the same chair with Joy's arms around her neck. They laugh and cry together. "This one is my favorite. I have it in my bedroom. On the table next to her chair. This chair. Come with me."

Ada follows her to the master bedroom. Cobwebs hang from the tips of the four-poster bed, unmade. The chair is in the corner, faded red fabric, all softness worn away. "I sit there when I read my Bible. Every morning and every night, most days."

"Why was . . . I mean, do you know why Julian happened by that day?"

"Providence, my dear. That's all I can tell you." Joy hesitates, squishing her face toward the center, all of it, her skin wrinkling around her nose. "Listen, dear, I'm guessing you don't have family, since you're here on Christmas Day. And I can see you're hurting something fierce. It's amazing, isn't it, how much pain comes from losing someone you knew so short a time?"

"How—"

"My first husband. Cancer ate him alive. He had it when we got married and didn't know it. Was gone not two years later. I didn't know he'd take half of me with him. That two becoming one flesh? It's the real deal.

"I didn't think I'd get over it. But I did. And I met Vinny. I ignored him for months, though, 'cause my first husband was Vinny too. Vinny One and Vinny Two, we joke now. But the Lord stitched me up and healed me something good, so I could love again. It happens."

"I believe you," Ada says. "Joy, can I take your picture?"

She shrugs. "Sure, why not? Got a camera?"

"It's in the car."

So Ada makes the trip again, from stranger's home to Julian's Jeep, collects the camera and the framed photo, and finds Joy again, still in the bedroom, though she's brushed her short, feathery silver hair and changed her sweater to a button-down jacket, free of baby drool and crusty white icing. The camera, cold from the car, feels less alien in her hands. Still heavy. Still *his*. But she's not as intimidated by its shiny blackness, its lights and automated hisses.

She tells Joy, "This might sound odd, but I was hoping

I could take the photo with this." She holds up the frame with Nona's image preserved behind glass.

Joy takes the frame, positions it on the red chair, Nona's chair, balanced on the bottom corner and resting cock-eyed in the seat, sides of the frame indenting the fabric of the arms. Then she stands behind the chair, leaning over to hold the frame with both hands as if it is her mother, and it's that day when Julian came, and what was best for her hurt her more than anyone should have to hurt. Ada snaps the photograph, and in the aftermath of the flash sees Nona's tears evaporate from her chair.

CHAPTER THIRTY-ONE

She knows she shouldn't, but Katherine goes to see Thomas.

He's living at the Clearwater Motel, an extended-stay place where the social service department also houses displaced families and those waiting for rooms in assisted living facilities. Then there are the men who are between women, the women who are between men, those who are unemployed, who are unable to pay security deposits or have bad credit. And, probably, those who earn money in less than legal ways. Katherine parks beside Thomas's car and locks her own, holds her purse more tightly than a running back secures the football, and climbs the outside stairway to the second-tier balcony. Room 230 is at the end.

Thomas opens the door. "I didn't think you would come."

She steps inside, the smell of take-out Mexican, shaving cream, Jim Beam, and unwashed clothing mingling in a haze of desperation, carried by the steam still lingering from a recent shower. "I didn't want to."

"Then you wouldn't be here," he says.

He's left several messages for her since Susanna asked him to leave. She told Will about each of them, going so far as asking if he wanted to hear. He didn't. So she says now, "I deleted it," and he understands the code. Thomas's voice in this morning's call sounded so much more needy.

Katherine loves to be needed.

"How are you?" she asks, moving a pile of folded white t-shirts from the chair closest to the door, and sitting.

"Well, my wife kicked me out. My son refuses to talk to me. I'm living in this crap hole." He unscrews the lid from the half-empty bottle of whiskey beside the television, pours an inch into the glass. Swirls it. "My life is pretty much a punch line."

"I'm sorry."

"Are you?" He gulps the contents of his glass. "That's great."

"Thomas—"

"You still have your family. How'd you pull that one off?"

"I told the truth," Katherine says. She won't tell him about Will's indiscretions, how their adulterous equality probably saved their marriage, or at least contributed to the lack of blame shifting and a willingness to be responsible for their own misdeeds. She doesn't mention the crash, how it changed everything. How it still ripples through each day, Evan's heart a second time, and becomes a thing to which all can be measured, and all is found insignificant.

"How virtuous."

"I didn't mean it—"

"I know," he says, and his body softens, rounding at the edges in a way only she sees because she knows him. He's butter, left overnight on the kitchen counter, so solid looking until a knife cuts through it.

She's his knife.

"What happened?" she asks.

"How'd she find out? Some friend saw you and I together a few too many times and told Susanna, so she asked." He picks up the whiskey bottle again, but changes his mind and instead finds a Sprite in the mini-fridge. Holds it up toward her. She shakes her head and he closes the door. "My honesty didn't pay out quite as well. But, I do have the Clearwater, so cheers." He pops open his can, raises it to the room, and takes a long swallow.

The cell phone buzzes in Katherine's purse. A text. She ignores it.

"You look nice," Thomas says.

"Don't do that."

"It's not a come-on."

"Fine, then. You look nice too."

He turns sideways and flattens his untucked oxford against his stomach. "And thinner, huh?"

"Now that you mention it," she says.

"The divorce diet," he says. "It should be patented."

She bites the inside of her cheek at the D word. "Are you sure there's no chance you two can—"

"Already heard from her lawyer."

Katherine's phone vibrates again.

"I really am sorry."

"I know."

Tears ooze into her eyes. If she blinks, they'll spill onto her face, so she tries not to, but her lids close on their own volition, and she's left with two warm, salty rivulets on either side of her nose, slipping around her nostrils and converging in her philtrum before she licks the wetness away. If she had known beforehand, but that's the nature of affairs—people don't think of the consequences, but constantly sidestep them. *Don't be seen. Don't get caught. Don't let those texts be read, those calls be answered by your spouse.* It's unfair. Thomas has lost everything. She has more than she deserves.

Thomas, as always, knows her mind. "It's not your fault. I did it to myself. Sometimes you get what you deserve, you know? And when you don't, that's called grace. Or, at least that's what they say over at this new church I'm going to."

Church. God. How many turn to the intangible in their nightmare times? She has no judgment over where Thomas seeks his comfort. Once it was beside her, in bed. Now it's religion. It's been such since creation. Feed the body or feed the soul. One helps in the forgetting, the other in the facing. She's been there. She'd rather forget, too, but sometimes it's not possible.

Another vibration from her purse.

"Kate. Do you still love me?"

If she's honest with herself, she knows she does. If she's

honest with herself, she doesn't feel a fraction for Will what she does for Thomas. It doesn't matter.

"I need my family."

He nods. "Yeah."

Her phone rings now, Will's tone, an obnoxious *wha-wha-wha* chosen by Evan, the sound a construction vehicle makes when it moves in reverse. She unsnaps her phone pocket and swipes the call on. "Hey."

"Where are you?" Will asks, sounding frantic.

"Why? What's wrong?"

"It's Evan. The school called. He's on his way to the hospital by ambulance."

"What happened?"

"I don't know. The nurse wasn't clear. Something about his chest and trouble breathing. I didn't wait for more. I'm on my way there."

"I'll meet you. It'll take me twenty minutes."

Will hangs up. Katherine jams her phone in her coat pocket—her new coat, still wool but gray this time, subdued and inconspicuous—and opens the door.

"Kate?"

"I have to go."

She skids on the stairs, the pointy heel of her boot catching on something unseen in the slush, grabs the metal handrail and continues to her car, starts it. Every light is red as she drives the main road through town; she shouts angrily at each one, "Come on, come on," but they ignore her. She can't help but consider this some cosmic punishment. She went to see Thomas. Something bad happens to

Evan. She reminds herself of the favorite argument of her college classmates, applied to everything from laboratory reports to dating. *Correlation does not imply causation.* She repeats it, her invocation.

Correlation does not imply causation.

Correlation does not imply causation.

Correlation does not imply causation.

Another red light. She swears. And then she starts to pray, the way every child begins, with *Dear God.*

She stops. She has nothing left to bargain.

With Evan the first time, she made her promises and did her best to keep them, giving to this unknown God what all people give when they make such bargains—their goodness. But she doesn't have any left, if she ever had it at all. There is no reason for God—should he exist, should he listen, should he act—to do a single thing to help her now. And yet, hope permeates her skin, warming her, a sensation so close to a lover's touch she blushes. And when she parks the car in the emergency room lot, she opens her hands, rests them in the solid center of the steering wheel, and whispers, "Please." Her prayer, one word sheathed around all she knows and doesn't know to say.

And she runs through the sliding doors of the hospital.

"I'm looking for my son, Evan Walker," she tells the intake nurse.

"Katherine." It's Will, waiting for her.

"Is he okay? What's going on? Will, tell me—"

"It's not his heart."

She slides her fingers down her face, pulling, gasping as

her eyes turn upward, toward the ceiling. Toward heaven. "Thank you," she breathes, and then to Will, "Where is he?"

"Come on. Back here."

He holds her elbow, steers her around a laundry cart, a blood pressure cuff on a stand, but it's not necessary because she feels so easy here, in this place where milliseconds and plaid curtains separate life and death. The familiarity will never leave her.

She finds Evan on a bed, and her eyes read the monitor above the bed, the only room in the small hospital equipped for cardiac patients, the one where heart attacks come, where her son must come. His oxygen saturations are bouncing around the mid-80s, an acceptable level for him but an indication of a serious problem in any one of them. His heart rate and respiration are normal. But his face. Bruised around his left eye and cheek, eyelid drooping, lip split and swollen. Blood in his hair.

She brushes his knee, the top of his head. "Oh, baby, what happened?"

"You happened," Bryce says. She hadn't noticed him in the corner.

"I don't—"

"He got his head kicked in by a bunch of guys who called you a whore."

"Bryce," Will says.

"No, Dad. She did this to him. They kicked him in the chest, because they knew . . . they knew about . . . and he couldn't breathe, and I . . . the nurse sent me in the ambulance with him so he wouldn't be alone, and I thought . . ." He hiccups, chokes on his saliva.

"Bryce, I can't apologize more than I have."

"You're not going to," Will says. "Because this isn't only about you."

"Will," Katherine says, shaking her head.

Bryce jumps from the chair, it screeching backwards, slamming into the wall. "She's the one, Dad. She—"

"Then I am too," Will says. "Your mother hasn't done anything I haven't."

Silence, and then Bryce says, "What?"

"You heard me. I had an affair too. Your mother didn't want to say anything because she didn't want you mad at both of us. She didn't want you, both of you, to feel like you had no one. But you know what? You have us. We screwed up big time, but we're here, and we're going to put this family back together, piece by broken piece, no matter what it takes. You hear?"

Bryce turns his head.

"Did you hear me?"

"Yeah," Bryce says. He looks at both Will and Katherine. Blinks. Nods. "Yeah."

"Jesus," Evan croaks, his enlarged lips hardly moving.

"What?" Will asks.

"Sometimes it takes falling onto Jesus."

Will scrapes his stubble with his fingernails, brows creasing, and he rattles the change in his pocket. "Uh, yeah. Okay. Well, whatever it is, we'll figure it out."

Katherine rolls Evan's hand in hers, and she remembers

when she would kiss his knuckles, counting between each loud, sloppy puckering sound, making mistakes as she went. *One, two, nineteen, eighty-seven.* And he would giggle and say, "Nooooo," correcting her math. "It's three, Mommy. It's four."

"Are you sure?"

"Yes. You taught me. You can't forget already."

"Oh, you're right. Let me try again. One, two. Four hundred and thirty-six," she'd say, bringing on another eruption of giggles.

When Will and Bryce aren't around, and he's not on painkillers with wire tentacles sticking to his chest, she'll ask him what it means to fall onto Jesus. But for now, she lifts his hand and gently brushes her lips against the nubbin of bone where his pointer and hand join, and Evan manages a wry half smile and whispers, "One."

CHAPTER THIRTY-TWO

She's not driving to Wyoming, where the emaciated boy in the photo lives. He's still alive; Ada found several stories in his hometown paper online, detailing his recovery. And Julian's photo essay, painstakingly recording how his treatments ravaged both him and his mother—physically, emotionally, and financially, in hopes of saving his life.

His name is Greyer DiGiulio, the youngest son of a single mother, never long with the father of either of her sons. His older brother Joshua was diagnosed with leukemia and died within a year. Doctors discovered Greyer with the same cancer at eleven, the same age his brother was. Natalie DiGiulio didn't know how she would live through it all a second time. Ada had reached her on the phone.

"Julian called and asked if he could chronicle Grey's story, and I said yes, not because I wanted him there, but because I really needed money. I did my research. I knew who he was. Anything Julian Goetz did was going to get national attention, and I figured we'd have a much better chance of fund-raising with his name behind our story. I still had outstanding bills from Josh, my credit cards were maxed, I'd used all my paid leave so every day I needed to be home with Grey we had no income. Friends and family did the best they could to support us, but none of them were much better off than we were.

"So Julian came and took pictures, and was as unobtrusive as possible. And then he was done." Ada recognizes the romantic treble in Natalie's voice; she'd fallen in some semblance of love with this photographer who was privy to the most intimate moments of their lives. She tells how, like Joy Robertson, she received a substantial check in the mail after Julian won the Pulitzer for Greyer's story.

"Ten thousand dollars," she said. "I knew that was how much the Prize paid out, and I thought it was generous of him to donate it all to us. But when I went to put a little of the money on Josh's back bill, the hospital told me his outstanding balance had been paid in full. Anonymously. I'm almost positive it was Julian, but when I asked him, he just told me to thank God.

"So I did. I do. And I light a candle at mass every Sunday for Julian Goetz."

* * *

She doesn't want to go back to the brownstone, yet, but the time is close. She won't be able to find the boy in the photo from the Middle East. That leaves only one more photo, the homeless church service beneath the bridge in Albany, the city adjacent to Trent. Ada is afraid. Dark skin. Filthy skin. Track-marked and oozing and diseased skin. Her still-developing sense of independence doesn't include bravery.

The bridge crosses the Hudson, a different river from the one that caught Julian's body when it fell back to earth. Engineers and medical doctors reassured the families, given the type of explosion, the altitude, the way the airplane broke apart, their loved ones most certainly were already dead before the water consumed them. Do the words bring comfort? To some, perhaps, but not to her.

She carries the framed photograph beneath her arm, the camera strapped around her neck but zipped under her coat so no one can grab and steal it. She sees three fires flickering in barrels, people in a large circle around them, some standing, some cross-legged on the damp, graveled ground, some on cushions or folding chairs or piles of rags. A well-worn path cuts through the snow, carved by feet and shopping carts and dragged trash bags full of earthly possessions. She feels as though her rib cage will swing open and her heart burst out, it pummels her chest wall so forcefully. Her armpits tingle. Each breath fights its way up her trachea, clawing, kicking, tumbling from her lips with ragged determination.

She walks toward the river.

Some people look at her and murmur, but most focus on the preacher, a pale man wearing two knit caps and a peacoat, scarves laced around his legs. He stands on a pile of wooden pallets and talks to those gathered.

"What does it mean, then, to take up our cross and follow him? You may say, 'We carry enough crosses,' but are they ones he calls you to carry, or ones you bear up all on your own? You may say, 'We are hungry and thirsty,' but is that hunger and thirst for righteousness? You may say, 'We are poor,' but is it a poverty of spirit?

"You may be thinking, who cares about righteousness and the spirit and crosses. All you know is your stomach is empty and your toes are black from frostbite, and you think no one cares. Christ cares. You want him to prove it? He did prove it. He died for you. Even if every person who walks by you today spits on you, tramples you, judges you for your homelessness or addiction or unemployment or your smell, they are not Jesus. They do not speak for Jesus. He says you are loved. He says you are worth his life."

The man holds up a loaf of bread. "And so, when we eat this, we do it to remember that we have value to him, that he sees us even if not one other single person does. We can be like him, even if others are not, because we remember his sacrifice."

He gives the bread to the person on his right, who rips a piece from the loaf and passes it to the next person, and the next. Ada stands behind the circle, but when the bread comes close to her, a woman slaps the man holding it and points to her. He turns and waves it at her. *Take and eat.*

She's never taken Communion before. In her community, only men were allowed, and the reasons were twofold, according to the prophet. Because in the biblical accounts of the Last Supper, only men are mentioned as being present; any other talk of love feasts or the breaking of the bread, her father said, are only meals and not Communion. And because the men are the intermediaries between God and their wives, their daughters; therefore the sacrament carries no meaning for women. Holy Zion freely offers bread and wine to any and all in the congregation, but they only serve Communion once a year, at the Passover, as is their understanding of when it should be celebrated.

Take and eat.

She approaches, the loaf in his grubby hand, the meaty part of the bread speckled with grit. She twists off a small bit of crust and backs away. The man shuffles to the next person and hands the loaf off, and it continues around the circle until all have some. The man on the pallets tears the remainder in half. "This is my body, broken for you."

A woman limps around to each person, sticking a paper Dixie cup in his or her hands. Another woman fills the cup with grape juice, the bottle shaking so badly as she pours, it sloshes over the rim and onto the fingers of more than one of those beneath the bridge, including Ada. When all the juice had been poured—juice! She's never heard of such heresy—the pale man says, "This is my blood, which is shed for the forgiveness of sins. Drink it, all of you."

So they do.

As does she.

The crowd breaks apart, some dropping their cups on

the ground and moving to their makeshift cardboard homes and beds situated more deeply under the bridge. Some surge closer to the burn cans, looking toward the road leading to the water, seemingly waiting. Others collect the cups, tossing them into the fire or stacking them into their belongings. People eye her with all manner of expressions she's unable to read because of their appearance—beards and matted hair and cloths over their faces—and her fear. She wants to turn and leave, but her body won't obey and she's relieved by it.

Not far to go now.

The pale man approaches. "Can I help you find someone?"

She shakes her head.

"Then what can I do for you? Not that you're not welcome here. You're just looking a teeny bit out of place." He holds his finger and thumb a centimeter apart when he says *teeny*, peering through the thin space at her, his other eye closed.

"I'm Ada Goetz."

His smile vanishes. "Julian," he says, more breath than word.

She nods. "You knew him."

"Going on ten years," the man says. "I'm Camden Cooper. Are you cold?"

"Very."

She thinks he'll lead her to an inside area, but instead he beckons her closer to one of the fires. "Gladys, a chair please," he calls out.

Someone shouts, "Sure, Preach," and moments later

the largest woman Ada has ever seen—tall, wide, thick—approaches, two beach chairs swinging on her wrist. She wears a short, tight dress despite the cold, and strappy gold shoes, dirt staining the toes of her creamy hosiery, a color much too light for her skin. If it weren't for the clothes, Ada would think her a man.

Gladys opens the chairs and wanders off. Camden offers the least broken one to Ada, and she sits, crossing her legs for warmth. He offers, "I can find you a blanket," but she shakes her head, not wanting unknown filth and germs on her. He laughs a little and says, "A clean one."

"Oh, I didn't—"

"Ada, it's fine. No one's pretending it's the Ritz down here."

"I'm sorry."

"No, I'm the one who's sorry. For your loss. Yeah, he's somewhere out there worshipping before the throne of the Almighty, but, man, it's Julian, and . . ." His voice clouds, and he sniffs, grunts the mourning from his throat. ". . . and it's Julian. So I guess I'm sorry for my own self too."

Camden feels through the pockets of his coat, removes a crushed box of cigarettes, shakes a butt into his hands. He holds it in his lips, lights it. After a short drag, it extinguishes. He flicks the remaining filter into the barrel. He jerks his head at the frame she still holds. "What are you clinging to so tightly there?"

She turns the photograph over in her lap.

"I've seen that one," Camden says. "People come down here with all kinds of frames, you know? Pictures of their loved ones in them, runaways and addicts and crazy uncles, asking if anyone has seen them, thinking they might have fallen off the face of the earth and landed here."

"And you?"

"I'm here by choice. Sounds crazy, I know, but that's how it is."

"You live here all the time?"

He nods, points over his shoulder. "That pile of junk is all mine."

Ada can't respond to his words. She doesn't know how. To her, the souls beneath this bridge are here for their sins: addiction, prostitution, or illnesses related to those things. Mental instability, which her father would declare either brought on by the worldliness in which they drench themselves, or by demons that will release them only through repentance. *Jesus ate with sinners and tax collectors*, Julian reminded her. Again, two Gods—her father's and her husband's. She's drawn toward the one Julian taught her and Pastor Ray preaches, and most members of Holy Zion seemingly embrace, but she's still afraid if she gets too close, she'll learn he's the fire-breathing beast of the Revelation and she'll be burned to ash.

She brushes those thoughts away and asks, "How did you meet?"

Camden shakes his head. "I use the term *meet* loosely. Julian was down here taking pictures and I tried to steal his camera. Yeah, while it was around his neck. I was so strung out I didn't know why I couldn't just grab it and run. And Julian, he just laughed. At least I think he did. Maybe that's the haze of cocaine talking. But what he did do is buy me breakfast from that cart right across the street there. We sat and talked until I passed out. I woke up a day later with twenty bucks and Julian's card in my pocket. I immediately went and spent all the money on booze and drank myself into a stupor.

"Some time later, and I can't tell you how long, I was arrested for destruction of property. Took a baseball bat to a line of cars. Again, I can't tell you why. I still had Julian's number and I thought, *What the heck?* So I called him and asked him to come bail me out. He showed up to my arraignment instead. Somehow he managed to convince the judge to remand me to rehab. I was one ticked cokehead, let me tell you. I screamed all sorts of profanity at him, spit on him while the guards were dragging me out. And you know what he said? 'God loves you too much for this.'

"Now I've had many people get all religious on me, and I pretended to listen because it usually came with a free meal or a blanket or something. But, and I can't describe it any better than this, Julian's words sounded different. On that day, at that moment, the Holy Spirit decided to use his words to open my eyes. I worked that rehab, and it was hard. I came out clean, and it's been ten years and it's still hard, every single day. Especially here, because I can get it so easily—though by now the regulars know not to offer. Every now and then when things get bad, I admit to hitting the booze and getting wasted. I'm not proud of it, but that's reality."

"If it's about money—"

"Ada, sweet Ada," Camden says, and she sees compassion and fire in his eyes, the echo of the flame in the garbage can, the image of Christ. "Julian told me about you. He loved you from the moment he saw you. He wanted to bring you here, to meet me, all of us, but was waiting. He said you weren't ready yet. But here you are."

A white van appears, creeping down the access road to the river. The ragtag collection of men and women move toward it in unison, as if the ground suddenly tipped in its direction and they are rolling like glass marbles. The back and side doors open, and well-dressed volunteers hand out foil-wrapped sandwiches, cups of coffee, clothing and toiletries and other items.

"The mission," Camden says. "They come every day with food, and then on Sundays with these extras. They're doing the Lord's work, I don't begrudge them that. They have a shelter they run, too, and I believe most of them honestly care. But they don't understand, Ada, not like I do. They haven't been homeless. They haven't been afraid to go to sleep because it's so cold they think they'll freeze to death if they do. They don't use the Hudson for their toilet and wash water. They have their own struggles, to be sure, but not these struggles. And if they did in the past, they're far enough removed from it that my small flock here under this bridge, they don't care. They think, *I have a bed now, and clothes and food and a shower and a job. I'm not like you anymore.*

"So that's why I stay, Ada. Because when I say God loves them no matter what, they know I have the same *no matter what* as they do. Street cred, that's all. And I'm here until the good Lord tells me it's time to move on."

The understanding again refuses to come to her. Camden Cooper, a minister to the homeless and a former drug addict still given to bouts of debauchery? *This I say then, Walk in the Spirit, and ye shall not fulfill the lust of the flesh.* Her father quoted Galatians at them daily. And second Corinthians. *For what fellowship hath righteousness with unrighteousness? And what communion hath light with darkness?* How can such paradox survive in one half-starved man?

I take the photos, Julian told her once. *I don't try to figure it all out. God's done that all for me.*

"Can I take your picture?" Ada asks.

"Okay now," he laughs, "Julian didn't tell me you were a photographer too."

"I'm not. It's, well, it's this thing."

He stands near the fire barrel, holding the frame, and she shoots the photo. Gladys marches over—Ada is certain she has stubble on her upper lip, her chin—and she poses next to Camden. Then another person, and another, until half the bridge people are assembled and Ada has to move backward to fit everyone in the frame because she doesn't know how to zoom out.

"I'd like a copy of that," Camden says. "Maybe fifty copies. People here will want one too."

That Ada understands without him explaining. Photography is a civilized pursuit, something of holidays and grandbabies and special memories. The camera gives humanity.

She shakes his hand, and the hands of several others, enduring foul-smelling hugs as Camden introduces her as Julian's wife. Then they grow bored, and achy from standing, and they want to inspect the goodies given to them by the mission volunteers, and she's left alone with Camden again. She says good-bye, and he removes a dirty string from his neck, places it over her head. A plastic cross dangles from the bottom.

"I baptized him here, you know. Julian. In this river. He hadn't been, before then." And Camden wanders back toward the water's edge, kicking the damp stones.

* * *

She's not through the door of the brownstone twenty minutes before Hortense arrives, barging in with her own key, not ringing the doorbell. Ada had to use the spare key hidden in the backyard, the one in the film canister with the rock glued to the lid that Julian buried in pea stone beneath the drippy gutters; her own house key was with the Jeep key, on the ring she last saw dangling from her father's hand.

Ada expects questions, braces for them, but Hortense drops her purse on the floor and folds Ada against her, not unlike the day Julian died. When Hortense pulls away, she presses her wrists into the fleshy part of Ada's upper arms and jostles her, the way Ada's mother did to her when she wanted her attention, shaking her hard enough so her head was forced upward to look into her mother's face. The way

Ada did to her younger siblings when she was cross with them, or frightened by something dangerous they had done.

"I thought you went back," Hortense says, and then embraces Ada again—for her own sake, not for Ada's.

"No." She doesn't have the energy to tell Hortense how she tried and failed. Not now.

"Then where have you been?"

So Ada tells her, as she rehangs the frames, three of the images now a story within a story, less about the subjects photographed and more about the photographer. She straightens the picture of the emaciated boy. "I talked to Greyer DiGiulio's mother. He's in remission. But I couldn't drive all the way to Wyoming to take his picture."

"Why would you want to?" Hortense asks.

"Because . . ." Ada hesitates. She never intended to show *her* photographs to anyone, but finds herself opening the bag on the sofa, turning on the camera, and giving it to Hortense, who inspects each one, while she watches. This is the first time she's looked at them too.

"That's you," Hortense says, tapping the screen. She enlarges the image of Joy, standing behind Nona's chair, and points again. Ada sees it, her body—spectral, malformed—mirrored in the glass protecting Julian's original work. Anyone else would have known to step out of the way, to angle her body and the camera so her reflection wouldn't be seen.

"You're there again." Hortense says. "And in this one too."

Julian once told her some cultures believe cameras steal the souls of those photographed, trapping it within the bounds of the two-dimension paper image. But in portraits she took, Ada sees *her* soul. A piece of herself, captured forever with the fragments Julian left for her to find there, in his work. Her father told everyone in the community that the heathens had no excuse to disbelieve since the Lord Almighty etched himself upon all things at the time he formed it. But she knows now each act of creation imprints the creator on the created. It's here, before her eyes, in these photographs.

"I think you should go to Wyoming," Hortense says, switching off the camera. "There's something here. We could . . . you could do something with it."

"The pictures aren't any good."

"Yeah, they suck. But who cares about that? It's what you're trying to say."

"There's no message in these."

"There always is. Why did you think to take them to begin with?"

"I don't know. It was a spur of the moment idea."

Hortense shakes her head. "Nope."

"It doesn't matter anyway. Even if I did travel to see Greyer, there's still this other one." She touches the first in the collection, the Middle Eastern flag burning with the boy's hair aflame.

"But, Ada—"

"Hortense, I'm sorry. I don't mean to seem impolite, and especially after everything you've done for me, but I've spent the morning under a bridge. I'm freezing. My feet are soaked. I've lived on vending machine snacks and fast food.

I've driven I don't know how many miles. I just want to shower and sleep, if that's okay."

"Sure, it's okay," Hortense says, and her painted lips curl up at the ends, a crescent moon, red, like ones Ada has seen in the sky on the hottest summer nights. Then the woman squints at her, inspects her, and shakes her head. Another chuckle. "Yeah, more than okay."

Hortense scoops up her purse and, before leaving, spins back one more time, arm in the air; if she'd had fingers, she'd be pointing one of them. "Oh, one more thing." She gives Ada an orange Post-it; it's stuck to her stub. "This kid came by looking for you while you were gone. Evan . . . Walker, or something. His address and phone number are in there. You can ask Ray White about him, but he was really desperate to talk to you."

"Okay. Thanks."

Hortense looks again, the curious smile still there. "Julian would be thrilled," she says, and once she's out the door, Ada sags. Her feet, damp in her tights, leave footprints on the wooden floor. Not quite a month unlived and the house smells of must and emptiness. She opens windows, despite the chill outside. The cold air holds a similar solitude, perhaps because the molecules move so slowly, they never touch. Even the atomic world knows loneliness.

She showers, notices a jelled lump of fat above each hip bone, testament to her diet over the past weeks. Her breasts seem fuller; she lifts them, drops them, and the bounce feels heavier than usual. She turns to the side, tugs the extra skin at her navel, stretches it as far as possible, and then she lets go. It snaps back with a jiggle, blotchy from all her pinching. She likes how she looks with the extra weight. She thinks Julian would have liked it too. He worried he was hurting her each time their bones ground against the other, pelvis and ribs mostly. She never noticed but he wasn't nearly as pointy as her.

She wears his bathrobe over her flannel nightgown. His wool socks on her feet. And instead of sleeping in the guest room, she turns down the blankets on Julian's bed. Their bed. She hasn't changed the sheets since before the crash, so his scent rises up to her, released from beneath the down comforter. She loosens all the tucked-in sides and rolls up in the layers of bedding so she's surrounded by him. But she doesn't cry. Camden is right, the tears are only for the living, and she's done weeping over herself.

CHAPTER THIRTY-THREE

His face is almost completely healed, only a thick scab near the corner of his eyebrow that pulls his skin when he squints or wrinkles his forehead. His mother grabs him when he walks by and smears a blob of Neosporin on the spot. "You don't want it to scar," she says.

"Like it matters," Evan says. "I have a million scars."

"Not on your face."

He tries to remember what he can about the fight. He'd been going to Spanish, without Grace. Usually they walked together but they weren't speaking, still, since the afternoon on the bus when he sat with the kids from First Baptist. It wasn't a planned shunning; the next day she didn't sit with him on the morning bus, and he ignored her on the afternoon route, and once through the weekend both had decided independent of the other they wouldn't be the first to give in. So be it, and a week and a half later, neither had acquiesced.

It was a few tenth-grade jocks. Not the upper-tier ones, who were smart and popular and the better athletes of the school. The fringe jocks, second-string players, the ones still on the modified or JV teams, with grades hovering at the eligibility cutoff and a referral every now and then to the vice principal's office for unruly lunchroom antics. These boys searched out reasons to be angry and aggressive, which is why sports appealed to them, even as they lacked ability. Biggish fish, small pond, and all that. In another, larger district, the boys who beat up Evan wouldn't have made the mascot team.

They came down the hall, one of the three jocks stopping for a drink at the fountain and then spitting a mouthful of water at a girl passing by. The other two laughed and shoved and then noticed Evan.

"Hey, Seth," the redhead shouted, "here comes the home wrecker's spawn."

Evan was startled. He didn't see Seth at all, who was at his locker somewhere behind Evan. He'd gotten so used to keeping his head turned away and mind occupied with petty distractions while passing this area of the corridor, he'd intentionally forgotten his friend stopped in this area after every period—Seth one of the few students who refused to carry extra books for other classes because he regularly forgot them here and there, under chairs and on top of towel dispensers in the restroom.

"Don't start, McGowan," Seth said, and Evan noticed him now, off to the side and equidistant between the boys and Evan, the third point of a triangle. *Too much geometry,*

Evan recalls thinking, but didn't have time to consider much of anything after that because the redhead sauntered toward him and knocked his books from his arms.

"So, Walker, what do you think about your mama being a whore?"

Evan had never been in a fight. He didn't know how to begin, but when this beefy kid called his mother *that* word, Evan couldn't ignore it. He lowered his head, an undersized, underweight linebacker in Pee-Wee Football, and rammed his shoulder into McGowan's gut.

He heard the *Oof*, and then swearing and stampeding, and the other two boys, one arm trapped by each of them, were holding him upright. McGowan punched him in the face.

"Stop," Seth said.

"Shut up, Bailey. He has it coming. If you weren't such a chicken we wouldn't have to do it for you." And McGowan hit him again, near the mouth this time.

"Evan!" Grace now, and she pulled at the arms of the kid on his right, trying to force his grip to release. "Let him go."

"The girl has more balls than you do, Walker. Both of you." McGowan laughed. "You still have that bad heart? Maybe we should check that out?"

He saw the red-haired, red-faced boy coming at him, and his captors pulling him down, then he felt it, a crushing jolt as McGowan jammed the bottom of his sneaker into his ribs.

The boys dropped him.

Against his cheek, the floor felt cold and gritty and

then slippery. *With my blood.* He moved his head the tiniest bit, feeling the wet warmth beneath it. Then he noticed he couldn't breathe.

Grace saw it. She screamed for help. Seth knelt beside him, rolled him onto his back. "Breathe, Evan. Come on." Suddenly a crowd gathered around him and Seth tried to wave them back, but they pushed in and the heat of their bodies washed over Evan, a sauna of scented hair spray and chewing gum, and he clutched his throat, suddenly afraid, after everything, he'd die right here on the high school floor.

Please, no.

"Move, move. Move now."

The crowd jostled and opened, and the nurse strapped an oxygen mask over Evan's nose. He drew a frayed breath, then another. It hurt, but he could manage it. Grace stood against the lockers, sobbing, Seth's arms around her, and then Bryce was there, out of nowhere like Superman. And the paramedics. Then he was loaded into the ambulance with his brother and carried away to the hospital.

He stayed home from school for a week, Grace visiting him every day, bringing his homework assignments and giving him the gossip. Seth called. "I just can't come by," he said. "Your mom. I can't see her."

"I know."

"I didn't want those guys to do that."

"I know that too."

"You know everything."

He doesn't know if he and Seth will be friends again. He won't ask, yet.

The beating skews the social scales, again, sympathy tipping it toward his side, and he's no longer a pariah. Grace had been right. Short memories. New scandal. Eventually no one has the self-discipline to care anymore.

He doesn't return to the Baptist lunch table.

"Your room is worse than a sty," his mother tells him. "Clean it."

"I'm injured," Evan says.

"Clean it gently."

He does still hurt, every move, every breath, but the pain is receding. He sorts his clothes into piles—probably dirty, mostly clean, and unsure. He fills his hamper with the dirty laundry, stuffs his drawers with the clean items, and hesitantly sniffs each article of clothing in the questionable pile, deciding most of those can be put away too. As he forces the last pair of jeans into the dresser, he finds a rumpled sheet of notebook paper folded in the back pocket. Opens it.

daviddickenson@firstbaptistfirststreet.org

555-4288

For the parts of the Bible you want, that talk about Jesus,

look at Matthew, Mark, Luke, and John

Evan has a Bible. The Methodist church gave one to every kid in his confirmation class. He hasn't opened it in the two years he's had it. It's still wrapped in plastic in the bottom of his closet; he digs through the summer shorts he tossed in there instead of packing them away at the end of last season, the too-small shoes, his sleeping bag with the broken zipper, dozens of photography magazines. He bites a hole in the cellophane, pulls it open with his teeth, static attaching the wrapping to his chin, and then his hand when he brushes it from his face. He settles on his bed and flips the book open to the table of contents, figures he'll start with Matthew since it's listed first, and after skipping through the long list of names and the birth of Jesus—he knows about *that* already—he reads.

CHAPTER THIRTY-FOUR

The doorbell rings as Katherine zips on her boots over her jeans, and then slips a stack of thin, metal bangle bracelets on her wrist. She figures it's the UPS man because he's at the front of the house, and everyone they know comes through the back door, directly into the kitchen. Which, at the moment is in utter disarray as she and Will have been removing wallpaper, and it's tedious and messy work. The online videos showing how to painlessly take it down with a steamer and spray bottle of vinegar? Yeah, all lies. They've not finished one corner yet, each small section requiring scraping, soaping, sponging, more spraying, and some solution left overnight which dissolves the glue and also pocks the drywall behind it. Will suggests demolishing the walls and building new ones. "It'll be faster, easier, and probably cheaper."

"Wait until we paint the cabinets," she tells him.

Earrings next. One on, and then the other, but she can't

find the back for it. "Evan, come on," she calls, crouching on the floor. "We have to go."

The doorbell rings again.

She swears, unable to find the bitty silver nut, so she takes out both earrings and, on the way through the dining room, drops them into the Depression-era candy dish on the sideboard.

"Evan!"

"Coming," he shouts back from his bedroom upstairs.

They have family counseling in twenty minutes. Will and Bryce are meeting them there.

Whoever is at the door knocks now. Katherine groans and thinks, *Give it a rest already.* She opens to find a young woman there, dwarfed in a puffy, calf-length coat and faux shearling-topped snow boots. "Can I help you?"

"I'm sorry to disturb your evening, ma'am. My name is Ada Goetz and I was hoping I could speak with Evan Walker."

The world implodes, every scrap of matter spins, spins, spins as if trapped in a tornado, funneling down to the point of origin, until it disappears, sucked into another plane of existence, and all that remains is stark, white silence.

And then vibrations. Evan, clattering down the stairs with his jacket flying behind him, his gangly legs, his sneakers on his hands as if they were feet and he plans to walk on them. And then he talks to her, his mouth moving without sound, and she has the sense he's within a bubble she must pop before his words can be free, so she extends her pinky and pokes it toward him, into this invisible bubble, and her hearing returns.

"Mom?" Evan asks, face contorted with concern.

"Evan." She clears her throat. "This is Ada Goetz."

"You're on your way out," Ada says.

Katherine looks at her son, who carries the same expression she must, this blanched, tight-jawed kind of calm that appears on bodies in morgues, spread on gurneys in wait of their autopsies—stiff with *rigor mortis* beneath a disingenuous, sleepy ease. Only Evan's eyes betray him, his lids pulled back as far as they'll go, jerking his pupils to one side in communication. Her own eyes sting with too much openness.

Ada hunches deeper into her too-big coat. "I shouldn't have come unannounced."

"No," both Katherine and Evan say at the same time. The young woman blinks at the forceful puff of the word in her face.

"What we mean, is, you're not intruding. Please, come in," Katherine says.

"Are you sure?" Ada feels the discomfort between them.

"Yes, absolutely. I apologize. We were going out, to . . . the store, but it's nothing that can't wait."

"Yeah, nothing," Evan parrots.

"Thank you," Ada says. She cautiously steps over the threshold, struggles from her boots, sheds her coat, and Katherine sees a girl, not a woman, someone who isn't much older than Bryce, wearing a long corduroy skirt and oversized cowl-neck sweater, drowning in her clothes.

"Come, sit down. Evan, take her coat," Katherine says,

an edge in her voice, the razor of a dictator. Ada flinches, smoothing her skirt beneath the back of her thighs before settling on the love seat, on the end closest to the front door. "Can I get you a drink? We have water and soda, tea. I can put on coffee."

"No, I'm fine."

"I'm going to make tea. Won't take long. Evan, could you call your dad and tell him we won't be meeting him at the store?"

"He'll want to know why."

"You're right. Well, then come help me in the kitchen a minute. You know I can't reach the tea bags."

They both hurry into the other room. Katherine runs the water and turns on the vent fan above the stove to mask their voices. Evan says, "You can't reach the tea bags?"

"It was the only thing I could think of."

He holds out his phone. "Dad's called twice."

"Dial him back and give it to me."

She fills the teakettle and drops it on the stove, cranks the burner to high. The wet bottom sizzles, and a burnt smell fills the kitchen, some remnant of last night's dinner still on the element. She takes the phone from Evan and says, "Hon, you and Bryce go ahead without us."

"What's wrong?" Will asks.

"Nothing's wrong. We just . . . look, I'll explain when you get home. I can't right now."

"Kate."

"Ada Goetz is sitting in our living room."

"Who?"

"Exactly." The kettle screeches. "Will, I have to go." She hangs up.

"That went well," Evan says.

She fills three mismatched mugs—each faded by the dishwasher, two with half-visible cartoon drawings of cows lamenting their lack of morning coffee, and one with a pithy saying about bacon's perfection—with the steaming water, drops a tea bag in each, and nudges Evan. "Carry yours."

"I don't want any."

"Just take it."

He follows her back to Ada, and she says, "It's super hot," as she gives the mug to her. Ada nods and worms her cold fingers into the handle, pressing against Katherine's tea-heated ones, the temperature difference shocking. *That's death, his death*, Katherine thinks, *soaked into her*. The absurdity of it all comes over her as she shuffles coasters onto the coffee table. No amount of hospitality will resurrect her husband, and if it could, what has Katherine done but throw a mug of cheap Lipton at this poor woman, no sugar, no milk, pastry, not even her good teacups, displayed in the china cabinet across the room.

"I did try to call before I came," Ada says, setting her mug on the coaster. "It said the number had been disconnected."

"We dropped our house line," Katherine says. She and Evan sit opposite Ada, on the sofa. "Just recently. We all have cell phones now."

"I don't want to take up more of your time than necessary."

"Please, don't worry about it. We have all night."

Ada glances back and forth between the two of them, absorbing their tension. "I think," she begins. Hesitates. "I spoke with Ray White, Evan. He said you had spoken to him while I was . . . away. I promise you, he kept everything you said in confidence, but thought . . . well, he thought it might be good for me to come see you."

Evan looks at Katherine. She nods. *Tell her. Tell her everything.*

"I was, I mean, I am a really big fan of your husband. No, fan isn't the right word. He . . ." Evan scratches his knees, twitches, wading through his thoughts. "He's been an inspiration. To my photography."

Ada smiles. "That's really nice to hear," she says, and Katherine recognizes the dishonesty in the curve of her mouth, not intentional, not malicious, and most likely not even known to her. Katherine's seen it so many times before, when mothers she'd met during her hospital stays with Evan, or through this support group or that fundraiser, smile at the memory of their children taken too soon and say things like *Even though she was only here a short time, she taught me so much* and *He touched so many lives and I know he was put on this earth for a purpose.* And they believe their words. But she knows every single one of them would trade almost anything for another five minutes with their child. So Ada smiles at Evan, taking comfort in yet another person inspired by her husband, another life he touched, but in places perhaps she doesn't admit she has, she'd take a living Julian Goetz who did nothing but love her, over a dead Julian Goetz who touched a million people with his camera.

Well, at least Katherine would.

"I went to the funeral," Evan continues, and she stops her head from spinning toward him because she did not know this. "I saw you there, leaving there, but I didn't get to talk to you. So I just wanted to tell you that. How I felt. I wanted you to know. I thought, well, I know it doesn't mean all that much, but maybe it would help somehow. Just a little."

"It does, Evan. Honestly."

"I didn't mean for you to come all the way up here. It's a long drive, and all."

"I've gone farther," she says, and stands. "And I've also taken enough of your time. Thank you again for inconveniencing yourselves for my sake."

Katherine coughs, a fake, dry sound, but Evan refuses to look at her. He won't tell Ada. He won't sacrifice his mother. It's her choice.

The young woman and her son exchange email addresses now. She wants him to keep in touch. He scurries around to find some paper, a pen with ink. The first two ballpoints don't write; he scribbles on the magnetic grocery list, leaving only deep gashes that can be felt, not seen. "Mom, are there any pens that work in this house?" he asks, and she snaps and points at her briefcase, a gift from Will when she earned her real estate license. Not a real briefcase with popping latches and legal pads. This one is glazed calfskin, mottled red with gold-tone zipper pulls and a shoulder strap. Gorgeous.

When she unwrapped it, she couldn't believe Will had chosen something so perfect or spent so much money. She later learned Robin picked it out.

"Front pocket," she says, and he finds a blue highlighter. "Not that."

"It works," he says, and prints his email on the paper, slowly, each letter formed and legible and large. Then he tears off the top sheet and gives it to Ada. She folds it into the pocket of her skirt and writes her address for him.

Katherine's skin prickles with pseudo-sweat, a clammy sheen of anxiety but no actual perspiration. She can keep silent. Her confession gains this woman nothing. All she owns, every person she loves, those things she holds valuable, she can pile it at Ada Goetz's feet, washed in Katherine's tears of contrition, dried with her hair.

Julian Goetz is dead.

She has nothing to give Ada, but she needs something from her. She needs forgiveness. She needs it, and has no right to ask. In this moment, though, she realizes if she doesn't seek it out now, she will never have peace. She will live with the guilt of knowing not only that her selfishness killed a man, but she's harboring a lie, and it will peck away at her, until all the flesh has been torn from her bones, and she'll be no good to anyone.

"Mrs. Goetz," she says. Beside her, Evan shakes his head, but she continues, "I met your husband. The day of the plane crash. I was supposed to be on his flight. It was overbooked."

"Julian told me. He was bumped, too, at first."

"I wasn't bumped."

Ada blinks. Frowns.

"I offered to give up my seat. To your husband." Katherine draws quick, empty breaths, the way a fish struggles for air when outside water, entire chest cavity heaving, mouth opening and closing, but still suffocating. "He said . . . he said . . ."

"He wanted to be home for my birthday." And then Ada smiles. "Stubborn man. Nothing was going to keep him off that plane."

Katherine cries with her lungs, her throat, not her eyes. No tears. Each inhalation is a wheeze of torment, and she covers her face in shame. Evan drapes his spindly adolescent arm over her neck.

"Mrs. Walker," Ada says. "Mrs. Walker, it's okay."

"I'm so sorry. Please forgive me. Please."

And Ada, peeling Katherine's hands from her face, says, "There's nothing to forgive." She hesitates, smiles uncertainly, and scrunches her shoulders. Then she wriggles into her oversized boots and her oversized coat, and disappears from the house.

What about me?

Suddenly, uneasiness replaces Katherine's penitence. She couldn't have imagined this response from Ada Goetz. She left room for only two options, forgiveness or hatred. Not indifference.

"Mom?"

"She didn't forgive me." And then an unreasonable anger creeps up from the emptiness of Katherine's stomach.

Without this absolution, how will she be able to start over, washed clean and able to escape the burden of her choices that day in the airport? "How could she not forgive me?"

"She doesn't even blame you, Mom."

"She needs to forgive me." The sentence comes from her, a hiss, and then a pitiful bubbling sound. "I need her to forgive me."

Evan shakes his head. "Not her. Someone else."

"Who?"

"Wait here. I'll be right back. There's something you need to read."

He tumbles up the stairs as only Evan does, bumping shins, reaching out for the steps above him with his arms, his motions ape-like. She hears him above, running the hallway to his room, banging and scraping, and then him stampeding back to her, a book in his hands, paper cover curled open. A Bible. Katherine presses her lips tight and, in a silent sucking motion, pulls the saliva from her mouth. Everything behind her teeth is so dry it collapses and she can't tell her tongue from her cheek from her palette. She swallows the warm, frothy spit. She won't say what she thinks, that this is a waste of time, a collection of myth and escapism and mistranslated histories. Prayer is one thing, or going to a church service, hearing some sermon encouraging happiness and fulfillment, and then eating a slice of crumb cake with friends she sees only on Sunday. But searching some ancient instruction manual for advice on modern living? No. It's what people do when they cannot handle situations of their own making. *The Zoloft of the masses.* A chuckle puffs her cheeks but cannot escape her clamped jaw, so it dies without sound.

Then Evan turns the thin pages; they crackle like tissue paper, like a gift being unwrapped. Her soul shifts. She'll listen, if only for him.

CHAPTER THIRTY-FIVE

There's nothing left for her now, it seems, and she feels almost as trapped as when she lived in the community. It's disillusionment, something she's not experienced before because she's never allowed herself to hope outside the boundaries of her father's rules for her. She expected *something* to happen at the end of her quest. She believed she heard from God to go, find these strangers hanging on her wall, and she did so in obedience. Now? She's home again, rattling around the brownstone amongst Julian's things, and there is no *next*.

Sunday. The Lord's Day. She has no desire to visit Holy Zion after being away so long. People will want to know how she's doing and where she's been, and all the questions dizzy her to the point of not knowing her own name. She dresses in her clothes from yesterday, draped neatly on the back of the chair; she has so few clothes and wears each outfit three times, unless she's spilled on it, or it's noticeably soiled in some way. She makes breakfast. She eats. She cleans the dishes, dries them, and stacks them back in the cupboard. Only twenty minutes has ticked away. Time moves slowly in the in-between.

She grabs the car key, ties on her boots, and backs the Jeep from the garage. She figures she'll go to church, but she drives past it and, even though she controls the vehicle, she's surprised not to have stopped. She continues to drive north on Route 37 because it goes through three states and she'll tire of driving before running out of road.

Instead of thinking, she notices things. Church doors, decorated for a wedding, and women in sleeveless dresses shivering on the steps of the old stone cathedral. Dozens of old Christmas trees at the end of driveways, waiting to be hauled away. Fire hydrants and broken telephone poles and banners advertising preschool enrollment. Then she sees the sign for the orchard, closed this time of year, but she knows where this particular turnoff leads—to the country, where Julian took her to drive.

She flicks on her directional.

She doesn't fly like the day they were together. It's January and ice clings to the pavement here and there. With miles between the farmhouses, it's likely no one will find her if she spins out of control and crashes. But she goes fast, and she opens the windows despite the cold, all four of them, and gives winter permission to wash her clean with its frosted fingers.

And she shouts a wordless cry of frustration and wonder and sadness, heavy with questions, pleading with the unknown. Her breath condenses and trails after the sound, out the window, both dispersing in the gray air. *What next? What next?*

Silence.

She slows the car, parks in the middle of the road, and steps from the Jeep. Brown pasture grass patched with snow rises away from the pavement. Nothing else. Ada breathes deeply and, without consideration, climbs onto the hood of the car, then to the roof, and shouts again.

Her voice echoes back.

* * *

It's almost ten at night, and Hortense calls and tells her she's coming to the house with someone, so get decent. Ada hadn't been asleep but reading in bed in a nightgown, and she most certainly won't see anyone in her bedclothes, even with Julian's bathrobe—despite both Hortense and Mark being comfortable enough to run from bedroom to dryer clad in only underwear while she sat at their kitchen table. She's also been flustered by random people clearly in their pajamas in public places—eateries, the public library, and the bank. To some things she will never grow accustomed.

The doorbell rings multiple frantic times without space between. She lets Hortense inside, and the young man with her.

"Nazih?"

"Hello, Mrs. Goetz."

She sighs. "Do you think you'll ever call me Ada?"

"No, I do not believe so."

"You know each other," Hortense says.

"You've been here for dinner while Nazih has been here, too, Hortense," Ada says, brow wrinkling. "You know we know each other. Is something wrong?"

Hortense nods. "Go on. Tell her."

"What?" Ada asks.

The young Yemeni man walks past her, places his palm over the burning boy in the hallway's first photograph. "This is me."

Ada watches Nazih remove his hand. From the angle the moonlight filters through the windows into the brownstone, from her position in the hall, she can see the oily print; it shimmers with an iridescent luster, and she thinks she won't ever wipe it away. This is one of the college students who attends Holy Zion, who has eaten in her home, who left messages after Julian's death asking if he could help in any way—calls she didn't return. But she would never have known the image and Nazih are the same. Too many years between them, too much smoke obscuring the boy's face, too many times Ada avoided this photograph because it haunted her so deeply.

"I do not know the entirety of the story because Mr. Goetz did not speak of it. But I will tell you what I can. Somehow, Mr. Goetz knew I wanted to come to the United States as a student. I only can surmise he must have had someone watching for my name. I did not realize he knew it. I did not know who he was until I saw this photograph.

"I received an offer to attend Trent Polytechnic and was informed I would have all my tuition paid by a scholarship. When I arrived, Mr. Goetz contacted me; he hosted several students for dinner each week, and I was welcome to attend. I admit I came only for the food and because I wanted to learn how to be more American. The first night I arrived before all the others and Mr. Goetz showed me this image. It did not hang on the wall then. I did not believe he still thought of me. I imagined Western journalists cared nothing for the people in those faraway places; they came only because we give them much to cover for their news.

"He provided the scholarship for me but would not let me thank him. He said I owed him nothing, it was for Christ. I thought, who is this Christ to ask a man to give so much to a stranger? And who is he that a man would obey? That is why I began to attend the Holy Zion church, to learn about this God-man I had been taught was the reason for so much suffering and hate. Now I, too, follow him."

So she takes his picture, right there, pulling the frame from the wall for him to hold, and the camera has become less shocking in her hands, the honeymoon over but still newlyweds, still learning, awkward but no longer embarrassed. She doesn't fumble with the power switch or try to remember which symbol on the dial means point-and-shoot mode. She doesn't startle at the sound of the shutter or the burst of flash. She looks and shoots, and Nazih's image appears in the viewing window.

"Not bad," Hortense says.

Ada swings the camera around and captures a photo of

a surprised Hortense. They inspect it and laugh, her face half-blurred and half missing. "Sorry," Ada says.

Hortense plucks the camera from her hands. "You do it like this," she says, and she holds it out, balancing it on the flat of her wrist, the lens facing both of them. "Press the button. With your outside arm."

She does, and they're together in a single image, both looking straight ahead, and smiling.

* * *

And so life continues.

Hortense contacts Greg Eisen and tells him about Ada's journey with—through—the photographs in the hallway. He proposes the idea to several magazines and all show interest. So he gathers Ada and photographer Roberto Alvarez, and they retrace her original steps. Greg hears the stories of Julian for the first time and she hears them again, and Roberto takes new pictures. "We can't use yours, Ada. They're not crisp enough for print," Greg tells her.

"They're bad, Greg. Just say it."

He laughs. "They're awful."

"We can't all be Julian Goetz," she says, repeating something she's heard from Hortense time and again.

"True that."

"Some of us can be pretty darn close," Roberto says.

Greg laughs again. "Keep telling yourself that, Alvarez."

She's not offended, and her original concept—each subject holding, interacting, with his or her portrait—remains.

In fact, the only difference is skill; the poses remain remarkably the same. Ada does get to meet Greyer DiGiulio as well, and before Roberto works his magical flash, she takes her own picture of him, healthy, shirtless in the grass, the emaciated boy of the image far off but never forgotten, held above his head. And yes, her reflection appears in the glass.

They fly to and from Wyoming on a Union North flight, which Ada correctly assumes was booked for dramatic effect. And while Greg draws parallels and plays up his fears in the magazine story, Ada hardly thinks of Julian, except to wish he'd been there to share this first with her. Perhaps her mind knows her heart can't handle such thoughts—*this is the elevation where Flight 207 exploded, these are the last sounds Julian heard, this is the napkin he wrote on, the peanuts he ate*—and protects her from them. Perhaps God knows. Either way, they're all home safely and Greg's narrative article, *The Five: A Faith Legacy of Julian Goetz*, captivates readers and brings a frenzy of requests for interviews and appearances by Ada. She declines them all, and lets Hortense deal with the rest of it.

Her father must have seen the story, and that knowledge brings her satisfaction. Too much, probably.

And so life continues.

She receives her invitation to Terrance Brimworthy's wedding, still a couple months off, and asks Hortense to go with her as her date. She agrees, but hints Ada should bring Nazih instead. "You have noticed how much attention he's been paying you?"

Ada hasn't. She can't imagine being with someone

else and doesn't want to try, not yet. But she thinks of Joy Robinson and her two Vinnys, and expects she won't be single forever. Julian wouldn't want that for her, anyway. And if it happens to be Nazih, she imagines he'd be pleased with that, too, because it is one more thing pointing toward heaven, a strange and wonderful tale of a photographer who took a picture of a boy halfway around the world, who learned the boy's name and tracked him and found a way to fulfill his dream of coming to the United States, only to have this boy, now a young man a year younger than Ada, be the kinsman redeemer for his widow. Who but Julian's God can knit together such happenings?

She has come to love this God she once feared, the one she but saw through a glass dimly, twisted and deformed by her father's words and actions into something wholly unrecognizable. The people of Holy Zion have been patient with her, and gracious, forgiving Ada for her initial suspicion of their dark skin and raised hands and boisterous *amens* punching though the sermon. She attends two Bible studies, one with the ladies, and one with the young adults—yes, with Nazih, who has switched to addressing her as Ada. From the women she learns steadfastness and hospitality and patience. From the youth she learns passion and questioning and vulnerability. From both she learns community.

And Hortense. Something shifts with them. Ada is no longer Julian's ward to her. And while they're not quite friends, they quietly move in that direction. Ada has days she misses Hortense being around, not because of loneliness—she's never had trouble being alone—but because being around Hortense brings her pleasure. And when Hortense shows up unannounced, more and more she's asking her to get a bite or do a little shoe shopping rather than checking in like a babysitter. Less and less she associates Mark and Hortense with Julian. They still tell stories about him, crazy antics they swear are true even though Ada has difficulty believing it, but they don't possess him in the same way.

They belong to her now too.

And so life continues, but it moves so slowly, even clumsy Ada has no trouble keeping up. She doesn't know what comes next. She takes her GED exam and passes. Nazih brings catalogues from the college and she pages through them but has no desire to learn about psychology or biology or education. She can't imagine having some job where she sits at a desk all day typing and answering phone calls, or lectures children, or microwaves hamburgers. For today, she washes the sheets and the last of Julian's dirty laundry, and packs his clothes for donation. She keeps two shirts that smell like him, folds them into a food storage bag, the kind with the plastic zipper, and every few days she opens it only enough for her to press her nose inside, and she inhales him, closing it quickly so his scent has less chance to dissipate, so she'll have him as long as possible.

She boxes most of his photo equipment for Evan Walker. They've kept in touch over email, him sharing some of his photos and asking her advice about a girl he likes. Grace, her name is. She tells him she's the last person to give relationship tips, but is excited to meet her when they come this weekend to pick up everything. She'll let him look through Julian's studio and library and take whatever else he can use.

She keeps Julian's spare camera. She still takes pictures. It begins as a journaling exercise, one photograph a day showing how she feels. At first it's mud puddles, cinderblock walls scarred with graffiti, headstones in the cemetery on Fifth Avenue, a spider squashed on the stoop outside her building—one she accidentally stepped on earlier in the day. All brown things and gray things and dead things. Hortense set up a blog for her to post her photos, and after several months, as she scrolls through them, she sees color between the clouds. A yellow dandelion. Children on swings, heads back, bare feet out, mouths open. Strawberry ice cream. Tomatoes in the farmers' market. Hortense's purple sandals. The browns are still there, but they're becoming less as she heals.

One thing she's unable to do is pray. Not in a direct, God-you-better-listen-now way. Even the corporate prayer time at church panics her, and she leaves the sanctuary shaking because certain phrases remind her of the prophet. Nazih says prayer is a conversation. If she's not ready yet to talk, she can try listening. So she does. Every morning before rising from bed, she stills herself and strains to hear God. She wants his voice in her spirit so desperately, needs it like bread, but it doesn't come, not like that morning in the Jeep when he told her to trust him.

And then it does, not in the silence of the morning, but as she hurries out to the women's Bible study. Her hand touches the knob of her front door and it sparks with static electricity.

Stay.

Unmistakably him. She doesn't understand it, but she stays in the brownstone. Pacing at first. Then snacking while half-entertaining herself with the computer. Then scrubbing the bathtub because it needs it and she hates doing it, taking a toothbrush to the grout, shining the basin with cut lemons and baking soda. Even using a toothpick to scrape out the black buildup in the crevice where the faucet meets the wall. And when she rinses it all away and thinks, *I could have been to the church and back twice over by now,* she hears a car door slam beneath her. Shaking off her rubber gloves, she runs to the next room and looks out the window.

A taxicab waits at the curb, and two people stand on the sidewalk, holding hands, faces tight with uncertainty, overwhelmed by the competing gangsta rap blaring from at least four different stoops, the shirtless teens with dark skin, the tattoos from neck to navel, the ladies in shorts smaller than underwear. The young man wears jeans and a button-down shirt, long-sleeved despite the August heat, though he's rolled the cuffs to the elbows. The woman can't be more than eighteen, her hair thick and long in a ponytail past her waist, her skirt covering her tennis shoes.

"Judith," Ada shouts, and the woman looks up.

"Ada?"

"Just wait right there. I'll be right down. I'll be right there."

Trust me.

READING GROUP GUIDE

1. With which character did you most identify—Ada or Katherine? Why?
2. Was there a particular scene in *Still Life* that proved emotionally powerful for you? How did this scene make you feel, and why was it moving?
3. If *Still Life*'s story line were actually to happen to you, how would you react? Have you ever felt guilty because a choice you made had consequences beyond what you could have imagined?
4. When listening to the news after Julian's last photographs are published, Ada considers the following: "As death closes in, all is stripped away until each individual's purpose on this earth remains, and their authentic self is laid bare. No more lies. No more façade . . . For Julian, it was more than clicking off photographs. He was a truth-shower. In the end, he

could be no other." What do you believe your "authentic self" would be shown to be?

5. Why do photographs speak to people so deeply?

6. *Still Life* could be characterized as a story about damaged people having to deal with the aftermath of an unimaginable tragedy. Have you faced unexpected situations in your life that moved you to change something about your circumstances? How do these pivotal moments force us to look more deeply into ourselves?

7. Why does grief have such transformative power? How has God used grief to draw you closer to him?

8. Would you recommend *Still Life* to a friend? What would be your most compelling reason for why someone should read this story?

ACKNOWLEDGMENTS

Thank you, to those who made *Still Life* possible:

Everyone one at Thomas Nelson Publishing who has worked on my behalf, and especially my encourager and editor, Amanda Bostic;

Bill Jensen, my agent, without whom my career would be nonexistent, since most days this introvert won't answer the phone, let alone think about attempting to manage the ins and outs of the publishing world;

Rachelle Gardner, who line edited both *Still Life* and *Stones for Bread* and made the whole process mostly painless;

Ashley Matthews, who to my shame I've forgotten to mention in two previous acknowledgements, and whose willingness to "play marbles" with Claire for hours on end enabled me to have precious time to write. Also our family's current mother's helpers, Sadie Clements and Sara LaGue—you both are such blessings to us;

J.M., who graciously shared her own experience of

being born without hands so I could authentically write Hortense's character;

Laura Combs, MS, LMHC, who gave clinical insights and advice for situations in the novel;

My parents, the best "Papa and Grandma" my children could have;

Gray, Jacob, Claire, and Noah—you are *my* heart;

And Chris: "Where you go I will go, and where you stay I will stay. Your people will be my people and your God my God. Where you die I will die, and there I will be buried. May the Lord deal with me, be it ever so severely, if anything but death separates you and me."

A solitary artisan.
A legacy of bread-baking.
And one secret that could collapse her entire identity.

". . . a quietly beautiful tale about learning how to accept the past
and how to let go of the parts that tie you down. . . . entwined with a
meaningful spiritual journey and amazing bread recipes that will appeal
to the beginner and satisfy even the most seasoned baker."

—*Romantic Times*, 4 1/2 stars, TOP PICK!

Available in print and e-book

ONE

'm young, four, home from nursery school because of snow. Young enough to think my mother is most beautiful when she wears her apron; the pink and brown flowered cotton flares at the waist and ruffles around the shoulders. I wish I had an apron, but instead she ties a tea towel around my neck. The knot captures a strand of my hair, pinching my scalp. I scratch until the captive hair breaks in half. Mother pushes a chair to the counter and I stand on it, sturdy pine, rubbed shiny with age.

Our home is wood—floors, furniture, spoons, bowls, boards, frames—some painted, some naked, every piece protective around us. *Wood is warm*, my mother says, *because it once was living*. I feel nothing but coolness in the paneling, the top of the long farm table, the rolling pin, all soaked in January.

At the counter, the smooth butcher block edge meets my abdomen, still a potbellied preschooler's stomach, though my limbs are sticks. Mother adds flour and yeast to the antique dough trough. Salt. Water. Stirs with a wooden spoon.

I want to help, I say.

You will, she tells me, stirring, stirring. Finally, she smoothes olive oil on the counter and turns the viscous mound out in front of her. *Give me your hands.* I hold them out to her. She covers her own in flour, takes each one of mine between them, and rubs. Then, tightening her thumb and forefinger around a corner of dough, she chokes off an apple-sized piece and sets it before me. *Here.*

I poke it. It sucks my fingers in. *Too sticky*, I complain. She sprinkles more flour over it and says, *Watch. Like this.*

She stretches and folds and turns. The sleeves of her sweater are pushed up past her elbow. I watch the muscles in her forearms expand and contract, like lungs breathing airiness into the dough. She stretches and folds and turns. A section of hair comes free from the elastic band at the back of her head, drifting into her face. She blows at it and, using her shoulder, pushes it behind her right ear. It doesn't stay.

She stretches and folds and turns.

I grow bored of watching and play with my own dough, flattening it, leaving handprints. Peel it off the counter and hold it up; it oozes back down, holes forming. I ball it up like clay, rolling it under my palm. Wipe my hands on the back pockets of my red corduroy pants.

My mother finishes, returns her dough gently to the trough. She places my ball next to her own and covers both with a clean white tea towel.

I jump off the chair. *When do we cook it?*

Bake it. Mother wipes the counter with a damp sponge. *But not yet. It must rise.*

To the sky?

Only to the top of the bowl.

I'm disappointed. I want to see the dough swell and grow, like a hot air balloon. My mother unties the towel from my neck, dampens it beneath the faucet. *Let me see your hands.* I offer them to her, and she scrubs away the dried-on dough, so like paste, flaky and near-white between my fingers. Then she kisses my palms and says, *Go play.*

The kitchen is stuffy with our labor and the preheating oven. The neighbor children laugh outside; I can see one of them in a navy blue snowsuit, dragging a plastic toboggan up the embankment made by the snow plow. But I stay. I want to be kissed again and washed with warm water. I want my mother's hands on me, tender and strong at the same time, shaping me as she does the bread.

ABOUT THE AUTHOR

Photo by Allen Clark

Christa Parrish is the author of five novels, including the 2009 ECPA Book of the Year *Watch Over Me* and the Christy Award-winning *Stones for Bread*. She lives in upstate New York with her husband, writer and pastor Chris Coppernoll. They have four children in their blended family.

* * *

Visit her website at christaparrish.com
Facebook: Christa-Parrish
Twitter: @breakingthesea